LINDA RATHGEBER & DAVID NICHOLL

PLAYING WITH FIRE

Tapping the Power of Macromedia® Fireworks® 4

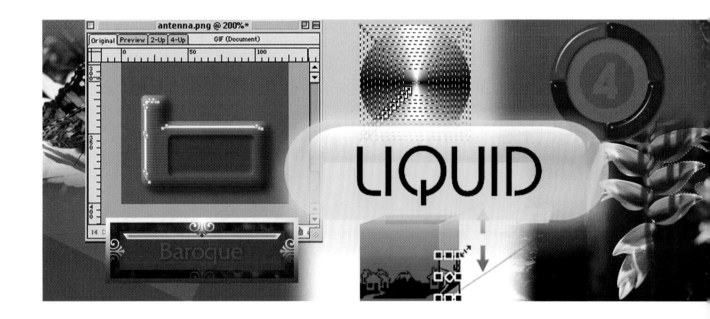

Hungry Minds™

Best-Selling Books • Digital Downloads • e-Books • Answer Networks • e-Newsletters • Branded Web Sites • e-Learning

New York, NY ▲ Cleveland, OH ▲ Indianapolis, IN

Playing with Fire: Tapping the Power of Macromedia® Fireworks® 4

Published by
Hungry Minds, Inc.
909 Third Avenue
New York, NY 10022
www.hungryminds.com

Library of Congress Control Number: 2001089316

ISBN: 0-7645-3549-8

Printed in the United States of America

10 9 8 7 6 5 4 3 2 1

1K/SZ/QW/QR/IN

Distributed in the United States by Hungry Minds, Inc.

Distributed by CDG Books Canada Inc. for Canada; by Transworld Publishers Limited in the United Kingdom; by IDG Norge Books for Norway; by IDG Sweden Books for Sweden; by IDG Books Australia Publishing Corporation Pty. Ltd. for Australia and New Zealand; by TransQuest Publishers Pte Ltd. for Singapore, Malaysia, Thailand, Indonesia, and Hong Kong; by Gotop Information Inc. for Taiwan; by ICG Muse, Inc. for Japan; by Intersoft for South Africa; by Eyrolles for France; by International Thomson Publishing for Germany, Austria, and Switzerland; by Distribuidora Cuspide for Argentina; by LR International for Brazil; by Galileo Libros for Chile; by Ediciones ZETA S.C.R. Ltda. for Peru; by WS Computer Publishing Corporation, Inc., for the Philippines; by Contemporanea de Ediciones for Venezuela; by Express Computer Distributors for the Caribbean and West Indies; by Micronesia Media Distributor, Inc. for Micronesia; by Chips Computadoras S.A. de C.V. for Mexico; by Editorial Norma de Panama S.A. for Panama; by American Bookshops for Finland.

For general information on Hungry Minds' products and services please contact our Customer Care department within the U.S. at 800-762-2974, outside the U.S. at 317-572-3993 or fax 317-572-4002.

For sales inquiries and reseller information, including discounts, premium and bulk quantity sales, and foreign-language translations, please contact our Customer Care department at 800-434-3422, fax 317-572-4002 or write to Hungry Minds, Inc., Attn: Customer Care Department, 10475 Crosspoint Boulevard, Indianapolis, IN 46256.

For information on licensing foreign or domestic rights, please contact our Sub-Rights Customer Care department at 212-884-5000.

For information on using Hungry Minds' products and services in the classroom or for ordering examination copies, please contact our Educational Sales department at 800-434-2086 or fax 317-572-4005.

For press review copies, author interviews, or other publicity information, please contact our Public Relations department at 212-884-5000 or fax 212-884-5400.

For authorization to photocopy items for corporate, personal, or educational use, please contact Copyright Clearance Center, 222 Rosewood Drive, Danvers, MA 01923, or fax 978-750-4470.

Hungry Minds™   is a trademark of Hungry Minds, Inc.

To all of the bright and talented people who make up the Fireworks community around the world. We hope that you find what we've done with this book both useful and inspirational.

Linda Rathgeber:
In memory of Bernd, who once asked the liberating question, "Where did you get the idea this wasn't supposed to be fun?"

David Nicholls:
For Trish, who was as puzzled as anyone by how two authors could write a book without ever having met in person, but trusted me and gave unfailing support when most needed.

FOREWORD

Before Fireworks was a product, there were vocal Fireworks customers. The very first version of Fireworks was developed after a series of meetings with vocal customers who were unafraid to tell us exactly what they wanted in a Web graphics product. Their opinions were vital to the development of our very first public beta, and feedback from the public beta was used to refine version 1.0.

In the years since we introduced Fireworks 1.0, we've continued to communicate with our users at trade shows, at our offices, at their offices, and over the Internet. Seeing people use the software, often in unexpected ways, delights us. Hearing their criticism challenges us to improve. Every version of Fireworks has been shaped by users' feedback; without them, Fireworks wouldn't be the product that it is today.

It's especially enjoyable – and incredibly flattering – when someone goes beyond using Fireworks and becomes an advocate for the product – an "Evangelist," in Macromedia parlance. That's exactly what Linda has done. Linda built and maintains a wonderful Web site full of Fireworks tips and techniques and seems to answer every question posted on our newsgroup. Enthusiasm like hers makes our team work harder.

Linda has put the same energy into the book you're reading now. When you're finished you'll know lots of great Fireworks techniques. You'll be able to use the software more quickly and effectively, allowing you to worry more about your design and less about how to accomplish it.

Hopefully, you'll also come away with some of Linda's enthusiasm for Fireworks. I think it's unavoidable.

Thank you for picking up this book and learning more about Fireworks. Please be sure to let us know what you think. Your suggestions for improving Fireworks can be sent to wish-fireworks@macromedia.com. Without you, it wouldn't be the product that it is today.

And thank you, Linda, for your ceaseless efforts on our behalf.

Jeff Doar
Programming Leader, Fireworks 4
Macromedia, Inc.

PREFACE

Four years ago, I was editing and producing graphics for a magazine called *The Holistic Resource*. David was working in the desiccated arena of government science policy on another continent. As chance, and the marvelous technological achievement we call "The Internet," would have it, David was also dabbling in Web design and had published an article on his site I knew would be perfect for our next issue. A knock on his virtual door led not only to my acquiring an immensely popular article, but also to the cover photo for the issue as well. It also led to our sharing the computer graphics tricks each of us had discovered on our own and hoarded.

Several tens of megabytes of e-mails later, David had taken the plunge and was working as a freelance Web designer. Inspired by his brass and trial versions of Macromedia's Dreamweaver and Fireworks programs, I soon followed. My experience with Fireworks turned into a love affair that found its expression in the Fireworks forum and on a Web site called Playing with Fire.

What we've learned, and hope to communicate with this book, is that Web graphics are like magic tricks. They must create an immediate impression, yet take a back seat to content and be very short on download time. The sleight of hand necessary to perform this magic is built into Macromedia's Fireworks 4, which, in our opinion, is the best overall graphics design tool for the Web.

As will be evident from the examples in the book, Fireworks vector/bitmap duality is wonderfully flexible. Apart from straight graphics capabilities, it offers the designer sophisticated JavaScript/HTML coding for rollovers and Dynamic HTML effects that, until a year or two ago, would have required the skills of a JavaScript guru.

Most of the examples are in an easy-to-follow step-by-step tutorial format that you can practice with the book open next to your computer. Many of the images and editable PNG files are included on the accompanying CD-ROM, which also contains trial software, commands, textures, and styles by numerous Fireworks experts. Also included is a set of powerful, fully functional plug-in filters that enable you to tackle extraordinary special effects, generously provided by Ilya Razmanov (aka Ilyich the Toad) from Russia. Watch out for this lad, he's *very* good.

We hope the lessons in the book inspire you to explore all the possibilities of Web imaging with Fireworks 4. May you acquire skills that give your imagination wings.

ACKNOWLEDGMENTS

We'd like to thank all sorts of people, but first of all, the great people of IDG Books and Hungry Minds Inc. Writing the book took place at a complex time for the companies publishing it. IDG Books merged with Hungry Minds, Inc, and the resulting changes meant that we lost our original project editor, Marti Paul. I'd like to thank both Marti and her associate, Lane Barnholtz, for starting us off in the right direction, and Mica Johnson who picked up the ball and kept it rolling. One bright and constant star was our acquisitions editor, Michael Roney. Michael's confidence in our vision and his efforts during the corporate changes are the main reason the book exists.

Our gratitude to Joseph Lowery, whose introduction to Mike Roney led directly to our accepted book proposal, to Mark Haynes, Jeff Doar, Doug Benson, David Morris, Dennis Griffin, Eric Wolff, Karen Silvey, Erica Burbach, John McDonald Jr., Vernon Veihe, and John — he's everywhere, he's everywhere—Dowdell of Macromedia.

Many generous and talented people have contributed tutorials to this book. Their names belong here, too. They are Bob Haroche (U.S.), Brian Baker (U.K.), Den Laurent (U.K.), Eddie Traversa (Australia), Japi Honoo (Italy), Kevin French (U.S.), Kleanthis Economou (Canada), Lanny Chambers (U.S.), Sandee Cohen (U.S.), and Wanda Cummings (Canada). And, if you haven't checked out Sandee Cohen's *Fireworks 4 Visual Quickstart Guide* or Al Sparber's *Dreamweaver Magic* — you should!

Thanks also to Ben Summers (U.K.) for pep rallies and helpful advice over the past year or two. We're pleased to be able to include a trial version of his excellent graphics compression and animation utility, Ignite, on the CD-ROM featured in Chapter 8.

On a personal level, thanks to Trish Nicholls, Lillian Jenkins, Frank Ray, Helen Hyams, Dorothy Liuzzo, and Gary Liuzzo, for their encouragement and support during the writing of the book and the months of work leading up to it. David would also like to put on record his appreciation of the benefits of Indian and Ceylon Tea, which contributed to the effectiveness of more than one late-night writing session.

Lastly, thanks to you, reader. It is for you we have performed this labor of love, sweat, and tears.

CONTENTS AT A GLANCE

CONTENTS

CHAPTER   2
COLORING YOUR WEB   **29**

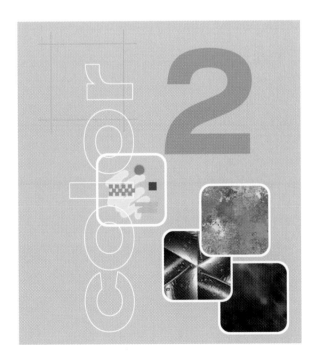

CHAPTER   **3**
MANIPULATING TYPEFACES IN FIREWORKS   **47**

CHAPTER **4**

ADDING ACTION TO YOUR PAGES   **65**

CHAPTER 5

PROCESSING AND KNEADING PHOTOGRAPHIC IMAGES 91

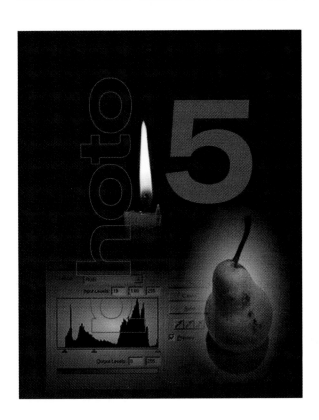

CHAPTER   6
A LITTLE RAZZLE DAZZLE   125

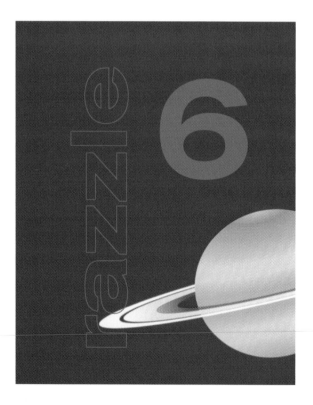

CHAPTER   7
ANIMATING TECHNIQUES   159

CHAPTER 8
KEEPING COMPANY WITH OTHER SOFTWARE   183

drawing

1

CHAPTER 1
BUILDING BLOCKS — DRAWING SHAPES IN FIREWORKS

As you discovered if you read the Preface a few pages back, this book has an unusual genesis. It's not your run-of-the-mill computer how-to book that explains what the manual skimmed over. It's about using the software — in this case, Macromedia's Fireworks 4 — to arrive at complex and beautiful graphic elements for your Web pages. The program manual shows you how to operate the software. Our objective is to show you how to solve problems and communicate to you the sheer fun you can have with Fireworks while working toward your artistic goals.

Most of the lessons in the book were developed in response to questions posted to the Macromedia Fireworks news groups by real users. Some of the lessons are difficult, but they teach you extraordinary things. The effort you put into working through the lessons will be repaid by the rapid development of skills used by Web designers on a daily basis. You also gain the confidence to explore the phenomenal capabilities of Fireworks.

To start with, we'll tackle geometry — how to draw and manipulate shapes to build practical "Web things" you can use. If you are new to Fireworks, load the program and dabble with the preset, geometric shapes — rectangles, polygons, and ellipses. Go ahead. We'll wait. (If you don't currently own a copy of Fireworks 4 you'll find a fully functional trial version of the program on the CD-ROM at the back of the book.) After you have some fun, come back and we'll lead you through some of the more sophisticated drawing and shaping techniques that Fireworks supports. Bézier curves, dividing, distorting, and punching shapes are all within your reach.

"There's nothing remarkable about it. All one has to do is hit the right keys at the right time, and the instrument plays itself."

J. S. BACH

ROUNDING SQUARE CORNERS

Q. "How do I draw one of those fancy inverted L-shaped things with the rounded corners like you see on the Harvard Business Review site?"

HECTOR C.

1.1

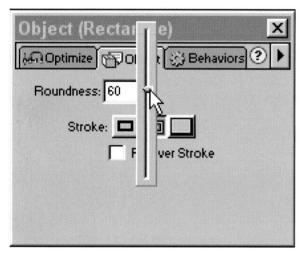

1.2

One of the graphic elements you see on high-caliber Web sites is the extended rectangular box, essentially a large, inverted L shape that wraps around text to contain headings and menus. The Harvard site, *www. hbsp.harvard.edu/products/hbr/index*, uses a bold, sweeping, inverted L-shaped element to add visual interest to an otherwise sober-looking, business-oriented design. The addition of an arrowhead to the L directs the viewer's attention to the main menu, helps to balance the design, and contributes to a feeling of assertiveness.

The new Rounded Rectangle tool, plus Fireworks' powerful Modify menu will have you creating these L-shaped elements in a snap.

STEP 1 Double-click the Rounded Rectangle tool (1.1) and drag out a wide, shallow rectangle. If you prefer to change the default corner radius of 30%, use the roundness slider in the Object panel or simply highlight the number by clicking it and then type a new one (1.2).

STEP 2 Drag out a second rectangle at right angles to the first and align its left corner with the top corner of the first rectangle (1.3). Choose Modify➤Combine➤Union. The two rectangles are fused together into one object (1.4). We'll use the Pen tool to round the square inside corner.

STEP 3 Activate the Zoom tool and click the top-left corner of your shape. Pull a vertical guideline to the point where the top edge of your shape begins to bend into the curve. Pull a horizontal

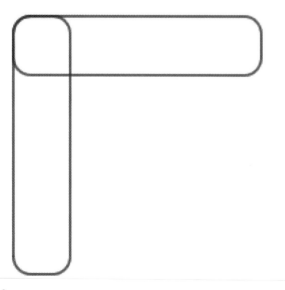

1.3

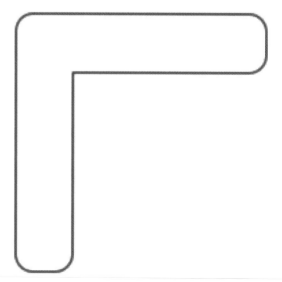

1.4

guideline to the point where the left edge of your shape begins to bend into the curve. Make sure that Snap to Guides is selected (View➤Guides➤ Snap to Guides).

Click the Line tool. While holding down the Shift key to constrain the angle, drag diagonally from the point where the vertical guideline intersects the top edge of your object until your cursor intersects the opposite line (a). Repeat this procedure from the point where the horizontal guideline intersects the left edge of your object (b) (1.5).

STEP 4 If you are not using precise cursors, switch to this option by choosing Edit➤ Preferences➤Editing. Check the box labeled Precise Cursors. Click OK.

To form the curve, click the Pen tool and place the cursor on point (a), where the line dragged from the vertical guideline crosses the edge of the other side of the object. Hold down the Shift key and drag to the inside corner of the object. Release the mouse button and click on the point (b), where the line dragged from the horizontal guideline crosses the object. Click. Working in a clockwise direction, click-advance until you have drawn a square path that returns to the original Bézier point. Click it to close the path (1.6). Choose Modify➤Combine➤Union. The curve is fused to the object (1.7). Fill as desired.

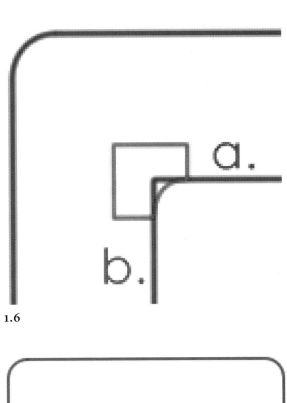

1.6

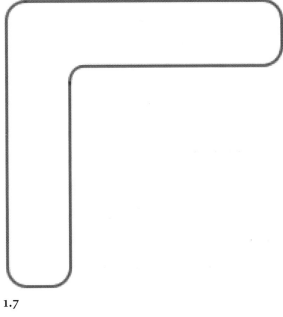

1.7

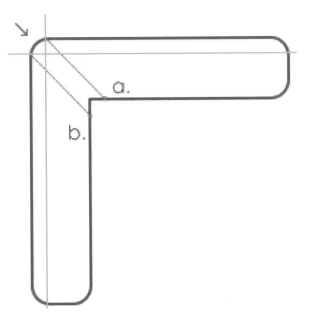

1.5

TRIANGULATING YOUR WAY

Q. *"How do I draw a triangle that I can fill? If I draw three lines I get a triangle, but I cannot fill it."*

MIKE C.

The simplest way to draw a triangle is with the Pen tool. Select a color for your rectangle and place the cursor at one of the imaginary points of the triangle. Click and release the mouse button to drop the first

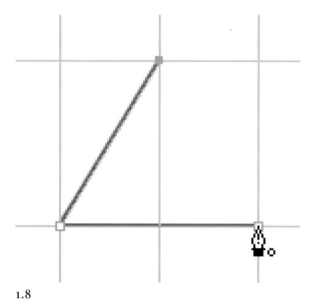

1.8

Bézier point. Move (but don't drag) your cursor diagonally to the second point. Click-release. (Note that if you drag while clicking, you'll draw Bézier curve segments.) Move your cursor to the third point. When you move the Pen tool cursor back to the original point you will see a small circle at its bottom right. Click this point to close the path. The triangle fills with the color you selected (1.8).

A second way to draw a triangle is to double-click the Polygon tool and reset the number of sides to 3 in the Object panel (1.9). Hold down the Shift key and drag upward with the cursor if you want the apex at the top. Drag downward if you want the apex inverted.

Here's an interesting technique suggested by a visitor to the Fireworks Forum (*news://forums. macromedia.com/macromedia.fireworks*). Drag out a square. Note that the Fireworks Rectangle tool draws rectangles as grouped objects. Before you can act on one of the corner points of the square, you must first ungroup the objects that make up the square. Choose Modify➤Ungroup. Click the bottom-left corner of the square with the Subselection tool and press the delete key. The corner point is removed, and the gap between the bottom-right and top-left points is automatically closed, creating a triangle. To rotate the apex to the top, choose Modify➤Transform➤ Numeric Transform. Choose Rotate from the drop-down list, enter –45 for the degree, and click OK.

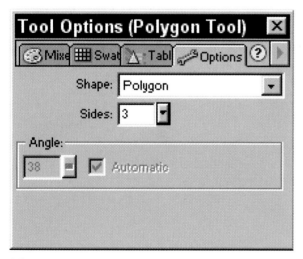

1.9

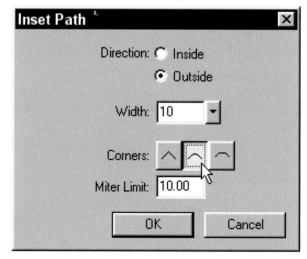

1.10

Q. "I am sure this is probably a simple question, but how do you draw a triangle with rounded corners?"

GEORGE S.

To round the corners of the triangle, choose Modify➤Alter Path➤Inset path. For direction, choose Outside. The width setting is your choice. For corners, choose the middle button. Leave the Mitre Limit set at the default 10.00 (1.10).

DIVIDING ELLIPSES

Q. "I'm trying to create a graphic of a circle broken up into three equal pie slices (these are not hot spots or image slices), each slice a different color. So 1/3 of the circle is red, 1/3 is blue, 1/3 yellow. This is so simple with crayons. How is it easily done in FW?"

BOB H.

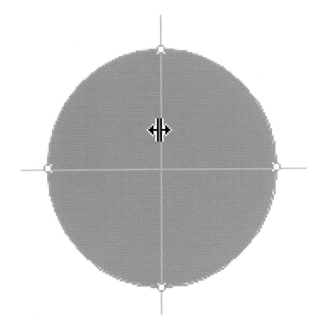

1.11

Instead of breaking down or cutting your circle into pie slices, you punch it.

STEP 1 Drag out a circle and choose Commands➤Document➤Center in Document. The color doesn't matter because you change it later. Drag vertical and horizontal guidelines to the center of the circle (1.11).

If you click the circle with the Subselection tool before pulling the guidelines into place, the Bézier points pop up, indicating the exact positions for the guidelines.

Double-click the Polygon tool. In the Tool Options panel, choose Star, 3 sides, and 2 for the angle. Place your cursor where the guidelines cross in the middle of the circle, hold down the Shift key, and drag upward along the vertical guideline to the top. Be sure to extend the tips of the star shape beyond the edge of the circle (1.12).

Choose Modify➤Combine➤Punch. The star shape will be punched through the circle. To split the wedges apart so that you can fill them independently, choose Split from the Modify menu. Color the wedges.

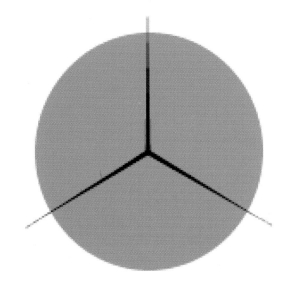

1.12

STEP 2 Because the angle you use for the star shape left gaps in the center (1.13), you need to close the gaps. Zoom in to 800% and choose View➤Guides and uncheck Show Guides to hide the guideline. Click the Subselection tool and then click one of the wedges. Drag the Bézier point at the apex of the wedge toward the center. Notice that even though the guides have been hidden, the points snap to them. Repeat with the other two wedges. Finally, choose Modify➤Group. Your shape is now ready to manipulate further or to export (1.14).

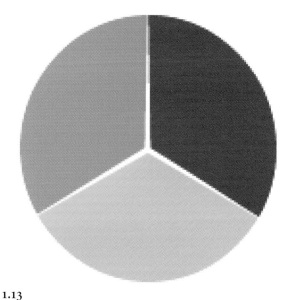

1.13

1.14

PENNING WITH FIREWORKS' REDESIGNED PEN TOOL

Q." Does anyone know of any good tutorials for drawing and editing paths in FW using the Pen tool and, in particular, manipulating points on Bézier curves? Maybe it's just me but I always struggle with Bézier curves trying to get the smooth shapes I want."

MARTIN S.

The Pen tool is one of Fireworks' most useful and powerful features. You can use the Pen tool to create, alter, and join paths. Learn to use it well, and it can become your best friend. Artist Kleanthis Economou is featured in this section, passing along some expert, first-hand knowledge of this versatile tool.

Before you get started, you'll want to enable the Pen tool options that make it easier to see what you are doing. Double-click the Pen tool to open the Tool Options panel (1.15). If it's not visible in your workspace, you can find it under the Window menu.

Checking the Show Pen Preview box in the Options panel enables you to preview the path segment you are about to create. Checking the Show Solid Points box sets the current anchor as a white rectangle, leaving the other points as filled blue rectangles. If the box is not checked, the colors are inverted. These settings define the appearance of all the anchors in Fireworks.

UNDERSTANDING PATHS

Before you use the Pen tool, we should discuss paths in Fireworks. A *path* is a sequence of connected line segments that define a shape. The path may be open or closed, depending on whether or not the beginning and ending points of the line are joined. Circles, squares, and octagons are examples of closed paths.

A straight line is also a path, but it's an open one. It consists of two endpoints, origin and destination, which define a line segment. If you add another point somewhere along this path, you have two line segments. The point added to the middle becomes the destination endpoint for the first segment, and the origin endpoint for the second segment.

The positions of these points, are defined in terms of *x* and *y* coordinates on the canvas.

Four points define a Bézier Curve: two endpoints and two control handles (1.16). Moving the control handles changes the shape of the curve.

Fireworks defines two control handles for each point. These are the preceding and the succeeding handles (1.17). The preceding handle influences the segment that has its anchor at the destination endpoint of a segment. In other words, the segment leading up to the anchor. The succeeding handle influences the segment that has its anchor at the origin endpoint of the segment — the segment that continues on from the current point.

CREATING SIMPLE PATHS

The easiest way to draw a path is by creating a sequence of points on the canvas. Select the Pen tool and position the cursor on the canvas. The cursor changes to a pen with a small x at its bottom-right corner. This x is one of several visual cues to aid precision when using the tool. It means that you are about to start a new path. Other symbols are defined as you continue.

Click and release the left mouse button. Doing so creates the first point in the path, or the *origin endpoint*. Move your mouse to a different location on the canvas, click, and release the left mouse button to plot the next point. Repeat this step as many times as you want. Each time you click, you add a new point to the path and draw an additional segment.

> **NOTE**
>
> Note that the Pentool's visual cues are not available if you are using precise cursors.

> **NOTE**
>
> *Bézier Curves*, the computer equivalent of the draftsman's French Curves, were invented in the early days of Computer Aided Design by French mathematician and automotive engineer, Pierre Etienne Bézier (pronounced Bezz-ee-EH). Bézier curves are used in computer graphics to produce curves that maintain the same shape when the image is rescaled.

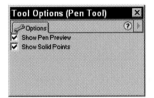

1.15

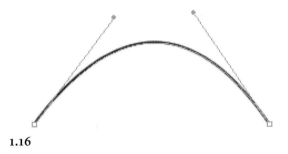

1.16

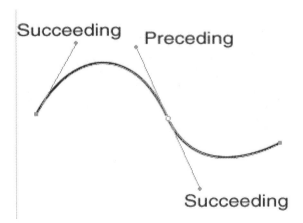

1.17

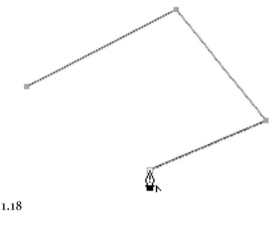

1.18

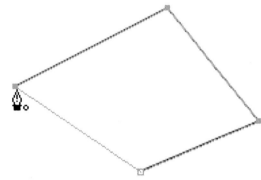

1.19

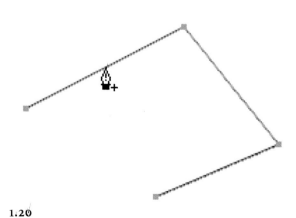

1.20

Release the left mouse button but keep the cursor over the point, and you'll see another Pen tool visual cue — an inverted *v* (1.18). This inverted *v* tells you that you can use the control handles of the point under the cursor to alter the curve by clicking and dragging. The same cursor appears each time you position the cursor over a point. Don't worry about this yet. Just note how the cursor changes. Later in this chapter, you find out how to use the control handles to alter the shape of the curve.

CLOSING A PATH

As mentioned earlier, a path is closed when the origin and destination endpoints join. Fireworks employs a another visual cue to help you see when you are about to close a path. As you move your cursor towards the origin endpoint of an open path, the Pen-cursor displays a small circle (1.19). If you click when you see the circle, the path closes.

ADDING POINTS TO AN EXISTING PATH

After you have drawn a path, you may want to add new points to existing segments. That's precisely what we did when we rounded the inside corner of the inverted L shape in the first exercise. Select the path and move your Pen tool over a path segment. You will see a small plus sign (1.20), which signifies that if you click the path you will add a point at this position. The existing segment is broken into two new segments. The path will appear unchanged, but Fireworks has created the control handles for the new point.

REMOVING POINTS FROM A PATH

To remove a point from a path, move the Pen tool over the point. When you see a little minus sign below the right corner of the pen cursor (1.21), left-click the point. The point disappears, a *x* replaces the minus sign, and a new segment is created from the previous and following points. Another way to remove a point is to click on it with the Subselection tool (the white arrow) and press the Delete key on the keyboard.

MASTERING THE CONTROL HANDLES

When you use the Pen tool to create paths, as you select or add a point, you can alter its control handles to change the shape of the path.

To alter the point's control handles, click and drag on the point. The Pen cursor changes into a wedge shape, and you can see both the succeeding and preceding handles (1.22). The active handle that your cursor controls is always the succeeding handle, the one that influences the next segment that you will draw. The preceding handle is opposite from the succeeding handle, and it influences the previous segment.

If you alter the control handles of the first point on a path, although you will see both handles, Fireworks 4 only keeps the succeeding handle. The succeeding handle will influence the next segment you are about to add, and the preceding one will be reset. (In previous versions of Fireworks, the preceding handle would remain as well.)

If you don't want to alter the previous segment you've drawn, but you do want to change the following one, you can hold down the Alt key as you click and drag the Pen tool (1.23). Doing this forces Fireworks to alter the point's succeeding control handle only, and it leaves the preceding handle unchanged.

If you made a mistake, move the cursor over the point and single-click again. Doing so resets the succeeding handle, but it does not alter the preceding one. You can also use this method to create only a preceding handle with the Pen tool for this point. The Subselection tool enables you to alter the control handles of a path with finer control and more options.

Now that you've used the Pen tool a little, play with it and all the options. It's a powerful tool that enables you to create an infinite number of subtle shapes. If you get confused, the Fireworks help file will set you back on track. Have fun!

Thanks to Kleanthis Economou for these Pen tool tips and tricks.

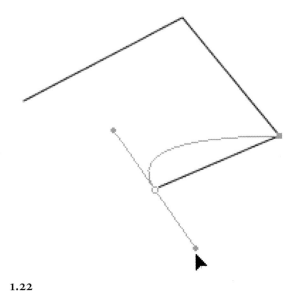

1.22

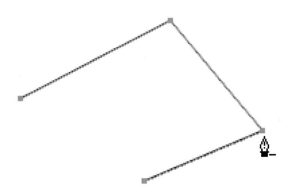

1.21

1.23

Q. "I seem to have a mental blockage with the Pen tool. If I want to draw a series of curves, for example a sine wave, I get the first one right but while drawing the second one, the shape of the first changes. This maneuver has stumped me. Some advice on how and where to click and drag would be appreciated."

PHIL S.

The shape of the second curve may be changing because the first curve hasn't been completed yet. Let's have a look at the way the Fireworks Pen tool handles drawing the peaks and troughs of a sine wave.

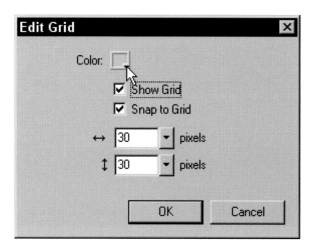

1.24

STEP 1 Open a 180 x 180-pixel canvas. Make sure that the Rulers and Grid are turned on by choosing View➤Rulers, and View➤Grid. Zoom in to 200%.

The default color for the grid in Fireworks is black. To make it easier to see what you are doing, change the grid to a lighter color. To change the grid settings, choose View➤Grid➤Edit Grid. Click the Color box and change the color to #99CCCC. Change the size of the grid to 30 x 30 pixels (1.24).

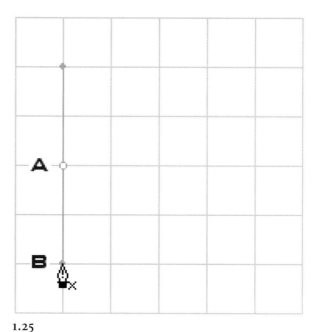

1.25

ARTIST:
Kleanthis Economou

ORGANIZATION:
Project Fireworks at *www. projectfireworks.com*. I live in Halifax, Canada and work as a Web Applications developer. I also do graphics work for the Web and print.

COMPUTERS:
I became interested in computers around the age of 12. My first was a Spectrum ZX80 (the one with the cassette player for a drive). After that, I moved to a Commodore 64, an Amstrad 128, an Amiga 500 and eventually, at the age of 16, I got my first PC — an 8088 with 640KB of RAM and 40MB hard-drive.

My current machine is a PIII 600Mhz, 512MB RAM, running Windows 2000 Pro. My monitor is a Sony FW900 (24-inch FD Trinitron display).

CONNECTIVITY:
I'm connected to the Internet by a 3Mbps DSL line.

PRIMARY APPLICATIONS:
Applications that I use most are Fireworks, Dreamweaver, UltraDev,

STEP 2 Click the Pen tool to activate it. Click the
middle, horizontal grid line where it intersects one
of the vertical grid lines. While holding down the
Shift key to prevent any accidental, sideways slip-
page of your movements, drag downward two
squares (from position A to position B in 1.25).
Release both the Shift key and the mouse button.
Move (don't drag) the tip of the Pen tool across
two squares and up two squares, to position C.
Your cursor should now be parallel with the first
point you added (1.26). Hold down the Shift key
and click. Drag upward two squares to position D.
(1.27). Release both the Shift key and the mouse
and this completes the trough of the sine wave.

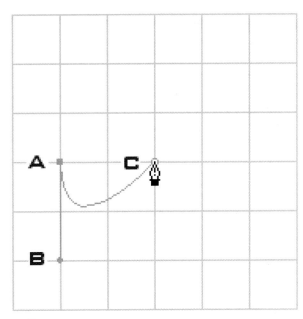

1.26

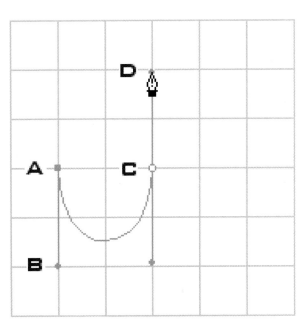

1.27

FreeHand, Flash, Director, and my
favorite text editor (sometimes, I think,
more than anything).

FAVORITE THING:
Well that's a difficult one. From the ones I
can mention in public, I'd say creating
designs that match the mood of my
favorite songs.

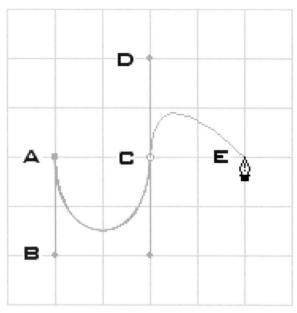

1.28

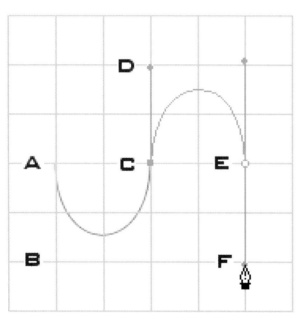

1.29

STEP 3 Without dragging, move two squares over and two squares down. The tip of the Pen tool should now be at position E, parallel with the first and second points you added (1.28). Hold down the Shift key and click. Drag downward two squares to position F. (1.29) Congratulations! You have just completed your first, perfect sine wave. To end the pen session, move the tip of the Pen tool back to the last point and double-click it to create an endpoint.

CREATING COMPOUND SHAPES

Q. *"I need to create an ellipse with two smaller ellipses at the ends and with half-moon cutouts at the top, bottom and sides. I hope that was clear. Is there a quick way to do this in Fireworks?"*

TIMOTHY E.

All kinds of odd shapes can be joined together in Fireworks, creating new objects that can be acted upon as a single unit. Begin by opening the View menu and enabling Rulers and Guidelines. Under Guide Options, choose Snap to Guides.

STEP 1 Activate the Ellipse tool and drag out an ellipse. Switch to the Subselection tool to make the Bézier points of the ellipse pop up. (See the section, "Dividing Ellipses" earlier in this chapter.) Use the Bézier points as guides to center-align vertical and horizontal guidelines.

Drag out a smaller ellipse and align it so that the left and right Bézier points line up with the horizontal guideline and its top and bottom Bézier points line up with the outside edge of the large ellipse. Clone the small ellipse by choosing Edit➤Clone and then use your arrow keys to move the clone to the opposite side of the large ellipse (1.30).

To combine the three ellipses into a single object, choose Edit➤Select All, Modify➤Combine➤Union (1.31).

STEP 2 To prepare for the half-moon cutouts, pull vertical and horizontal guidelines to the four outermost Bézier points (1.32).

Drag out a small, shallow ellipse and align the Bézier points with the cross that's formed by the guidelines at the top of the object. Clone the new ellipse and use your arrow keys to align the Bézier points of the clone with the cross that's formed by the guidelines at the bottom of the object. Drag out a small, deep ellipse and align the Bézier points with the cross that's formed by the guidelines at the right side of the object. Clone the ellipse and move the clone to the opposite side (1.33).

STEP 3 Shift + select the large object and the small ellipse on the right side. Choose Modify➤Combine➤Punch. The small ellipse is punched through the large one. Repeat the punch technique with the other small ellipses. You can now manipulate your shape further (1.34).

TIP

If you hold down the Shift key while using the arrow keys to move an object across the canvas, the object will advance ten pixels at a time instead of just one.

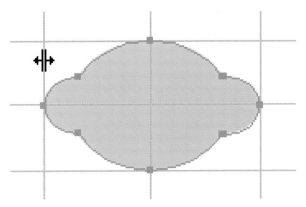

1.32

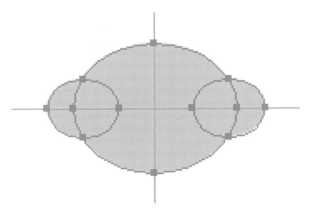

1.30

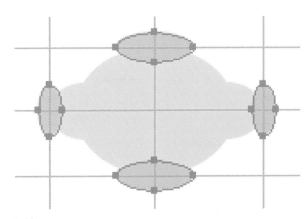

1.33

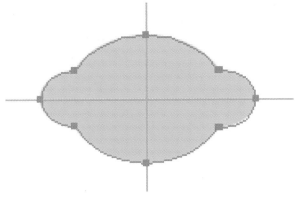

1.31

1.34

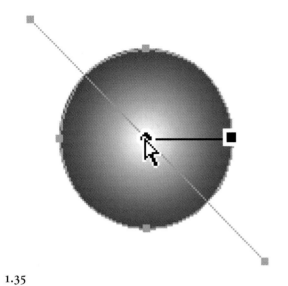

1.35

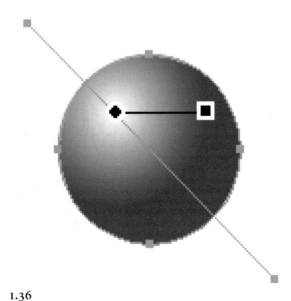

1.36

1.37

DRAFTING 3D ELLIPSES, CYLINDERS, AND RECTANGLES

Q. *"How do I make a 3D sphere in Fireworks?"*

MICHAEL L.

No matter how you rotate a sphere, it's still a circle. The interplay of light and shadow on the surface is what gives it depth.

Drag out an ellipse and give it a radial fill (1.35). While it is still selected, place your cursor on the pivot point (round handle) of the gradient rotation bar and move the pivot point to where you want the light to strike the surface of the sphere (1.36). Add a shadow if you want and export as a JPEG (1.37).

Q. *"What's the best way you've found to give a rectangle with rounded corners a cylindrical look?"*

CORY E.

The problem with using a rectangle with rounded corners is that it's a two-dimensional shape, and you want to create the illusion of a third dimension. A better way to draw a cylinder is with two ellipses and a rectangle.

STEP 1 Pull four guidelines onto the canvas to define the rough outline of the cylinder. Make sure that Snap to Guides is selected by choosing View➤Guides➤Snap to Guides.

STEP 2 Activate the Ellipse tool and drag a straight line from one vertical guideline to the other. Drag the cursor downward to create a shallow ellipse. Clone the ellipse and use your arrow keys to move the clone to the bottom guideline. Exchange the Ellipse tool for the Rectangle tool and drag out a rectangle between the two ellipses (1.38).

> **TIP**
>
> The shadow for a sphere is a flattened ellipse with a linear fill.

STEP 3 Shift + select the rectangle and the bottom ellipse. Then choose Modify➤Combine➤Union. The ellipse will be fused to the rectangle, forming the rounded bottom of the cylinder. Select the top ellipse and choose Modify➤Arrange➤Bring to front (1.39).

STEP 4 The last step in creating a realistic looking cylinder is adding gradients to the cylinder body and top. The colors we've used for the gradient, from the dark edge to the center highlight are #000000, #6A654D, #A8A480, #D0C4B0, and #FFFFFF (1.40).

Add the gradient to the cylinder body first. Stretch the gradient so that the highlight is to the right of center. Add the same gradient to the top ellipse but rotate the gradient so that the highlight is to the left of center. Open the Effect panel and choose Brightness/Contrast from the Adjust Color menu. Reduce the brightness of the ellipse to –30. To slightly blend the bottom edge of the ellipse into the cylinder body and reduce any stair stepping of its top edge, add a Gaussian blur. The radius of the blur should be between 0.4 and 0.6. Export your cylinder image as a JPEG (1.41).

If you want the top of the cylinder to appear closed, rotate the gradient so that the gradient highlight is at cross-angles to the highlight on the cylinder body.

1.39

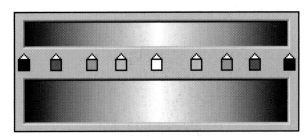

1.40

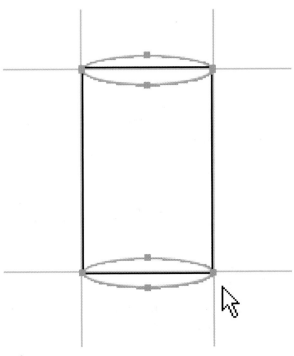

1.38

1.41

1.42

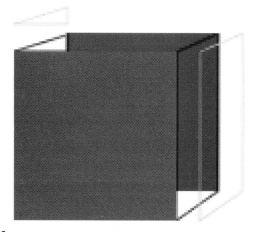

1.43

1.44

Q. *"I have a client who wants an animated Jack-in-a-box for a logo. I have clip art I can use for the clown figure, but how can I draw a 3D box so the clown is popping out of the middle? Is it possible with Fireworks?"*

ANDREW Q.

Fireworks isn't a 3-D rendering or morphing program, but by applying a perspective drawing technique, you can create a projection of a box that will enable you to move the clown figure between its front and rear parts.

STEP 1 Open a new canvas and drag out a square. Clone the square and color the clone a few shades darker than the original. You need to reduce the height and width of the clone by five pixels. Open the Info panel and highlight the width value of the clone with your cursor. Type in the new value. Reduce the height of the clone in the same way. Move the clone behind the original, and then move it about eight pixels higher and 20 pixels to the right (1.42).

STEP 2 Activate the Pen tool and zoom in. You'll need a clear view of the right edges of both squares.

Click with the tip of the Pen on the bottom-right corner of the front square. Move diagonally across the canvas to the bottom-right corner of the rear square. Click the corner. Hold down the Shift key and move to the top-right corner of the back square. Click the corner then release the Shift key. Move diagonally across the canvas to the top-right corner of the front square. Click the corner. Hold down the Shift key and move down to the bottom-right corner of the front square. When you see the little ring pop up at the lower-right side of the Pen cursor, click to close the path.

Finish the left side of the box in the same way, connecting the two corners with the angle formed by the overlapping squares (1.43). Add a solid fill to the penned shapes (1.44).

Q. "That was pretty easy. Now how would I wrap a texture or image around the box?"

ANDREW Q.

1.45

An image, texture, or text can be wrapped around the box by a combination of dividing it, then Distorting it around the corner of the box with Fireworks Skew and Distort tools.

STEP 1 If you could extend the shapes that make up your box past the edges of the canvas, the planes created by those extensions would eventually converge to a single point, the *vanishing point*. The lines from the vanishing point to the corners of the box are called rays. Making those rays visible shows you the exact angle that an image, text, texture, or anything wrapped around the corner of the box, needs to be distorted to(1.45).

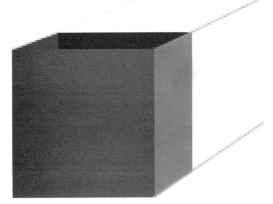

1.46

Use the Line tool to extend the lines that form the top and bottom edges of the right side of the box off the right side of the canvas (1.46).

STEP 2 Add the image you want to decorate the box with. We've used a ding font to create ours, and then converted it to a bitmap by choosing Modify➤Convert to Bitmap (1.47).

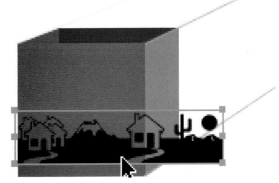

1.47

NOTE

Just as gradients can be used to create an illusion of depth, so can the right colors. Direct light, such as the light that falls into a room from a window, is cool. When it is reflected off the walls of the room its color is warm. We've used a warm, orange-red color on the front surface of our 3D box to suggest a reflected light. That makes it look closer. The color on the right surface of the box is a cool, violet pink. The coolness of the color suggests that the right surface of the box is being lit by a direct source of light from farther back in the space the box occupies. To the casual observer, the box simply looks red.

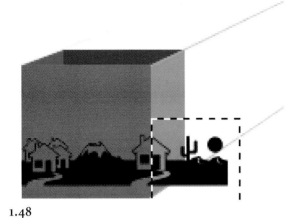

1.48

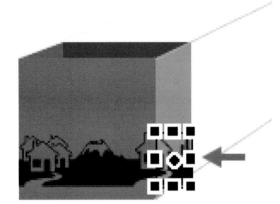

1.49

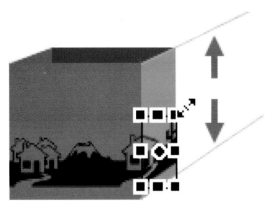

1.50

While the image is still selected, activate the Rectangle Marquee tool and starting at the right-front corner of the box, drag a marquee around it (1.48). Cut the selection to the clipboard, choose Modify➢Exit Bitmap Mode, and paste the selection back in. We've trimmed a bit off the right side of the pasted image to prevent it from becoming too distorted in the next step.

STEP 3 In real life, distant shapes maintain the same shape they would have if they were seen up close. It is only their proportions that appear reduced. To create an impression of distance on a flat surface, like the Fireworks canvas, it is necessary to distort the shape. This distortion is called *forced perspective*. Compressing the pasted shape toward the front of the box is the first distortion you will use to force perspective.

Activate the Transform tool, and use it to compress the right edge of the pasted image so that the right edge of the compressed image is aligned with the right edge of the box (1.49).

STEP 4 The second distortion you need to perform is to compress the height of the right edge of the pasted image. Exchange the Transform tool for the Distort tool. Pull up on the right-top and right-bottom corners of the pasted image until the top and bottom edges of the image are parallel with the ray lines (1.50). Delete the ray lines. Lighten the color of the transformed image (1.51).

1.51

PUNCHING NEW FORMS

Q. *"I want to create an interface that has cutouts with rolled edges. The idea is to then add raised panels with rolled edges to the inside of the cutouts so the lines around them look like they have been carved out. Any ideas?"*

DWIGHT M.

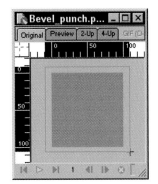

1.52

Fireworks enables you to punch one vector shape through another, which is the process that you use to create the cutouts. If the punched shape has a bevel applied to it as a Live Effect, the bevel is rendered on the outlines of the cutout as well. You take advantage of that bevel rendering in this exercise.

STEP 1 Open a new canvas and drag out a rectangle. Notice that the rectangle (1.52) extends beyond the actual surface of the canvas, so the Inner Bevel that is applied to the rectangle only appears around the edge of the cutout.

Open the Effect panel and choose Bevel and Emboss➤Inner Bevel. Use the Smooth Bevel option. Set the bevel width to 4 pixels and the contrast to 100%. You can leave the other options at their default settings.

STEP 2 Drag out a second rectangle. This one should be smaller than the first and inside the edges of the canvas. Its color should be a shade or two lighter than the canvas. Choose Edit➤Select All so that both rectangles are selected and then Modify➤Combine➤Punch. The smaller rectangle is punched through the larger one, and the bevel is added to the edges of the hole. To increase the depth, add a drop shadow (1.53). Add a bit of texture if you want.

1.53

STEP 3 The last step is to add the inner panel. Drag out a rectangle that is three to five pixels smaller than the hole punched through the original rectangle. To add the same bevel to the panel that you added to the outer rectangle, select the outer rectangle and copy it by choosing Edit➤ Copy. Select the new rectangle and choose Edit➤ Paste Attributes. Open the Effect panel and uncheck the Drop Shadow box (1.54).

STROKING IS AN ART

Q. "I'm trying to create an effect with Fireworks on a single stroke, where each tip of the stroke becomes faded and narrows to a fine point. I would appreciate any advice on how to do this in FW."

GARY S.

You can create the illusion of a faded, tapered stroke by performing the following steps:

STEP 1 Drag out a shallow rectangle as wide as you want your line to be and add a radial gradient. To adjust the gradient so that the line is solid in the middle and then fades toward the edge, open the gradient editor by clicking on the Edit button

1.54

in the Fill panel. Press the darker of the two color chips with your cursor (1.55).

STEP 2 When the cursor turns into a little hand, drag the color chip all the way to the left. Repeat with the light colored chip, but move it all the way to the right.

STEP 3 Reduce the height of the rectangle to one or two pixels. Your line will look tapered and faded (1.56).

Q. "I've got a circle stroked with basic/soft line. The stroke is dark gray, and the canvas is white. What's happening when I add a fill is that the outside of the stroke anti-aliases to the canvas color, which is fine. However, it looks like the inside of the stroke is also anti-aliasing to white, so there's a pixelly halo around the fill and the stroke. How do I fix this?"

ION R.

You are probably seeing pixels of the background color between the shape and the stroke because the stroke is narrow, and it is being rendered outside the path.

Select your shape and open the Object panel. In the Object panel, you find three buttons that enable you to specify how the stroke is rendered, relative to the path (1.57). Depressing the left button causes the stroke to be drawn inside the path. The middle button causes the stroke to be drawn in the middle of the

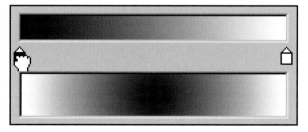

1.55

1.56

path. The right button causes the stroke to be drawn outside the path. Depressing either the left or middle button eliminates any bleeding of the canvas color between the stroke and the fill.

Q. "My goal is to place a two-pixel stroke around the perimeter of an imported JPEG. Selecting it and adding a stroke doesn't work. What am I doing wrong?"

DANNY A.

Fireworks strokes do not work on imported bitmaps, such as GIFs or JPEGs, because no path exists to attach the stroke to. You can use more than one way to add a two-pixel stroke or border to a bitmap, however. We'll use David's fractal fern image (1.58) to demonstrate these.

METHOD 1 Select the image and open the Effect panel. Choose Bevel and Emboss➤Outer Bevel. Change the color of the bevel from the default red to the color you want to use for your border by clicking in the color well. Doing so opens a palette from which you can select a new color. Adjust the width of the bevel to one pixel. Reduce both contrast and softness to zero (1.59).

1.58   *Fractal Fern by David Nicholls*

1.59

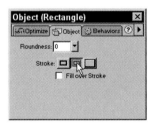

1.57

METHOD 2 The previous method slightly rounds the corners of the border. If you don't want the corners use a Glow instead of an Outer Bevel. From the Effect panel, choose Shadow and Glow➤Glow. Set the Glow width to one. Increase the opacity of the glow to 100%. Decrease the glow softness to zero (1.60).

METHOD 3 Drag out a rectangle the same size as your image and give it a one or two pixel wide stroke. Move the rectangle behind the image (Modify➤Arrange➤Send to Back). Cut the image to the Clipboard and select the rectangle. Choose Edit➤Paste Inside. The image becomes the fill of the rectangle and is surrounded by the rectangle's stroke.

METHOD 4 Expand the height and width of the canvas by one or two pixels. To do this, choose Modify➤Canvas Size. In the Canvas Size dialog box, enter the new dimensions for height and width and click on the center Anchor. Click OK to close the Canvas Size dialog box.

Q. "I am trying to quickly add a one-pixel white stroke and a shadow to a photograph, giving it a border and depth. I tried making a Style, but that only added the shadow not the stroke. How I can make a Style to do this so I can quickly add them to pictures of various sizes?"

TRAVIS A.

It is possible to create a style that will add both a white border and a drop shadow to a photo, an imported GIF, or a Fireworks vector image that you've converted to a bitmap (1.61).

STEP 1 Expand the canvas by 20 pixels. Add a background color to the canvas by choosing Modify ➤ Canvas Color. The background color of the canvas should be the same color you will be placing the image against on your Web page. If you leave the canvas set to the default of Transparent, the border and drop shadow will automatically be anti-aliased to white when you export the image. They will not blend properly into your page.

1.60

1.61

STEP 2 Select the image, open the Effect panel, and choose Shadow and Glow➤Glow. Change the color of the glow from the default red to white. Move the contrast slider to 100%. Decrease the edge softness to zero. Set the glow width to one pixel. Add the Drop Shadow.

STEP 3 While the image is still selected, click the button at the top right of the Styles panel and choose New Style. Uncheck everything but Fill Color, Effect, and Stroke Type. Give your new style a name and click OK (1.62). Your new style will automatically adjust to any image size.

Styles are stored in Fireworks' memory, but because styles are Live Effects, they remain permanently editable. If you want to change the colors of your border and shadow for other images, return to the Effect panel to make the necessary changes.

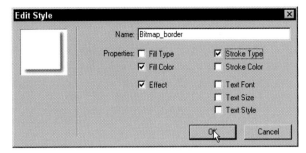

1.62

Q. *"How can I get a dashed stroke on an object in FW? I want to make one of those cheesy coupon-looking things, and I can't find the option on the stroke palette."*

MARK M.

Type out a string of dots in the Text Editor. Arial Rounded is a good choice for this use because its dot character is round instead of square, as they are in most font faces. Attach the text string to the object path by choosing Text➤Attach to path. You can adjust the placement of the text string on the path by increasing or decreasing the Kerning, Leading, Horizontal Scaling, or Baseline Shift until you like the way it looks.

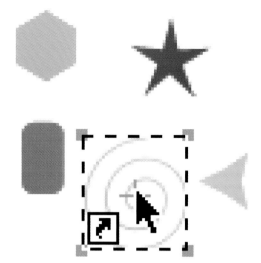

1.63

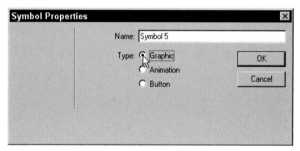

1.64

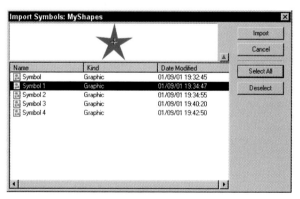

1.65

CREATING LIBRARIES OF REUSABLE SHAPES

Q. *"Is there some way I can create a library of shapes I frequently use and access it from the Fireworks menu?"*

RAPHAEL J.

Anything that can be turned into a symbol in Fireworks, such as text, vector shapes, and small animations, you can add to the menu of items that you access via the Insert menu.

STEP 1 Open a small canvas (100 x 100 pixels). Zoom in and begin adding small shapes, such as arrowheads or ding fonts to the canvas. These shapes can be all one color or a variety of colors. Keep the shapes as small as possible. Because they are vector shapes, you can resize them later without loosing their outlines (1.63). As you finish drawing each one, convert it to a symbol. Choose Insert➤ Symbol and click the radio button next to the word Graphic in the dialog box that pops up (1.64). Note that if you have used fonts they should be converted to paths before converting them to symbols.

STEP 2 From the File menu, choose Save As and browse to the Fireworks Libraries folder. Our Fireworks Libraries are located at C:\Program Files\Macromedia\Fireworks 4\Configuration\ Libraries. Give the file a name and click OK. Exit Fireworks. When you reopen the program, your custom library is ready to access by choosing Insert ➤ Libraries. Locate the title of your Library in the list and click on it. The Import Symbols dialog window loads your new Library (1.65).

Keep in mind that Fireworks loads your custom Libraries each time that the program opens. Too many Libraries or too great a file size may degrade the program's performance. A better option (and one that can still be accessed through the Insert menu) is to create a second Library folder (Libraries 2) in the Fireworks Configuration directory. You can then access the items in your new folder by choosing Insert➤Libraries➤Other.

color 2

CHAPTER 2
COLORING YOUR WEB

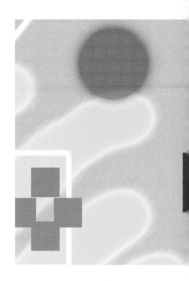

C olor is an obvious component of any Web site design. But color is also a design element that many artists — amateurs and more than a few professionals — get wrong.

One of the first shocks graphic artists encounter as they transfer their skills to the Web is that they may have to live with the 216 Web-safe colors visible on all 256-color systems. Unfortunately, these colors were generated by a mathematical formula and are not evenly distributed in the color spectrum to which the human eye is most sensitive (the blue-green area is short-changed). So Web-safe colors are not the whole answer to designing with color. The good news is that the vast majority of modern PCs and Macs are equipped with displays set to 65,000 colors or better.

WORKING WITH WEB-SAFE COLOR

Q. "I always use Web-safe hex color specifications because I can be sure that the color will be displayed properly. We've been having a discussion here at work about hex vs. the named colors like "gray." A book I have says that to save yourself headaches, you should use the "gray" attribute instead of the hex color number because hex colors render differently browser to browser. Does it matter?"

BILL P.

Named colors are the X11 color set that was created for the graphical user interface of Unix, Linux, BSD, and similar operating systems.

"Of all design elements, color most exemplifies the wholeness of design, the necessity to reason globally."
EDWARD R. TUFTE, FROM *THE VISUAL DISPLAY OF QUANTITATIVE INFORMATION*

The WWW Consortium proposed the inclusion of the one hundred and forty X11 colors in their Cascading Style Sheet specifications but they were not implemented in the final draft. Thus the Web-safe palette, based on a mathematical formula, was adopted instead.

Both Netscape and Internet Explorer have supported the named colors since 1997. They are rendered differently by Macs and PCs, however, and only the "VGA 16" subset of the colors is supported by other browsers, like Opera. For the curious, the VGA 16 colors are Aqua, Black, Blue, Fuchsia, Gray, Green, Lime, Maroon, Navy, Olive, Purple, Red, Silver, Teal, White, and Yellow. Regardless of being supported by browsers, it is technically incorrect to use them. For this reason, you should specify hex colors in your projects.

Q. *"If the pixel color value falls outside of the Web-safe ones, doesn't the browser then dither the color to get the right color on the screen?"*

MURRAY S.

Web-safe colors are the ones that look about the same in all browers and operating systems when the monitor is set up to display 256 colors. That doesn't mean the browsers are limited to displaying those

> **NOTE**
>
> Bit depth can mean two different things: the number of colors in a graphic image and the number of colors a monitor can display. Eight bits is 256 colors (2 to the power 8); Sixteen bits, or *high color* is 65,000 colors (2 to the power 16). Twenty-four bits, or *true color* is 16.7 million colors (2 to the power 24).
>
> Some display card manufacturers call 24-bit color "hi color" and reserve "true color" for what they call 32-bit color, but this is not an accurate use of the definition.

colors. The bit depth setting of the monitor is more important in determining what a user will see on-screen.

Browsers map an area of non-Web-safe color to the nearest color the system is capable of displaying or dither it. What happens is unpredictable. At 8 bits, dithering is almost guaranteed, and at 16 bits, mapping is more likely. Which colors the non-Web-safe colors are mapped to depend on the browser/OS combination. Because the JPEG format uses 24-bit true color, we can use a JPEG gradient as an example.

The gradient between one Web-safe color and another is made up of many thousands of colors. In some areas along the gradient, the colors are Web-safe. In other areas, they are not. At 8-bit color depth the gradient will dither because the browser/OS combination is forced to reduce millions of colors to 256 (2.1). Which 256 depends on which browser and which OS. (And the monitor manufacturer, and the video display card, and the video display drivers. But let's not get too complicated.) It's safe to say that Internet Explorer's 256 colors are in agreement with Windows 256 colors but not necessarily with the Netscape or Macintosh 256 and vice versa.

A 16-bit color display is more likely to band the gradient or display a combination of banding and dithering (2.2). The banding is caused by mapping the colors in the graphic to the colors the system/browser combination is capable of displaying. The image will look different in Netscape than it does in Internet Explorer. Its appearance will also depend on your operating system, and whether you are using a Mac or a PC.

A monitor set to true color displays a smooth gradient with no noticeable dithering or banding in the browser (2.3). Our monitors are all set to true color. Regardless of which browser we're using, we don't see dithering or banding of JPEGs. However, compression artifacts (those crinkly little objects you see around hard edges in over-compressed JPEGs) are easier to see.

GIFs are different because GIFs are limited to 256 colors, making them unsuitable for gradients or photographic images. Exceptions are small graphical elements using Fireworks WebSnap Adaptive color and full dithering (2.4). This controlled kind of dithering tiles the pixels of the image in a way that softens the transition from one color to the other and creates the illusion of more than 256 colors (2.5). Another option, though at a slight file size penalty, is to add noise. By *noise* we mean seeding the image with randomly colored pixels. You can do this by using a texture or by using a filter that is specifically designed for this purpose.

Q. "So does the erratic behavior of 8-bit color screens with different browsers and operating systems mean we are stuck with using a limited palette forever?"

DANIEL S.

No. Current statistics (early 2001) show that about 78 percent of regular Internet users employ equipment that displays high color. The numbers for true color Internet users are rising steadily. As quickly as the Internet changes, we predict that within the next three or four years it will be possible to drop the restrictive, Web-safe palette altogether. If our site statistics showed that our visitors were viewing the site in true color, we'd feel safe using any color we wanted, knowing that our design would be rendered reasonably close to what we were seeing on our own machines, with no noticeable dithering or remapping. Nonetheless, there are other, very good reasons for limiting the number of colors you use on a Web page.

LIMITING COLORS CAN BE A GOOD THING

Q. "Almost all of the books that I've read on Web graphics recommend using not only Web-safe colors for GIFs, but also limiting the number of colors on the pages altogether. I can understand the need for using Web-safe colors, but why should I stick to only a few colors?"

JIM M.

The number one reason for limiting the number of colors in a GIF is to reduce the amount of time it takes for a browser to download, decompress, and display the image.

Remember that although a GIF or JPEG file stores the image information very efficiently, it must be decompressed for display on-screen, which takes up video memory. You should use the same color table for each GIF used on a Web page when specifying an Adaptive palette. Here's why.

The Adaptive palette options create a unique color table for each image by sampling the more commonly used colors in the image. Palette conflicts may be generated on Windows machines because Windows loads the palette before it loads the image. As each image in a sequence of images with different palettes is loaded, the screen's color table is updated, which causes flashing on machines with slow graphics adapters. The Fireworks Create Shared Palette command provides the ideal solution to this problem. You find this option under Commands➤Web➤Create Shared Palette (2.6).

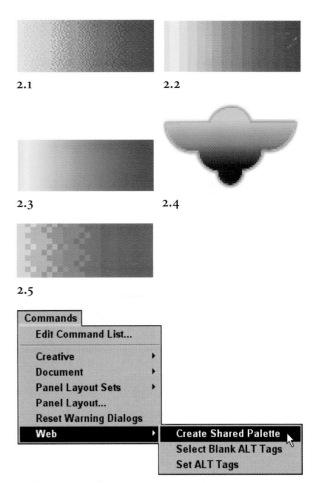

2.1

2.2

2.3

2.4

2.5

2.6

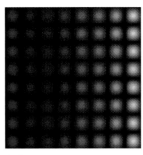

2.7

2.8

Perhaps the most important reason for limiting colors is not technical but psychological to create focus.

Whether we are conscious of it or not, our eyes gather in everything within our field of vision. An overload of color information confuses the eyes and can lead to eye fatigue (2.7). Strategic placement of color within the field of vision gives the eyes a place to rest and focuses the viewer's attention on important information (2.8).

COLOR SCHEMES FOR YOUR WEB SITE

Q. "I'm a programmer, not an artist, but the company I work for wants me to create a Web site. Can you suggest some good color combinations?"

JEREMY T.

In general, you can create a harmonious color combination by avoiding the shotgun effect of colors that are too different, like saturated blue and orange, or colors that are too similar. Like other aspects of visual communication, color affects the senses in different ways. An individual's reaction to a color, or combination of colors, relates to his or her particular associations. What pleases one may not please the other. Table 2.1 presents some color combinations that we find pleasing.

TABLE 2.1	**COLOR SCHEMES**

SWATCHES	HEX NUMBERS
Figure 2.9	Canvas #000000, red/violet #999933, gold #CC9900 Accents: light gold #FFCC00, white #FFFFFF
Figure 2.10	Canvas #003366, dark blue #666699, medium blue #9999CC Accents: pale blue #CCCCFF, red/violet #993366
Figure 2.11	Canvas #666600, dark green #999900, light green #CCCC00 Accents: yellow # FFFF99, red #990000
Figure 2.12	Canvas #006666, dark green # 009999, medium green #66CC99 Accents: pale green #99FF99, white #FFFFFF
Figure 2.13	Canvas #660033, violet # 993366, taupe: Web dither # FFCCCC, #99CCCC Accents: black #000000, white # FFFFFF
Figure 2.14	Canvas #003333 , #006666, tan #CC9966, peach: Web dither #FFCC99, #CCCCCC Accents: brown #996600, green #669966
Figure 2.15	Canvas #330033, dark green #336666, gray #CCCCCC Accents: violet #993366, medium green #669999
Figure 2.16	Canvas #006699, medium blue #6699CC, white #FFFFFF Accents: black #000000, light blue #99CCFF
Figure 2.17	Canvas #999966, light green #CCCC99, white #FFFFFF Accents: dark green #666600, darkest green #333300
Figure 2.18	Canvas #666666, pale gray #CCCCCC, white #FFFFFF Accents: gold #FFCC00, coral # FF6666
Figure 2.19	Canvas #FFFFFF, cocoa #996666, pink #FFCCCC

Continued

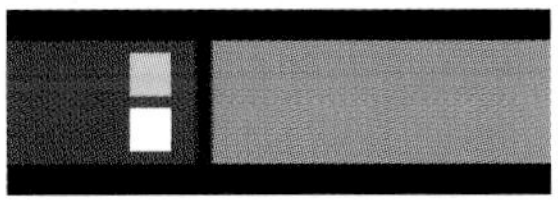

2.9

2.10

2.11

2.12

2.13

2.14

2.15

2.16

2.17

2.18

2.19

2.20

2.21

2.22

2.23

2.24

2.25

2.26

2.27

2.28

TABLE 2.1   **COLOR SCHEMES**
                       (*CONTINUED*)

SWATCHES	HEX NUMBERS
Figure 2.20	Accents: tan #CC9966, charcoal #333333 Canvas #FFCC66, pumpkin #FF9900, black #000000
Figure 2.21	Accents: tan #CC9966, blue #666699 Canvas #663333, mustard #FFCC00, green #999900
Figure 2.22	Accents: yellow #FFFF00, white #FFFFFF Canvas #333366, medium blue #336699, aqua #66CCCC
Figure 2.23	Accents: purple #663366, white #FFFFFF Canvas #666633, salmon #CC6666, cocoa #996666
Figure 2.24	Accents: white #FFFFFF, brown #330000 Background: Web dither #666699, #666666, salmon #CC9999, aqua #99CCCC
Figure 2.25	Accents: aquamarine #99FFFF, dark blue #003366 Canvas #330000, medium pink #CC9999, yellow #FFCC66
Figure 2.26	Accents: pale yellow #FFFFCC, mahogany #663333 Canvas #330066, purple #996699, white #FFFFFF
Figure 2.27	Accents: tan #CC9933, green #336633, blue #666699, violet #663366, red #990033, orange #CC6633 Canvas #000000, gray green #999966, yellow green #CCCC66
Figure 2.28	Accents: white #FFFFFF, hot pink #FF0099 Canvas #003333 dark red #999933, coral #FF6666 Accents: white #FFFFFF, red #CC0000

CREATING TRANSLUCENT IMAGES FOR LAYERING AND DHTML EFFECTS

Q. "I'm hoping to get the effect of a semi-transparency. I've tried a variety of ways to export PNG transparencies. When I import the file into DW [Dreamweaver], I either get the original background color or it is changed to a different one but not transparent! What gives?"

CORY.C

PNG transparency is unsupported by the current generation of browsers. For now, your only transparency option for an inline image is the GIF format. Use the following Fireworks technique to convert almost any kind of image to a translucent GIF.

STEP 1 To begin, you need to create a new black screen texture. Open a 2 × 2-pixel white canvas. Zoom in to 800%. Click the Pencil tool and choose black, 1 pixel, and hard edge for the stroke. Click with the Pencil tool at the top-left corner and on the bottom-right corner. Your enlarged texture image (2.29) should not have the border I've added to make the image easier to see on the page. Choose File ➢ Save As and save it directly to the textures folder of your Fireworks directory. My Fireworks directory is C:\Program Files\ Macromedia\Fireworks 4\Settings\Textures. Close Fireworks and restart it.

STEP 2 Open the image you want to make translucent and change its canvas color to white (Modify ➢ Canvas Color). We use the blue, tritone image (2.30) for our demonstration. Drag out a black rectangle on top of the image. Make it the same size as your image, so that it covers the background area, as well. Open the Fill panel (2.31) and while the black rectangle is still selected, apply your new Black Screen texture to it. Move the intensity slider to 100%. While the rectangle is still selected, open the Layers panel (2.32) and choose the Screen blend mode from the drop-down list. All the black pixels of the texture will disappear, partially revealing the image. At this point the white pixels of the texture are still there and all remains opaque (2.33).

> **NOTE**
>
> Ellipses treated in this manner may have jagged edges and will look best against a texture, another photographic image, or a color of similar intensity.

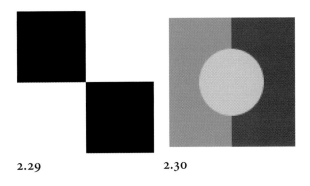

2.29   2.30

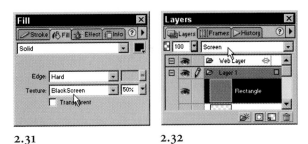

2.31   2.32

2.33

Open the Optimize panel. Select your optimization settings and then choose index transparency. The white background of the image drops out, taking the white pixels of the screen with it. A fine mesh of the image colors is left behind. (2.34) Your translucent image is now ready for Export. Translucent images can be layered over an image or the background of your Web page, allowing the color to bleed through (2.35).

REALIZING REALISTIC METALLIC GRADIENTS

Q. "Can you suggest how to create a realistic looking metallic gradient (maybe a steel one) using Fireworks? I just can't seem to get the right combination of colors"

MIKE P.

Getting the right combination of colors is easy if you know the Fireworks "open a photo of a metallic object and use the Color Picker in the Gradient Editor trick."

For this exercise you need to get an image of a metallic object with the right kind of finish into Fireworks. If you can't find the right type in your clip art collection, have a look through the rich variety of royalty-free images at photographer David Wourms' Web site (*www.wourms.com/freestuff/default.asp*).

STEP 1 As soon as you've found the right image (2.36), open it in Fireworks and make any necessary adjustments to the hue, saturation, lightness, darkness, and so on. Use the Magnifying tool to zoom in on an area of the image that has a smooth but short transition from a highlight to a shadow (2.37).

Open a new canvas and drag out a small, black rectangle. A 40 × 40-pixel-frame is adequate. Move the canvas with the rectangle next to the metallic image. Select the rectangle and open the Fill panel. Change the fill option of the rectangle to Linear and then click the Edit button.

STEP 2 When the Gradient Editor window opens, click between the existing color chips to add another chip. Click the new chip to change the cursor to the Color Picker. Use the Color Picker to select a pixel of the highlight color in the metallic image. The selected color will be added to your new chip. This chip will be the reference point for the other chips that you will add.

STEP 3 Add another color chip to the right of the highlight chip. Return to the photo with the Color Picker and select a pixel of color from the area immediately adjacent to the highlight. In the Gradient Editor, add a new color chip to the left of the highlight chip. This time, instead of selecting the color from the metallic image, use the Color Picker to copy the color from last chip you added by clicking on it.

Add two more chips, one to the left and one to the right of the two you added previously. Click the right chip and return to the photo. Select a color adjacent to the darkest region of the image. Copy the color from the right chip into the left one. Finally, change the colors of the chips on the far right and the far left — the two that were already there when you opened the Gradient Editor — by making a selection from the darkest region of the image.

STEP 4 Spread the color chips or rearrange them to style the gradient (2.38). To keep a permanent copy of your gradient, convert it to a Fireworks Style

2.34

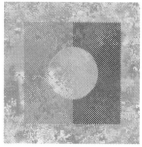

2.35

2.36

2.37

CLEARING UP ALPHA AND INDEX TRANSPARENCY ISSUES

Q. "I've created an image against a transparent background. When I export it, the transparent background becomes white. If I then make the background transparent again, either by selecting it with the Eyedropper tool or using Index transparency, all the white in the image disappears. What am I doing wrong?"

MARIAN J.

The background turns white when you export an image created against a transparent canvas because Fireworks assigns a white matte color to the image. The transparency information is still there. You can demonstrate this to yourself by changing the matte color a few times in Export Preview.

To a GIF, a transparent canvas means that one color has already been turned off. The GIF doesn't know which one it is because "transparent" isn't a color. When you use the Eyedropper tool to select the white matte in Export Preview, you are selecting white as the *second* transparent color. All white pixels in the image are then turned off, leaving holes wherever the white pixels were.

We thought it might be fun to present one solution to this problem as a kind of experiment.

STEP 1 Open a new document with a white canvas. Cover the left half of the canvas with a black rectangle. Drag out a brightly colored rectangle, roughly two-thirds the size of the canvas. Center it by choosing Commands➤Document➤Center in Document. Drag out a small white rectangle. Clone the white rectangle and change the clone to black. Arrange them so that the white rectangle is

2.38

in line with the black part of the background and the black rectangle is in line with the white part of the background (2.39).

STEP 2 Choose File➤Export Preview. Choose Index transparency from the drop-down menu. Both the white canvas and rectangle become transparent. Change the transparency setting to no transparency, and the white is returned to both (2.40). Open the drop-down menu and choose No Transparency.

Open the drop-down menu again and choose Alpha transparency. The white of the canvas disappears, leaving the white rectangle untouched (2.41).

The Fireworks PNG format uses the same RGB colors that are available to other formats but contains a fourth bit of information called Alpha. Alpha information is a way of associating variable amounts of transparency with the colors in the image. When you select the GIF format for an image but choose the Alpha transparency option, Fireworks assigns the Alpha channel information to the canvas (Index) color. The GIF, which doesn't recognize the Alpha channel information (but knows that something has

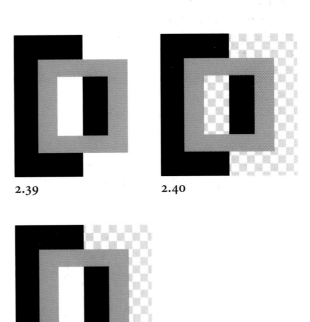

2.39   2.40

2.41

been turned off), leaves all the colors in the image turned on. This may not be the way the programmers intended us to use this feature, but it's darned useful.

ANTI-ALIASING WITH COLOR

Q. *"It seems that any time I try to rotate a line or a rectangle, the lines appear jagged (like a saw tooth edge). Horizontal and vertical lines appear smooth and this is the look I would like to achieve — a hard edged, smooth line. I have tried different levels of anti-aliasing but this does not make enough of a difference. I don't want to blur or feather the edge. What can I do?"*

TERESA H.

Let's have a look at what happens to angular lines when they are rendered in a matrix like the pixels of your screen. In a close-up of three, 1-pixel-wide black lines (2.42), Line A is perfectly straight because the pixels can be rendered down a single line of squares. Line C is perfectly straight because it can be rendered across a single line of squares. Line B, which is drawn at a 45° angle, must step diagonally from one line of squares to another along its full length.

Viewed at normal size, a line at a 45° angle looks relatively smooth because the steps are small and even.

It's when the angle is deeper or shallower than 45° that things get wonky (2.43). The lines must be rendered in combinations of steps and straight lines of two or more pixels. These uneven steps are more easily observed, even at small sizes (2.44).

Anti-aliasing helps by adding extra pixels to the line. These extra pixels are rendered in a color somewhere between the color of the line and the color of the canvas. However, if the contrast between the two colors is too great, the anti-aliasing cannot work as efficiently (2.45). One way to compensate for this is to feather the fill instead of anti-aliasing it. Use a feather setting of 1 and then tighten the feathering with the Sharpen filter by choosing Effect panel➤Sharpen➤Sharpen.

Another technique for softening the edge is to use a stroke. Choose Basic➤Soft or Soft Rounded and set the width of the strike to 2 or 3 pixels.

One rather arcane method that works well for simple shapes (and some text) is to draw the object at 36ppi on one canvas (File➤New, set the Resolution to 36ppi). Then copy and paste it into a second canvas set at the default resolution of 72ppi. When prompted, choose Resample. Click the resampled object to select it and then choose Modify➤Convert to Bitmap. Resize the object by typing a new height and width for it into the Info panel.

Lastly, when you need to use an object against more than one background color, you can create an illusion of smooth edges and avoid an anti-aliasing halo at the same time by choosing the right colors. The trick is to use colors for both the page background and objects that are in the same family. Here's how it's done.

> **STEP 1** Open a new, dark colored canvas. Add a white rectangle and rotate it about 10°. Even with anti-aliasing the rectangle still appears jagged (2.46).
> **STEP 2** With the rectangle still selected, click in the fill color box of the Tools panel box to activate the color selector. Touch it to the canvas. Open the Tool box color picker again and click the Color Wheel button at the top to open the system Color Picker. Note the position of the marker next the color gradient bar at the right side of the window. Choose a color a few shades darker or lighter and click it (2.47). The rectangle changes to the color you have selected.

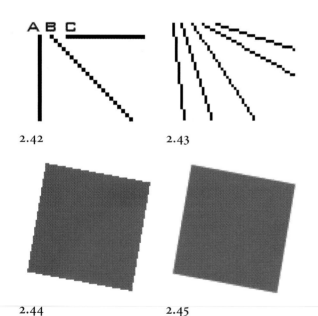

2.42   2.43

2.44   2.45

Because the colors are so closely related to the color of the canvas, the jagged edges of the rectangle seem to disappear (2.48). Other colors from the same part of the color wheel (in the case of our example, the rose/violet range) work just as well (2.49–2.51).

FILLING BITMAPS WITH COLOR

Q. *"I've scanned my client's logo and spent a lot of time changing the background color to white. Now he has decided he wants the color of the text changed from blue/green to blue/violet. I tried selecting it with the Magic Wand tool and filling it but the result isn't what I want. Is there a simpler way to do this?"*

JEFFERY K.

There is a much easier way to change the text color than selecting it with a Marquee tool and filling it.

2.46

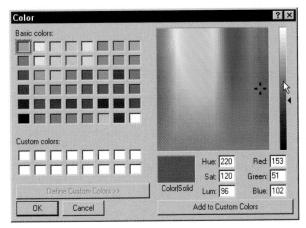

2.47

Select the logo (2.52) and open the Effect panel. Choose Adjust Color ➤ Color Fill. The default color for the Color Fill feature is bright red. Click the fill color box and change the color to blue/violet. (The color we have used is #666699.) Change the Blending Mode from Normal to Hue (2.53). All the green pixels of the logo are magically changed to blue (2.54).

2.48

2.49

2.50

2.51

2.52

2.53

2.54

2.55

2.56

2.57

PAINTING WITH LIGHT

This exercise binds together a number of Fireworks 4 techniques, provided by Eddie Traversa, with the singular goal of teaching you how to create resizable, abstract background images for your Web pages. Here's our man, Eddie . . .

STEP 1 Begin by opening a 1024×768-pixel, black canvas. Click the Layers panel Options pop-up menu and choose New Layer from the menu. Name (the arrow button at the top right of the Layers panel) the layer *background*. From the Layers menu, choose Single Layer Editing.

Locate the file called abstract 1.jpg on the CD and place it on the layer named *background*. The image needs to be positioned at the zero *x* and zero *y* coordinates. To move the image, open the Info panel, highlight the existing numbers, and type 0 for both.

STEP 2 Use the Opacity slider in the Layers panel to adjust the opacity of the background image to 60%. Use the Difference Blending Mode. If all you see is a black canvas, don't be alarmed. You are on the right track.

STEP 3 Create a second layer and name this layer *backgradient*. Drag out a rectangle that covers the whole canvas. Use the Transform tool to adjust the height of the rectangle to about 760 pixels and center it (Commands➢Document➢Center in Document). Open the Stroke panel and add a 5-pixel, soft pencil stroke to the rectangle and set the color to #827881. Switch to the Fill panel and enter #E1CFC2 for the fill color. Change the fill type from Solid to Linear. Notice that Fireworks blends the color of the solid fill with the color of the stroke to create the gradient. Return to the Layers panel and reduce the opacity of the rectangle to 23% (2.55).

STEP 4 Create another layer and name it *texture*. Drag out a 62×88-pixel rectangle on the new layer and set the color to #000033. Add a 75% Brushed texture to the rectangle (2.56). Duplicate the rectangle four times. Move the rectangles to random, but eye-catching positions on the canvas.

STEP 5 Insert a new layer and name it *hand_pose*. You'll be adding some elements that were designed in Curious Labs' Poser. These elements will form the focal point of the Abstract background image you are composing.

Let's work with the hand first (2.57). Locate the file named hand_pose.psd on the CD and import it to the canvas by choosing File➤Import. Browse to the file and click OK. Then choose Command➤Document➤Center in Document to center the hand image on the canvas. Change its opacity to 40% and select the Difference Blending Mode.

STEP 6 Now for our man. Locate the file named futureman_pose.psd on the CD and import it to the canvas. Use the Rectangle Marquee tool to slice the man in half from the abdomen down. Discard his bottom half (2.58). Yes, I know my vicious streak is showing!

Center the man's torso over the hand. Clone the torso (Edit➤Clone) and rotate the clone 180°. Align the top edge of the clone with the bottom edge of the original so that the two images appear as one (2.59). Change the opacity of the image to 25% and the Blending Mode to difference.

STEP 7 Now you can begin filling in the background with different elements.

Insert another layer and name it *bigcircle*. Drag out a 536 × 490-pixel ellipse. Add a 2-pixel basic, soft stroke. The stroke color is #827881. Change the fill color to #FFEBEA. Choose Linear for the fill type (2.60).

Return to the Layers panel and adjust the opacity of the ellipse to 15%. Duplicate the ellipse (Edit ➤ Duplicate) and resize it to about 214 × 184 pixels. Clone the resized duplicate and move one copy of the small ellipse to the top left of the big rectangle you created in step 3 (background). Move the second copy to the bottom-right corner of the rectangle (2.61).

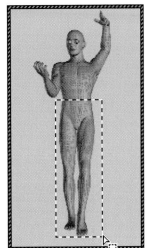

2.59

2.58

2.60

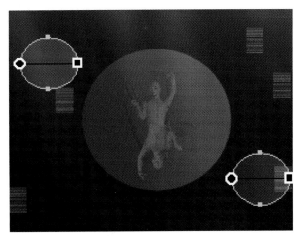

2.61

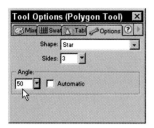

2.62

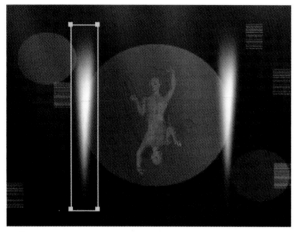

2.63

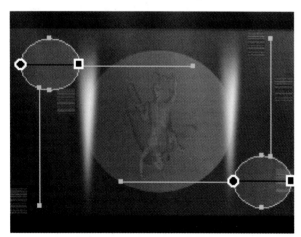

2.64

STEP 8 To make the background more interesting, you can add some light sources to it. Insert or add a new layer and name it *lightsources*. This next part is fun!

Activate the Polygon tool. In the Tools Options window, select the Star shape and change the number of sides to 3 and the angle to 50. Uncheck automatic (2.62). Drag out a 70 × 61-pixel triangle. (This may not make a lot of sense if you compare it to the light sources in the original background image, but bear with me for a few more steps.)

STEP 9 With the triangle still selected, open the Effect panel and choose the Gaussian blur filter from the Blur menu. Apply a blur radius of 8.3. You can play around with the setting. Generally, somewhere between 8-10 gives a good result. Select the Transform tool and stretch your triangle vertically to the edges of the *backgradient* rectangle. The triangle should appear to fade in from the top and bottom (2.63).

STEP 10 Some simple stuff now. Add another layer and name it *littlelines*. Draw a horizontal line, 410 pixels wide and 4 pixels high. Move it to the 9:00 position of the ellipse at the bottom-right corner. Duplicate the line and choose Modify➤ Transform ➤90 degrees CW. Move it just right of the 12:00 position of the same ellipse.

Duplicate both lines and move the horizontal duplicate to the 3:00 postion of the small ellipse at the top left. Move the vertical duplicate to just left of the 6:00 position. All four lines should extend from the edges of the ellipses toward the center of the screen (2.64).

STEP 11 The next step is to create some more rectangles. Create a new layer and name it *rectangles*. Activate the Rectangle tool and drag out a 650 × 250-pixel rectangle. Choose no fill. The stroke options are as follows: Basic➤Soft Line. Set the size to 2. The stroke color is #827881. Change the opacity of the line to 45%.

Position the rectangle off-center toward the left of canvas and then duplicate it. Duplicate it once more. This time position the rectangle closer to the top-right corner and duplicate it again. Your background is starting to take on some form.

STEP 12 Now we are going to add more rectangles to pad the background out further and provide some contrast. Create a new layer named *moresquares*. Add five rectangles of various sizes and scatter them around to interesting positions. Here size doesn't matter! The important settings are for stroke. Choose Basic ➤ Soft line and 2 pixels. The stroke color is #827881. For fill use #FFEBEA. Change the opacity to 20% (2.65).

STEP 13 What's needed now is some contrasting color, so let's add some. Create a new layer and name it *dashofcolor*.

Create 3 rectangles. The first one, which is 88 pixels wide, extends from the top to the bottom of the backgradient rectangle. The second one is about 350 pixels down from the top of the canvas. It is 26 pixels high, but extends the full width of the canvas. The third rectangle is placed at y-92 and x-76, and it is 78 pixels wide and 603 pixels high. The rectangles have no stroke. For fill color, use #660000. Reduce the opacity of the three rectangles to 40%. Use the Difference Blending Mode (2.66).

STEP 14 Are you still with me? Let's do text. Create a new layer named *textfill*. A sans-serif font, such as Bookman Old Style, looks good for this background. Set the font size at 45 and the color to #FFFFFF (white). Type the words **G O B E Y O N D** in all caps, adding a space between each letter and a couple extra between words. Position it at the top-left corner of the canvas. Set its opacity to 42% and use the Difference Blending Mode to create a silvery effect. Repeat the process for the word **T r a n s c e n d**. This time position it in the bottom-right corner of the canvas. The words should now be diagonal to each other (2.67).

Using the same font you used for the words, type out numbers 1-15, leaving a space between each number. Duplicate the numbers 10 to 15 times and spread them all over the backgradient rectangle. Apply the same Opacity and Blending Mode settings.

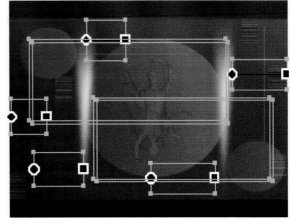

2.65

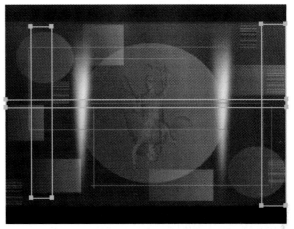

2.66

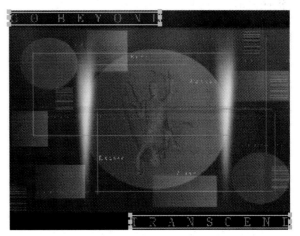

2.67

2.68

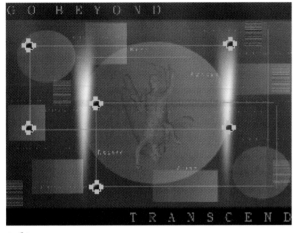

2.69

Type four new words: Excel, Exceed, Arise, and Awaken. Each should be typed separately, so they are contained within their own bounding boxes. Continue using #FFFFFF for the color. The opacity should be 63%. Use the Difference Blending Mode. Space the four words out inside the largest ellipse.

STEP 15 Just a few more final touches to wrap things up.

Create another layer and name it *morecircles*. Add a 36 × 32-pixel ellipse. Give it a fill color of #000033. No stroke. Open the Effect panel and choose Shadow and Glow➤Inner Glow. Leave the width setting of the glow at the default. Change the color from black to white (2.68).

Return to the Layers panel and change the opacity of the ellipse to 63%. Position it over the top-left corner of the double rectangle at the upper left of the canvas. Clone the ellipse and position the clone at the top-right corner of the same rectangle. Repeat for the other corners.

To add an element of the unexpected, repeat the process on the left side of the lower, right double rectangle (2.69).

ARTIST:

Eddie Traversa. Melbourne, Australia. Grad.Dip.App.Psychology, MA (counseling), PhD in progress. Currently working with Jeff Rouyer on a book called *Dynamic XHTML: The Developers Guide.*

WORK HISTORY:

A complete disaster because of my psychological issues with authority. I wonder why I keep fighting with my supervisor? I'm hoping to resolve this constant battle with my supervisor through the supreme spiritual encounter.

CONNECTIVITY:

Depends on whether or not my ISP lets me connect.

SYSTEM:

What system! My system is not to have one, as peeking into my office will quickly show you. If you mean my Jim Dandy machine, a Pentium 111 600 Matrox Millennium G400 dual head card 32 megs. Twin Hard drives, 18 gigabyte and a 9 gigabyte 128 megs of ram. I need more!! Creative Labs Sound Card 56k modem.

STEP 16 Next we'll add a checkered pattern beside the header. Add a new layer called *checks*. Drag out a 36 × 30-pixel rectangle. Set the stroke color to #827881, but choose no stroke. Set the fill color to #FFFFFF; then choose a linear gradient as fill type. Set the rectangle's opacity to 50%. Duplicate or clone the rectangle and arrange the copies into a checkerboard pattern (2.70).

STEP 17 Phew! Last step. Add a new layer and name it *secondback*. Locate the file named *abstract8* on the CD and import it into the new layer. Change its opacity to 30% and use the Difference Blending Mode (2.71). This last step adds some subtle, additional color.

Included in the CD-ROM is a link to Eddie's Web site that will resize your background to fit any browser window. All that's left to do now is to sit back and think up that next killer background.

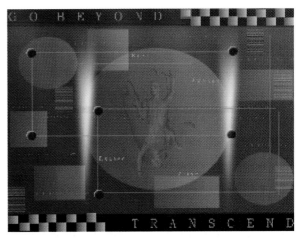

2.70

2.71

PERIPHERALS:

I have a little dog named God.

FAVORITE PLEASURE:

It's a toss up between watching my football team and sex. Hmmm, footy team I think.

type 3

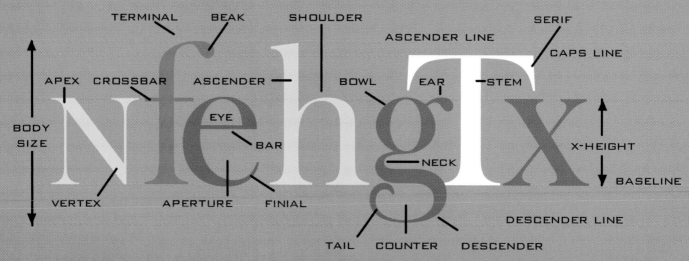

TERMINAL   BEAK   SHOULDER   SERIF

ASCENDER LINE

CAPS LINE

APEX   CROSSBAR   ASCENDER   BOWL   EAR   STEM

BODY   EYE

SIZE   BAR   X-HEIGHT

NECK

BASELINE

VERTEX   APERTURE   FINIAL   DESCENDER LINE

TAIL   COUNTER   DESCENDER

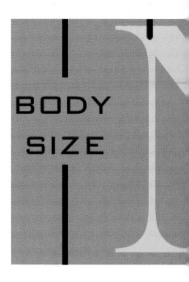

CHAPTER 3
MANIPULATING TYPEFACES IN FIREWORKS

Like print, the Web is fundamentally a visual medium, a great vehicle for delivering a combination of text and graphics. Yet the Web has striking limitations compared to print, especially in its ability to display typefaces, which are restricted to those installed on the average viewer's computer.

Text as art form, that is, unconstrained by the limitations of computer display fonts is still possible for Web pages. But to use it with any degree of flair, the Web designer must fall back on graphic text. With a powerful imaging tool like Fireworks, it is possible to create graphic texts — for headings and titles, and as design elements in their own right — that rival the best of the printed media. The tutorials in this chapter will show you how some of these effects can be achieved.

Our hope is that, armed with these techniques, you can explore an ever-wider range of possibilities. You, our fellow Web designers, are participating in the birth of a new art form. That's a very exciting place to be!

"Legend has it that one Johannes Faust broke into master Laurens Janszoon Koster's shop on Christmas Eve of 1441, stole all of his types and equipment, fled to Amsterdam, then on to Cologne and, finally, to Mainz, where a stranger named Johann Gutenberg soon invented movable type."

THE CURSE OF KOSTER

> **NOTE**
>
> Width settings for bevels, strokes, and shadows for the effects in this chapter are relative to the point size of the characters. If you use larger or smaller font sizes, you may need to adjust the settings to compensate for the difference.

POLISHING YOUR TEXT

Q. *"For some reason, no matter what I do, my text comes out looking kinda blocky or fuzzy. What can I do to make it look better?"*

GIL. D.

Screen graphics are measured in *pixels per inch* (ppi), with each individual pixel a dot of color in a grid, like the squares on a sheet of graph paper. The number of dots per inch is called the *resolution.* Changing the resolution is like zooming in or out from the graph paper.

In order to draw a curve or angle on the screen, your computer must lay the pixels out in stair-step fashion. At the higher resolutions used for print, the grid is small. A smaller grid means that more pixels can be squeezed onto the canvas, so the curves and angles of the fonts we use look smooth. At low resolutions, like the 72 ppi used for Web graphics, the pixels are larger and may cause the curve of a letter to become blocky or jagged. Fireworks uses anti-aliasing to overcome this problem.

Anti-aliasing smoothes jagged edges by subtly blending their color into the color of the background. Although doing so does blur the edge slightly, it makes the text more readable. The exceptions are Mini fonts, which should not be anti-aliased or auto-kerned.

A font itself can also cause jaggedness. Many of the fonts installed on our machines by word processing and illustration programs were designed for use at high resolutions. If the fonts were not carefully crafted, minor irregularities in the fonts were smoothed out by the laying on of hundreds (or even thousands) of dots of ink during the printing process. The inverse is true at low resolutions, where irregularities are emphasized, and delicate serifs, bars, and finials fade to ugly shadows when anti-aliased.

The best fonts for Web work are evenly weighted, with strong horizontal or vertical stress and high x-heights. Examples are Georgia, which is far easier to read on the screen than Times New Roman, and our favorite sans serif font, Akzidenz Grotesk Extended. You should also consider the quality of the font design. A well-hinted, skillfully designed font from a reputable house will save you endless aggravation and pay for itself in no time. Some good places to look for high quality fonts, including typefaces designed specifically for Web work, are

> Adobe Type Library — *www.adobe.com/type/main.html*
> Bitstream — *www.bitstream.com/*
> AGFA Monotype — *www.agfamonotype.com/*
> URW++ — *www.urwpp.de/english/home.html*
> Linotype — *www.linotypelibrary.com/*
> P22 Type Foundry — *www.p22.com/*
> The Font Bureau — *www.fontbureau.com/cgi-bin/index.cgi*

PostScript fonts seem to generate smoother outlines and scale better in Fireworks than their TrueType equivalents. Fonts used for graphic text, whether True Type or Post Script, benefit from increased spacing between the characters (called *tracking*). Tracking is not to be confused with *kerning,* which affects only two characters.

Fonts rarely scale well below 12 pixels. If you need a small typeface, use one that was designed that way instead of scaling down an existing font. There are some beautiful mini typefaces out there created by Web developers for use at sizes as small as 7 or 8 pixels. Jason Kottke's Silkscreen is a fine example of a mini-font (see *www.kottke.org*). Another useful one is Sevenet 7 (Mini 7 for the Mac), which you'll find at Joe Gillespie's marvelous site, Web Page Design for Designers (*www.wpdfd.com*). Thorsten Schraut, of *www.hi-score.de*, has created a baker's dozen of these tiny screen fonts.

Scaling fonts up to large sizes can cause as many distortions as scaling them down. Sometimes, you'll need to use a curvy font at a large size, and even the strongest anti-alias setting doesn't smooth it out. You can overcome this by applying a Gaussian blur. Use a setting of 0.4 to 0.7 (3.1).

Next, use the sharpen filter, also found in the Effect panel. I know that it sounds like you are simply undoing the blur, but it doesn't have that result. The difference after using this technique is impressive; and because it has all been done with Fireworks Live Effects, the text is still fully editable.

Another trick is to anti-alias text optically by placing it against a background color in the same family as the color you've given to the text. Finally, save plain text headers in GIF format anti-aliased to the color of your page. Texts with gradient effects are usually best saved in JPEG format.

CREATING METALLIC TEXT

Q. *"How do I create nice metallic effects for text in FW? I am fairly experienced but have never learned how to do this in any of my graphics programs. Thanks!"*

JAMEY

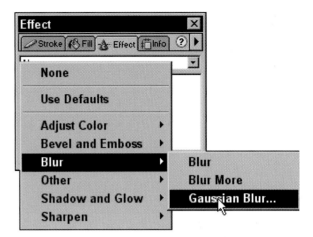

3.1

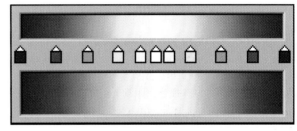

3.2

The Fireworks gradient editor and Live Effects make doing this a snap. Try the following:

STEP 1 Create the gradient by dragging out a rectangle and opening the Fill panel. Choose Linear from the drop-down list and click the Edit button. Moving from left to center, add the following colors: #5C2E03. #835603, #CBA859, #FFE681, #FFFFCC, #FFFFFF. Mirror the colors from the center to the right (3.2).

3.3

3.4

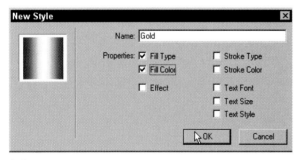

3.5

STEP 2 Converting the gradient to a Fireworks style is an easy way to keep it available for one-click application to text or vector shapes. With the gradient rectangle still selected, click the small arrow button at the top right of the Styles panel (3.3). Choose New Style from the pop-up menu (3.4). Give the style a name and check off the properties that you want preserved. Click OK (3.5).

STEP 3 The bold version of a serif face like Bengiat is perfect for this effect. Other good choices are Broadway, Normande, and Cooper Black. After you've found the right one for your project, type the text, and while it is still selected, click on the new gold style to apply it (3.6).

STEP 4 To position the gradient, move your cursor over the gradient control bar until you see the rotate symbol. Click and drag to rotate the gradient counterclockwise 90°. Place your cursor on the pivot point (the round handle) of the rotation bar and move the highlight of the gradient to about one third from the top of the text (3.7).

STEP 5 Apply the effects by opening the Effect panel and choosing Shadow and Glow➤Inner Glow (3.8). The color is #996600, width = 2, the opacity is 65%, and the softness is 4. Choose Brightness/Contrast from the Adjust Color menu and move the contrast slider to 18.

STEP 6 To add the finishing touches, open the Stroke panel and add a white, Basic, Soft Rounded stroke. The tip size should be 2. To center the stroke on path, where it needs to be for this effect, open the Object panel and click the middle stroke placement button (3.9). Add a light drop shadow if desired and export as a JPEG (3.10).

The set of textures that comes bundled with Fireworks can be used to add dozens of interesting surface effects to your gold text. A 50% Parchment texture, for example, adds a subtly aged finish. Horizontal Line texture 3 produces a ribbed finish. Here is the gold text with the addition of a 50% Metal texture (3.11). To simulate an acid-washed finish, use a 50% Vein texture (3.12).

EMBOSSING METALLIC TEXTS

Q. *"I've been attempting to draw sort of beveled 3-D metallic text. Does anyone know if there's an easy way to do this? Thanks in advance for any info."*

SCOTT M.

3.6

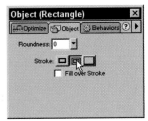

3.7

Yes, you can do embossed styles in Fireworks. The embossed text styles we are going to introduce in this exercise produce an almost three-dimensional effect and work nicely with lighter typefaces, including many brush and pen styles. Let's begin with a gold version.

3.8

3.9

STEP 1 Type out the text and add the gold style from the last exercise. Rotate the gradient counter-clockwise about 30° (3.13).

STEP 2 Open the Effect panel and add an Outer Bevel. The bevel style is Flat, width = 4 pixels, contrast = 100%, softness = 5, angle = 316°, style = Inset. Use a drop shadow to finish the effect. I've reduced the width of the shadow from the default 7 pixels to 4, changed the opacity of the shadow to 65%, and used a softness setting of 4 and an angle of 316° (3.14).

3.10

3.11

3.12

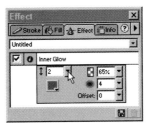

3.13

COPPER

Copper is an interesting metal to create a gradient for because its reddish-brown color is subject to dramatic alterations from natural aging and exposure to the elements. Think of the differences in color between a new copper penny, an old teakettle, or a garden sculpture weathered to green. The colors we'll use for our copper gradient are #531400, #804100, #FFCC99, and #FFFFFF (3.15). Add an Outer Bevel. Style = Flat, width 4 pixels, contrast = 100%, softness = 5, angle = 316°, style = Inset (3.16).

3.15

PEWTER

A pewter effect doesn't require blending many colors, and the temptation is to use a simple grayscale gradient. However, the natural aging of pewter objects often adds colors to the metal surface that are not

3.16

3.17

3.18

3.19

3.20

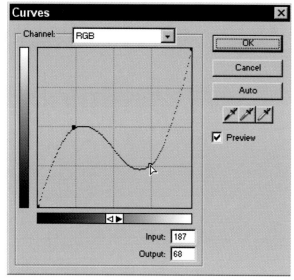

3.21

3.22

found in newly manufactured items of the same type. Your pewter text will look more realistic if you add a touch of blue to the grayscale gradient highlight, and brown to the dark end of the gradient to simulate a patina.

STEP 1 Drag out a rectangle and then open the Fill panel. Choose Linear from the drop-down list and click on the Edit button. Add the following colors from left to center: #000000, #333300, #F2F2FF, and #FFFFFF (3.17). Mirror the colors from the center to the right. Save as a style.

STEP 2 Add the style to the text. In addition to rotating the gradient, you might want to lengthen it to stretch the highlight over a larger area (3.18). With the text still selected, add an Outer Bevel. The settings are Flat, 4-pixel width, 100% contrast, softness of 4, angle of 316°. The drop shadow is 3 pixels at 50% opacity. Softness = 3. Angle = 316°.

STEP 3 Next, add an Inner Glow to refine the outline of the text. Choose Effects➤Shadow and Glow➤Inner Glow. The color is #CCCCCC. The Halo Offset is 3. Move the opacity slider to 90% and the softness slider to 4. Export as a JPEG (3.19).

BRIGHT SILVER

Very bright silver and chrome effects are more difficult to produce at low resolutions. The contrast in the gradient needs to be high and carefully positioned. Texts with bright metal effects also need to be drawn against a dark background, which forces severe limitations on their usefulness.

STEP 1 Type the text (the font we've used is Vivante) against a dark background and apply the pewter gradient from the last exercise. Move the pivot point of the rotation bar to the top of the text; then use the square handle to rotate the gradient clockwise 90° (3.20).

STEP 2 Open the Effect panel and choose Adjust Color➤Curves. Grab the diagonal line with your cursor and make the adjustments you see in Figure (3.21).

STEP 3 Choose Modify➤Convert to Bitmap. Return to the Effects panel and choose Sharpen➤ Unsharp Mask. Adjust the sharpen amount to 59, the pixel radius to 1.6, and the threshold to between 20 and 25. Add a drop shadow if desired and export as a JPEG (3.22).

DRAWING GEL TEXTS

Q. "So how about gel text. Is there an easy way to do this in Fireworks? That would be cool."

FERIDOON M.

3.23

3.24

The font for a gel text needs to be soft and rounded. Arial Rounded Bold with a little horizontal scaling works well. Other interesting choices are Allegro and Comic Sans. An iridescent blue, like Tiffany glass, would be an appropriate color choice for this effect.

STEP 1 We'll need to create a new gradient and add it to the Styles panel, as described earlier in Creating Metallic Text. The colors, from left to right, are #94B5DE, #BEE7FF, #FFFFFF, #D3FFFF, #94B5DE, #4479B6, and # 000066 (3.23).

STEP 2 Type your text and add the Style you created from the gradient. Because the Style is based on a Linear gradient, the text will have a gradient rotation bar attached to it. Move your cursor over the gradient rotation bar. When the cursor changes a to a rotation symbol, click and drag the bar to rotate the gradient 90° clockwise. This should move the gradient highlight to within one-quarter of the top of the text. Drag the square handle of the rotation bar until the dark edge of the gradient meets the bottom edge of the text. Open the Fill panel and change the edge of the fill from the default Anti-Alias to Feather, 2 pixels (3.24).

STEP 3 Add the effects by opening the Object panel and clicking on the middle of the three buttons to place the stroke over the path. Add a white stroke: Basic➤Soft Rounded➤2 or 3 pixels. From the Effect panel, choose Shadow and Glow➤Inner Glow. Color = #000066, width 2 (or 3, depending on the size of your text), contrast 100%, softness 4. On the Effect panel, choose Adjust Color➤Brightness/Contrast. Increase the contrast to around 18. We're almost there.

STEP 4 Add a soft blue drop shadow: 4 pixels, color #666699, opacity 65%, softness 4, angle 316 (3.25). If you'd like the gel text to appear softer or more liquid, return to the Object panel and change the stroke placement to outside the path (third button from the left) (3.26).

3.25

3.26

3.27

3.28

3.29

3.30

CHISELING TEXT

Q. "I'd like to create an image of my company name and logo chiseled into stone. I tried doing so with various fonts, but I am not getting the look I am after. I really would like to see the letters embedded into the surface. Can you help with this?"

MARC F.

Use a serif font to get the look you're after. It is said that serifs (3.27) originated with the brush lines ancient Roman stone carvers painted on the surface of the stone before chiseling it. Another theory has it that serifs originated with wood carvers, who use them to prevent chipping at the ends of their gouges. Regardless of how serifs actually came about, a serif font will produce a more realistic result in this exercise. Some fonts that work well are Albertus, Fritz Quadrata, Trajan, Garamond, and Americana.

STEP 1 A chiseled effect requires three layers of text. The shadow layer: Type the name in black (3.28). Drag out a gray rectangle (#999999) and add a 50% Metal texture to it.

STEP 2 The beveled layer: The layer that will be used on top is next. To create it, clone the black text and move the clone one pixel down and one pixel to the right with the arrow keys. While the text is still selected, zoom in on the image and use the Eyedropper tool to select a midrange color from the background. Open the Effect panel. Choose Shadow and Glow ➤ Inner Shadow. Adjust the amount to 2 or 3 pixels, depending on the size of the text. As you can see, the shadow alone creates some depth (3.29).

STEP 3 The highlight layer: Clone the text to which you have just applied the shadow. Move it one pixel down and one to the right. Change its color to white or very pale gray. Return to the Effect panel and remove the shadow (which the program remembers from the last layer) by unchecking the box next to the effect name (3.30).

STEP 4 Positioning the highlight: While the highlight layer is still selected, choose Modify➤Arrange➤Send Backward. The barely discernible offsetting of the light and dark copies of the text are enough create a three-dimensional effect (3.31). Oddly, while most people see this text as an innie, some people see it as an outie.

DISTRESSING TEXT

Q. *"How do I make distressed text? You know, the kind that looks abraded or weathered away?"*

SCOTT F.

This effect is fun because it begins with the text the same color as the background it is drawn against (3.32). The word you can't see is Weird in Zurich Black Extended.

STEP 1 Cover the text with a black rectangle. With the rectangle still selected, open the Fill panel and choose the Onyx texture from the drop-down list. Move the intensity slider to 100% (3.33).

STEP 2 Choose Edit➤Select All; then choose Modify➤Mask➤Group as Mask. The Onyx texture seems to disappear. Fireworks knows that it's there, however. You'll know this stage has been completed successfully when the blue star-shaped adjustment handle appears (3.34).

STEP 3 Magic time! Open the Effect panel and choose inner bevel, Flat, 100% contrast, 3 for softness, and an angle of 135°. Choose Edit➤Select All; then choose Modify➤Convert to Bitmap. Return to the Effect panel and choose Adjust Color➤Brightness/Contrast. Move the brightness slider to 45 and the contrast slider to 100%. At this point, you may change the canvas color (3.35).

EMULATING NATURAL MEDIA

Q. *"My client wants something that looks like watercolor or pastel text. How about something more subtle and organic looking? Is it possible to create something that looks like Sumi-e in Fireworks?"*

SUZE B.

These effects are handsome, yet simple to do. They take advantage of the ability to manipulate the Fireworks default set of fill patterns by shrinking or stretching them, changing their colors, and layering them with extra texture. The number of variations possible is limited only by the stretch of your imagination.

3.31

3.32

3.33

3.34

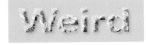

3.35

3.36

3.37

3.38

3.39

Pastel

3.40

STEP 1 Type some text. The font we've used for this example is Broadway. The fill color is # FF6633. The 1-pixel, Soft Rounded stroke is the same color as the fill (3.36).

STEP 2 While the text is still selected, open the Fill panel and change the Edge setting from the default Anti-Alias to Feather (3.37).

This simple effect (3.38) is the basis of a whole series of effects that emulate natural media.

Here is a method of creating an impromptu texture that we can use to add a hand-sketched appearance to the previous exercise. Varying the size, spacing, and number of tips will create anything from pencil-thin to heavy brushstroke effects.

STEP 1 Draw a vertical line and choose Random➤Dots from the list of stroke types in the Stroke panel. The stroke size should be 1 and the color should be black. Click on the button at the top right of the Stroke panel and select Edit Stroke from the pop-up menu. Change the Spacing to 70% and the number of Tips to 1. Convert the stroke to a bitmap (Modify➤Convert to Bitmap). Activate the Transform tool by clicking on it and dragging right to stretch the bitmap across the canvas (3.39).

STEP 2 Make a clone of the text (Edit➤Clone) and move it aside. Change the fill edge of the clone from feather to anti-alias. Rotate the texture counterclockwise about 40º and move it on top of the clone. Shift + select both the text and texture and choose Modify➤Mask➤Group as Mask. Move the now-textured clone on top of the original text but slightly out of register (so the pencil or chalk strokes look like they've been drawn outside the lines) (3.40).

To try a variation that evokes the texture of the paper the text might be painted on, use the following steps:

STEP 1 Type a word and fill it with a medium gray color, like #666666. Feather the fill color by four pixels and add a two pixel wide, Basic➤Soft Rounded stroke. Make the color of the stroke #333333.

STEP 2 Return to the Fill panel and choose the Scratch texture from the Fill panel Texture menu. Apply the Scratch texture to the fill of the text at 50% intensity.

To emulate the look of the stroke having been drawn on wet paper, switch to the Stroke panel and choose the Leaves texture from the Texture menu of the Stroke panel. Set the intensity of the Leaves texture to 100% to blot out large sections of the stroke.

Literally hundreds of variations on Natural Media styles are made possible by changing the color of the fill, changing the color and style of the stroke, using different pattern and texture combinations, and altering the amount of feathering.

DRIPPING TEXT

Q. *"How can I give a sludgy-looking text the effect of sludge dripping from it?"*

JOHN B.

Hmm. We're not sure what sludge looks like, but we'll give it a shot. For this exercise, we've chosen a funky-looking typeface called Pilot. Other fonts that would work well are Arial Rounded Bold, Bauhaus Heavy, Emblem, and Ray Larabie's Butterbelly. Butterbelly is the name of the font, of course, not a reference to Ray's physique :).

STEP 1 Type your text. Use no fill but add an Unnatural stroke. Really, that's what it's called! The style is Fluid Splatter, the color is #666666, tip size is 17, and the stroke edge softness is 100%. The text will be almost obscured by the splatter. Choose Modify➤Convert to Bitmap (3.41).

STEP 2 Type the text again, but this time, add a white fill. Move the new text to the center of the splatter bitmap. Select the spatter bitmap, clone it, and cut it to the Clipboard by choosing File➤Cut. Select the text and choose Edit➤Paste Inside. While the text is still selected, add a 1-pixel stroke. Add a drop shadow to lift the text away from the remaining splatter bitmap. If necessary, increase the brightness of the text (3.42).

ON THE CD-ROM

We've turned a few interesting variations on our basic Natural Media style into Fireworks Styles. You'll find pictures and a ZIP file of these on the CD-ROM at the back of the book.

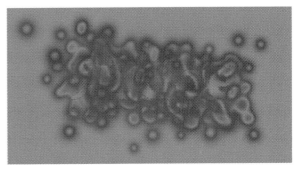

3.41

3.42

GLOWING TEXT

Q. *"I have been trying to come up with a neon-type effect in Fireworks. There doesn't appear to be a built-in style to achieve this look. Wondered if anybody has had the same challenge. I'd appreciate knowing of any way."*

JIM S.

The colors of neon lights are always very bright. The more contrast there is between your background and the text, the more the effect will look like neon. With neon lights, there is a glow produced by the reflection of the lamps off the surface they are plugged into. That glow is one of the effects we'll emulate. In addition, because neon lights are made of hand-bent tubes of glass with no sharp angles, you'll want to choose a font that replicates that rounded-edge characteristic. So the font you choose is as important to the final effect as the graphic technique. Some fonts that work well are Enviro, Freestyle Script, Kaufmann, and Ray Larabie's Neuropol.

STEP 1 Open a new document window with a black canvas. Type the text. I've used Neuropol at 60 pixels and stretched horizontally to 123%. Fill = 0, Color #990099, Stroke = Basic Soft Rounded, width = 6, placement is outside the path. The dark purple color will serve as a base for the glow (3.43).

STEP 2 Clone the first layer and change the color of the clone to #FF33FF. Reduce the stroke width to 2. Move the second layer on top of the first, slightly off register to the left (3.44).

STEP 3 Clone the second layer and add a glow. Choose Width = 2 pixels, opacity = 65%, softness = 12. We've used the default red color (3.45).

STEP 4 Move the new layer on top of the last one, but off center to the right by a pixel or two. Offsetting the middle and top layers will give the tube shapes more depth and a glassy look. Fine-tune the alignment of the three layers.

STEP 5 Draw some tiny I-beam-shaped black patches to represent the places where the ends of the tubes plug into . . . whatever they plug into (3.46). I cheated and used the capital I from a font called Jupiter. A hint of a brick wall behind your sign might be an interesting addition.

SHINING LEATHER TEXT

Q. *"How can I simulate the slick, black surface of patent leather?"*

KAREN D.

Whatever happened to patent leather anyway? The earliest known patent for this kind of leather dates back to the 18th century. It was made of horsehide that had been given a flexible, lustrous film by successive coats of pigmented lacquer in a base of boiled linseed oil. Modern patent leather finishes are made of pigments in a base of plasticized nitrocellulose or synthetic resin, making them more supple than the antique type. They also look like plastic, for which the following effects can double.

STEP 1 Type some text. Deutsch Gothic is an interesting choice of faces for this exercise. Add a 1-pixel, Soft Rounded stroke to smooth the outline. The stroke goes outside the path.

STEP 2 In the Effect panel, choose Bevel and Emboss➢Inner Bevel. Choose the Ring Bevel edge shape, set the width of the bevel to 3, the contrast to 100%, the softness to 3, and the angle to 309°.

STEP 3 To make the highlights look really shiny, we'll need to increase the contrast in the bevel more than the Inner Bevel preset effect allows. Still in the Effect panel, choose Adjust Color➢Brightness/Contrast. Increase the contrast to about 50. Add a soft drop shadow (3.47).

3.43   3.44

3.45   3.46

Modern patent leather is available in colors other than black and white. We've used #CC3300 (bright red) and a font called Jazz for a second example (3.48).

HALFTONING, COMIC BOOK STYLE

Q. *"How can I create text with a halftone screen on the edges like you see in old comic books?"*

JEREMY S.

We'll need to create a custom texture to generate the appearance of a halftone screen. This is fun to do in Fireworks, and your new creation can be exported from the program directly into the Textures folder of the Fireworks directory.

STEP 1 Open a white canvas, 4 x 4 pixels. Zoom in to 800% so you can see what you are doing; then drag out two rectangles on a diagonal line (3.49). Give the texture a name and save it to the Fireworks 4 Textures folder. (On my machine, the location is C:\Program Files\Macromedia\Fireworks4\Configuration\Textures.)

STEP 2 Type the text. Good font choices are Comic Sans, Dom Bold, Dom Diagonal, or Cooper Black. We've use Dom Diagonal for our example. Add a 3-pixel, Soft Rounded stroke. Open the Object panel and click on the first of the three buttons to move the stroke inside the path. Return to the Stroke panel and add your new texture to the stroke. Set it to 100% (3.50).

STEP 3 Open the Effect panel and choose Bevel and Emboss➢Outer Bevel. Change the color from the default red to black. Reduce the width to 1 or 2 pixels and move the contrast slider to 0%. Just for the fun of it, we've skewed and rotated the resulting image (3.51).

EXPERIMENTING WITH NEW PROCEDURES

Q. *"I guess this is off topic, but how do you come up with all of these special effects?"*

RICHIE B.

Confession time. Roughly half of the new effects we come up with are the result of trying to do an entirely different effect. For example, the glittery effect in the following exercise came about as the result of looking for a chunky metal effect to include as a variation on the gold text at the beginning of this chapter. It wasn't quite what we wanted (and we still haven't found one we're satisfied with), but it is interesting in its own way. We decided to include it because it works well with almost any kind of font.

STEP 1 Type some text. Drag out a rectangle large enough to cover the text and add the Aggregate pattern to it. Click on the Paint Bucket tool to bring up the adjustment bars. Slide both handles toward the pivot point to create a pattern (3.52).

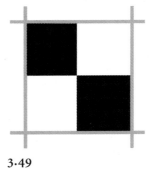

3.47   3.48

3.49

3.50   3.51

3.52

STEP 2 Place the patterned rectangle on top of the text. Click on the scissors icon to cut the rectangle to the Clipboard. Select the text and choose Edit➤Paste Inside. Open the Effect panel and apply an Inner Bevel. The default settings are fine. Choose Modify➤Convert to Bitmap (3.53).

STEP 3 Return to the Effect panel and choose Adjust Color➤Brightness/Contrast. Move the contrast slider to about 78. Next, use the Color Fill feature. The color is #000000, the Blend Mode is Tint, and the opacity is 48%. Add a soft drop shadow if you wish (3.54). Our variation is done with a Color Fill of #FF0000 instead of black (3.55).

PASTING FOR A TWO-TONE EFFECT

Q. *"How do you get this effect again? I have a black box and white box I want to take text and join it so the text is white in the black part and black in the white part."*

ROBERT G.

There are at least two different ways to do this in Fireworks. The first uses the gradient editor to create a two-tone image.

STEP 1 Fill the text with a black/white linear gradient. Open the gradient editor by clicking on the Edit button of the Fill panel.

STEP 2 Move the black chip directly on top of the white one or vice versa.

The second method uses a pasting technique that is more complicated but is a very useful one to master. Type the text on top of the box. Here's the box (3.56). Here is the text (3.57).

STEP 1 Align the text inside the box and drag out a white rectangle over the top half of the text (3.58).

STEP 2 Cut the white rectangle to the Clipboard. Edit➤Cut.

STEP 3 Click on the text to select it and choose Edit➤Paste inside. If necessary, use the star-shaped handle to fine-tune the alignment of the white rectangle inside the text (3.59).

PASTING WITH IMAGES

Images can also be pasted inside of text, and effects can then be applied to the whole (3.60).

STEP 1 Open a small image in Fireworks and type some text on top of it. Click on the image to select it, then copy it to the Clipboard (Edit➤Copy). Next, select the text and choose Edit➤Paste Inside. The text seems to disappear as soon as the image is embedded inside it.

STEP 2 In the Layers panel, click on the grayscale icon of the text to select it. We'll add a drop shadow the text to define its shape and lift it away from the background. Choose Shadow and Glow➤Drop shadow from the list of Effect panel effects (3.61).

STEP 3 For the shadow color, click on the color box in the Drop Shadow edit window and use its eyedropper tool to select the predominant color of your background image. When you've selected the color, click in the color box again, then click on the color wheel at the top of the palette. This will open the system color picker. Choose a color a few shades darker than the original one from the gradient bar at the far right of the Color window.

3.53

3.54

3.56

3.57

3.55

3.58

3.59

The following is a slightly more complex effect done with one of David's beautiful fern images and the bold, extended version a font named Akzidenz Grotesque (3.62).

STEP 1 Copy the image and paste the copy inside the text as we did in the previous exercise. Click on the area where the text was to bring up the star-shaped adjustment handle. This selects both the text and the image pasted inside it the text. Convert the selection to a bitmap.

STEP 2 In the Effect panel, choose Adjust Color➤Hue/Saturation. Check the Colorize box and move the Hue slider. We've moved the hue slider to 0 and the Saturation slider to 100% to generate a luminous, translucent red. We added a drop shadow to lift the text away from the background image (3.63).

WEATHERING WOOD

Q. "I'm doing a Web site for western film, and try as I might, I can't come up with the right look for the title. I need something like carved, weathered oak."

BEN H.

Fireworks comes with some pretty good tiling wood patterns that you can use as the basis of a weathered oak effect. In this exercise Fireworks converts text to paths that can be punched through a vector shape.

STEP 1 Drag out a rectangle and open the Fill panel. Choose the Wood pattern from the Fill panel Texture drop-down list. Clone the rectangle.

STEP 2 Type some text on top of the rectangles. Serifa, a slab-serif font created by Adrian Frutiger, is a good choice for this project because its blocky serifs are reminiscent of the wooden typefaces associated with America in the late 1800's. Adding a bit of vertical stretch to the text with the Transform tool gives it an even more authentic, western look (3.64).

STEP 3 Select the text and choose Text➤Convert to Paths. Then choose Modify➤Ungroup. Follow that with Modify➤Join. Wow! Look at all the Bézier points (3.65). Select the text; then click on

the background image and choose Modify➤ Combine➤Punch. It will be difficult to tell if this was successful because we cloned the background image, and you can't see the hole.

The important part is that the paths of the text have been transferred to the edges of the hole punched through the rectangle. Having the paths at the edges of the hole enables the application of Live Effects, like shadows and glows, to the inside of the hole, greatly expanding the range of effects that are possible in Fireworks. We'll explore some of those in the next steps.

STEP 4 Click on the image and open the Effect panel. Choose Inner Bevel. Set the bevel width to 4 and the angle to 316°. Inner Shadow is next, 4 pixels. Finally, choose Inner Glow. Change the color from the default red to black and the width to 4 pixels (3.66).

STEP 5 Choose Edit➤Select All. If you like, you can convert it to a bitmap. Return to the Effect panel and choose Adjust Color➤Brightness/ Contrast. Move both sliders to 40. To bleach or weather the wood, open the Hue/Saturation window and move the Saturation slider to the right until it reads −59 (3.67).

3.60

3.61

3.62

3.63

3.64

3.65

3.66

3.67

DESIGNING LOGOS

Q. *"Most of my clients already have logos they want me to incorporate into their site design. Occasionally I'll get a request to develop a new one. Eeiik! Where do I start?"*

KARLI S.

How about some techniques to experiment with? A little background information first.

The word *logo* derives from the Greek word *Logos* (λογοσ) meaning word, thought, speech. The thought we wish a logo to evoke is of a company or organization. If our design is successful, the logo is so strongly identified with the company that it can actually replace the company name in advertising. Think of Nike, Mercedes, and Coca-Cola. Some logos are pure symbols, geometric shapes, or images, while others are words in a distinctive style. So how do we go about designing one for use on a Web site?

Often your client will have a letterhead you can start with. Maybe he or she has a favorite symbol or animal that can be used. A case in point: David has a client — a financial advisor — who likes owls. The first step was to make a few pencil sketches of owls. After a second consultation with the client, one of the sketches was scanned as a bitmap, edited further, and colored. The client liked it so well that he has since used it on business cards, stationery, and even the glass door of his office. As is usually the case, the process was a combination of inspiration followed by feedback. Here's the final Web image (3.68).

A more conventional approach to designing a logo begins with the company name. Select a font that somehow characterizes the company name or business and experiment with Fireworks extensive text-manipulating capabilities in some of the following ways.

- Mixing cases (3.69, 3.70). Combinations of uppercase and lowercase letters attract attention. A logo made with all lowercase letters looks friendly and spontaneous. Using all uppercase letters evokes a feeling of power.
- Borders (3.71). Use a border to add visual weight, direction, and emphasis to the text of a logo. Use one of the shape tools or draw with the Pen tool to add lines and boxes. Add an interesting stroke.
- Change characters (3.72). Add new parts to letters or flip them to add a spark of originality to a font. The uppercase T (3.72) is actually two uppercase Ls, flipped and mirror-reversed.
- Back and forth (3.73). Reverse a letter or section of letters to focus attention on part of a word. Type each section separately, reverse one of them, and then align them.
- Baseline shift (3.74). This style is frequently used to evoke the feeling of a bygone era. Highlight a portion of the word in the text editor and shift the baseline up or down.

3.68   3.69

3.70   3.71

3.72   3.73

Ambrosia

3.74

■ Weight differences (3.75). Differences in the weight of the characters are an interesting means of accenting a syllable. This can be done by highlighting a section of text in the editor and either using a bolder version from the same font family or switching to a different, heavier-weight font.

■ Graphic accents (3.76). A graphic element used in place of a character, or part of a character, can make your logo more expressive. Ding fonts are ideal for this purpose.

■ Mixed fonts (3.77, 3.78). The contrast between two or more very different font types is another way of calling attention to your logo. Highlight the section you wish to change in the text editor and change the font.

■ Reflected text (3.79). This simple but sophisticated effect is an ideal one to use when you wish to create an atmosphere of serenity. Clone the text and flip the clone upside down. Use the Transform tool to reduce the height of the clone by approximately one-third.

■ Dropped character (3.80). Another whimsical attention-getter, you create this one by entering extra space between characters as you type. Reopen the text editor to type the dropped character; then use the Transform tool to rotate it.

■ Weld and punch (3.81). This is frequently used to add interest to simple monogram logos. Join two letters together in the text editor by reducing horizontal scaling. Convert to paths and ungroup. Type a third letter over the joint. Convert to paths and ungroup. Select all; then choose Modify➤Combine➤Punch.

■ Thickthin, softhard (3.82). Another nice monogram style, this one combines contrasting styles and weights of fonts.

■ Large, small (3.83). A third monogram style that nests a small letter inside a larger one.

■ Parent and child (3.84). A style often used in print. Type the parent letter. Use a contrasting type style and color for the child text. Rotate the child text and align.

3.81

3.82

3.75

3.76

3.83

3.77

3.78

3.84

3.79

3.80

CHAPTER 4
ADDING ACTION TO YOUR PAGES

This chapter is about actions and inter-actions: drop-down/pop-up menus, dis-joint rollovers, and other devices a Web page surfer can interact with and navi-gate by. Clients place high value on the Web designer's ability to provide interactive features on easily accessible and intuitive Web pages. The problem with designing such Web pages is that they require designers to be cross-browser gurus, equally as skilled in JavaScript and DHTML as they are in graphics. Fireworks removes a great deal of the pain in this process, allowing the designer to work with imagination rather than struggling with flaky code.

ROLLING WORDS AND IMAGES

Q. "I've designed the ubiquitous, top-left corner logo for a client. The image is a big at sign (@) with the name on the company centered on it. The secondary purpose of the logo is to serve as a hyperlink to the corporate home page. My problem is this. He is complaining that no one will click on it because there is nothing to indicate that it's a link. Is there anything for me in your bag of Fireworks tricks?"

FRANCIS E.

Well, your dilemma is a challenging one. Adding an underscore or .com to the text might prompt viewers to mouse-over the logo. Making the logo change color onMouseOver, and then again onClick, would reinforce the illusion. In case the viewer decides to

"You boil it in sawdust: you salt it in glue:
You condense it with locusts and tape:
Still keeping one principal object in view—
To preserve its symmetrical shape."

FROM *THE HUNTING OF THE SNARK* BY LEWIS CARROLL

read more of the page before exploring the link, a change in the color of the @ sign would serve as a reminder that the link is there. Try this fix as an image swap with an embedded, multistate rollover.

STEP 1 Locate the file named big_at.png on this book's CD-ROM and open it in Fireworks. Click the top-right button of the Frames panel and choose Duplicate Frame from the pop-up menu that appears. Click on the new frame. Frame 2 is where the @ sign changes color onMouseOver. Select the @ sign and change its color to black (4.1).

STEP 2 Duplicate Frame 2 to create Frame 3. Frame 3 is where the where the color of the text changes onMouseOver. Select the text and change its color to white. Duplicate Frame 3 to create Frame 4 (4.2).

TIP

The Object and other panels should be loaded by default when you open Fireworks 4. If the Object panel is not visible, open the Windows menu, and check Object.

4.1

4.2

4.3

4.4

STEP 3 Frame 4 is where the color of the text over the @ sign changes onClick. Select the text and change the color to #CC99FF (4.3).

STEP 4 The final goal is to get the text color to change back to its original value onMouseOut. Because the color on Frame 2 is the original color, simply use Frame 3 again rather than create a fifth frame.

ADDING HOTSPOTS, SLICES, AND BEHAVIORS

STEP 1 Select Frame 1 from the Frames panel and create a hotspot over the text. You can do this with the rectangular Hotspot tool or by selecting the text and choosing Insert➤Hotspot. Click on the @ sign and insert a slice (Insert➤Slice). Uncheck Auto-Name Slices in the Object panel and type in a name for your slice. This is not really necessary here but is a good habit to develop. Typing in names for the different slices simplifies identifying which slice you are working with in the Swap Image editor (4.4).

STEP 2 Click on the slice to select it and open the Behaviors panel. Click on the Add Action button (the + sign) and choose Swap Image from the pop-up menu that appears. When the Swap Image editor opens, you should see the name of your slice in the left window and the selected slice high-lighted in black in the right window (4.5). Under Show the swapped image from, choose Frame 2 (the default in this case). Leave preloading checked, but uncheck Restore Image onMouseOut. Click on OK. You should now see the onMouseOver event listed in the Behaviors panel.

STEP 3 Use the Select Behind tool (the second fly-out tool under the regular Selection tool in the Tools panel) to select the hotspot over the text. As the pointer hovers over the hotspot, you will see a red outline. Click on the hotspot and the red out-line lines turns blue, indicating that the hotspot is selected.

In the Behaviors panel, click again on the Add Action (+) button and choose Swap Image. The Swap Image editor will then open. Click on the slice in the right pane of the Swap Image editor. Change the frame number to 3. Uncheck Restore Image onMouseOut. Leave the Preload Images checkbox as is. Click on OK to close the window. The default event, onMouseOver, is the correct event for this frame.

STEP 4 If the text hotspot isn't still selected, select it again and click on the (+) button to open the Behaviors menu. Choose Swap Image. When the Swap Image editor opens, make sure that the slice is highlighted in the right pane of the window and change the frame number to 4. Uncheck Restore Image onMouseOut. Click OK. A second line is added to the list in the Behaviors panel. Change the event to onClick by highlighting the new line, clicking on the little triangle between the events and actions names, and choosing onClick from the pop-up menu (4.6).

STEP 5 There is one more behavior to add to the text hotspot. If the hotspot isn't still selected, select it again. Choose Swap Image from the Add Action (+) pop-up menu. Make sure that the slice is highlighted in the right window of the Swap Image editor. If necessary, change the frame number back to 2. Uncheck Restore Image onMouseOut. Change the event from onMouseOver to onMouseOut.

Preview the project in your browser (File➤ Preview in Browser or use the F12 key) to make sure that each rollover state is functioning as it should; then Optimize by selecting GIF in the Optimize panel. We'll describe exporting next, because there is code as well as graphics to be saved.

> **TIP**
>
> To make sure that you have selected a hotspot under a slice, open the Object panel. The word *Hotspot* should appear in parentheses next to the word *Object* in the panel title bar.

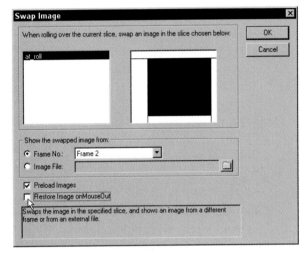

4.5

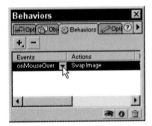

4.6

EXPORTING

Because this is a page element rather than a whole Web page, let's quickly run through how you would paste it into an existing Web page.

STEP 1 Choose Edit➤Copy HTML Code. The Copy HTML Code wizard opens. Because we are using Macromedia Dreamweaver as our HTML editor, we'll use the Dreamweaver option from the Choose your HTML Editor drop-down list.

(Other options are Front Page, Generic, and GoLive.) Be sure that you choose the correct setting. Click on the Next button.

STEP 2 In the next window, add a Base File Name for your slices. Clicking on the HTML Setup button in this window will allow you to select things like whether you want to use the HTM or HTML file type extension, whether to shim the table or not, and which color to give the empty table cells. After you have made your selections, click the Next button.

STEP 3 Click the Browse button of the new window to locate the folder that will hold the image files. After you select the folder, click the Finish button. The images will be exported to the selected folder, and the HTML code will be copied to the Clipboard.

STEP 4 To add the code and images to your Dreamwever page, place your cursor at the location of your Dreamweaver page where you would like the image to appear and choose Paste from the Dreamweaver Edit menu. That's it!

COMPOUNDING ROLLOVERS

Q. *"I am building a Web site for a wallpaper store that specializes in patterns for children's rooms. The owner wants to use figures from the wallpaper and demonstrate how those figures will look in different colors. I have created two rows of buttons. One row of buttons is just text. The other row is patches of color. Here's the hard part. I want the text buttons to roll over and open a sketch, and the color patches to remain static and color the sketch. All the sketches, whether colored or not, must be in the same place. Any thoughts on this?"*

PAULA N.

This interface requires attaching both a rollover behavior and a disjoint rollover behavior to the same trigger. In addition, a second set of triggers will target the same disjoint rollover space. Fortunately, this is not as complicated as it sounds, but you will need to follow the process carefully.

Locate the babypaper2.png file on the CD-ROM and open it in Fireworks (4.7). Click on the Frames panel tab and click-step through all 12 frames to see how the elements have been distributed. The words *flowers, toys,* and *stars* will become the text rollovers.

All three words change color on the second frame. When the viewer clicks on the text rollovers, the flower, toy, and star sketches will be swapped.

The circles of color will become the buttons that swap the different color images for the sketches, creating the illusion that the sketches are changing color and style.

After you have familiarized yourself with the distribution of the elements on the 12 frames, click on the Preview tab at the top of the canvas window and try the text rollovers by mousing over them and then clicking on them. Try out the color swaps by clicking on the color buttons. When you have finished playing with the rollovers and swaps, close the babypaper2.png file, locate the babypaper3.png file on the CD-ROM and open it in Fireworks.

ADDING THE FIRST HOTSPOTS

STEP 1 Hold down the Shift key and select all of the color buttons on Frame 1 and Choose Insert➤Hotspot. When prompted to choose between single and multiple hotspots, choose Multiple. Repeat this procedure with each of the three words.

STEP 2 Select all three of the hotspots over the aqua colored buttons and open the Object panel. Change the hotspot color to aqua. Select all three of the hotspots over the green buttons and change the hotspot color to green. Change the hotspots over the yellow buttons to — you guessed it — yellow. Those of you working in teams will find this kind of color-coding invaluable (4.8).

ADDING SLICES

STEP 1 Pull a guideline from the top ruler to the horizontal blue line. After making sure that Snap to Guides is selected (View➤Guides➤Snap to Guides), select the Pointer tool, double-click on the guideline and enter the number 96 in the

Move Guide dialog box that opens (4.9). Pull vertical guidelines between the words *flowers* and *toys* and between the words *toys* and *stars*.

STEP 2 Click on the Slice tool in the tool box to activate it and draw a slice over the top half of the canvas down to the horizontal guideline. Open the Object panel, uncheck Auto-Name Slices, and type **upper**. Draw three slices over the lower part of the canvas between the vertical guidelines. Click on the left slice, uncheck Auto-Name Slices, and type **flowers**. Click on the middle of the lower slices and uncheck Auto-Name Slices. Type **toys**. Select the lower-right slice, uncheck . . . you know the drill . . . and type **stars**.

STEP 3 Select all four of the slice guides. Click in the fill color box of the Object panel and choose #FFFFFF (white) from the color box pop-up window. Changing the slice guides to white will make the pale-colored objects on the frames much easier to see.

Select the slice guides and place them behind the hotspots. (Choose Modify➤Arrange➤Send to Back.)

ADDING BEHAVIORS

STEP 1 Click the hotspot over the word *flowers*. When the drag-and-drop behavior button pops up (the white circle with the cross hairs located in the center of the slice), click on it and choose Add Swap Image Behavior from the menu that appears. The Swap Image editor opens. In the right pane of the Swap Image editor, click on the slice over the top half of the canvas. Still in the Swap Image editor, choose Frame 1 from the Frame Number drop down menu, leave Preload Images checked, but uncheck Restore Images onMouseOut.

STEP 2 Click on the aqua hotspot over the word *flowers,* and then click on the drag-and-drop behavior button. As with the previous hotspot, choose Swap Image. In the right pane of the Swap Image editor, click on the slice over the upper half of the canvas. Change the frame number to 2. Keep Preload Images checked, but uncheck Restore Image onMouseOut. Follow the same

procedure with the hotspots over the green and yellow patches, changing the frames to 3 and 4 respectively, allowing preloading but unchecking the restore function. The rest of the sequence is as follows. Now pay attention!

The hotspot over the word *toys* swaps the upper half of Frame 5. The aqua hotspot above *toys* swaps the upper slice on Frame 6, the green hotspot swaps the upper slice on Frame 7, the yellow hotspot swaps the upper slice on Frame 8. The hotspot over the word *stars* swaps the upper slice in Frame 9, aqua-10, green-11, yellow-12. In each case, leave preload checked, but uncheck Restore Image onMouseOut. Open the Behaviors panel. One at a time, select all 12 of the hotspots and change the action from MouseOver to onClick. Phew! The rest is a piece of cake.

THE ROLLOVERS

Click on the drag-and-drop behavior button in the hotspot over *flowers*. When the Swap Image editor opens, click on the lower-right slice in the right window on Frame 2. This time, do not uncheck Restore Image onMouseOut. Repeat with *toys,* swapping the lower middle slice on Frame 2 and allowing the restore function. Once again, with *stars,* swapping the lower-right slice on Frame 2 and allowing the restore function.

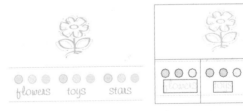

4.7   4.8

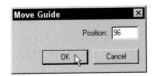

4.9

Optimizing and exporting

STEP 1 To optimize and export the compound rollover interface, choose File ➤ Export Preview. Choose the GIF format and use the all of the default settings. Click on the Export button. An alert box opens that says, "Slice objects will be ignored. To get sliced output and behaviors, chose 'Export Slices.'" Click the OK button. The Export dialog box opens.

STEP 2 Use the Save in drop down box at the top of the Export dialog box to locate the folder you want to deposit the HTML page in. When the contents of the folder are displayed in the window you can begin making your selections for the other options. Under File name, give the compound rollover interface a name. For the Save as Type option, choose HTML and Images. For the HTML option choose, Export HTML file. For the Slices option, choose Export slices.

Check the Put Images in Subfolder box and click the Browse button. Browse to the folder you want to deposit the images in. The Select Folder dialog box opens. When you have selected a folder, click the Open button to close the Select Folder dialog box and return to the Export dialog box. Click the Save button. Like magic, the HTML file and images are deposited in their separate folders.

POPPING MENUS, A NEW FIREWORKS TOOL

Q. *"I can't seem to find any tutorial or source file that will show me how to make a pop-up menu. Please, can someone help?"*

SCOTT K.

If you've seen run-time navigation menus on sites like MazdaUSA.com, Intel.com, and Microsoft.com, you may have wondered how to create this useful and dazzling effect. Macromedia has added a new pop-up menu command to the growing arsenal of Fireworks tricks. Developer and Macromedia Evangelist Kevin French is an expert on this feature and has agreed to share his skills with you.

One of the most exciting and talked-about features introduced in Fireworks 4 is the capability to create pop-up menus. A pop-up menu is a navigational element that is only visible when it is triggered by an event such as onClick, onMouseOver, and so on. Although there are as many ways to build pop-up menus as there are programmers willing to take a shot at doing so, the pop-up menus all perform the same functions. They allow you to include complex navigational elements on your Web pages in a clean, uncluttered manner. Fireworks will have you creating stunning pop-up menus in a matter of minutes, without writing a single line of code.

The objective of this tutorial is to build a navigation bar for a fictitious baseball site. All of the necessary files are included on the CD-ROM in the back of this book. I have also included a separate PNG file for the pop-up menu. The file is named menu.png. I have added the pop-up menu behavior to all slices that need it except for one. That will be your job. Feel free to use the pop-up menu behaviors that I have already created as reference points.

Locate the file menu.png and open it in Fireworks. Roll up your sleeves and get ready to build your first pop-up menu (4.10).

I have added the pop-up menu behavior to all slices that need it except one. That will be your job. Feel free to use the pop-up menu behaviors that I have already created as a reference.

STEP 1 If the slices are not visible, click on the Show Slices button at the bottom right of the Tools panel. There are already slices over the Home Plate, Photos, Trivia, and Contact buttons. You need to add a slice to the Stadiums button. Select the button and choose Insert➤Slice. (Without even knowing it, you have created the trigger element for the Stadiums button pop-up menu.)

STEP 2 Click on the Stadiums slice to select it. Notice a white circle with crosshairs in the middle of the slice. This circle is the drag-and-drop behavior button. Click on this circle button to open a menu of all behaviors that can be attached to this slice. Choose Add Pop-up Menu from the list (4.11). The Set Pop-up Menu Wizard opens.

The first screen of the Set Pop-up Menu Wizard (4.12) allows you perform several of the following functions:

Add/delete menu items
Indent/outdent menu items
Set the HTML target for menu items
Assign links to menu items
Edit menu items that have been added
View all menu items and their relationship to each other

Our Stadiums pop-up menu is going to be somewhat complex and will include the following menu items:

Yankee
    Monument Park
    Stats
        Capacity
        Dimensions
Fenway
Wrigley
Camden

Notice that this information is presented so that Capacity and Dimensions are submenus of Stats, and Stats and Monument Park are submenus of Yankee (4.13).

DEFINING CONTENT FOR YOUR POP-UP MENU

STEP 1 With the Set Pop-up Menu Wizard open, your task is to name the first menu item. Do this by typing **Yankee** into the field labeled Text.

STEP 2 Next, you want to assign a hyperlink to the menu item. You can either type the link into the Link field, or you can select links that you have

> **NOTE**
>
> A trigger is created when Fireworks attaches a JavaScript behavior to an element. The JavaScript behaviors instruct a browser to respond in a special way when it detects an event, such as the viewer mousing over a hotspot.

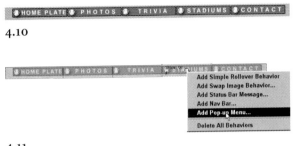

4.10

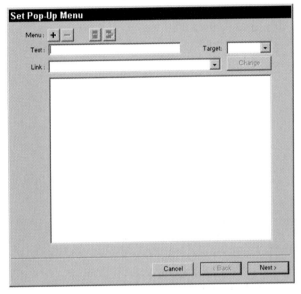

4.11

4.12

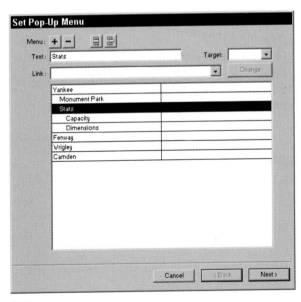

4.13

previously used by clicking the drop-down arrow in the Link field. Type **yankeestadium.htm** into the Link field.

STEP 3 If you were targeting an HTML frame, you would select that frame from the Target field or type the name of your frame into the Target field. In this case, we are going to leave the Target field blank. Selecting none from the Target drop-down menu produces the same effect.

NOTE

The Link field of the Set Pop-up Menu Wizard only allows a maximum of 50 characters for a hyperlink. If you have a link that requires more than 50 characters, you must first add the hyperlink to your URL Library. After the link is in the URL Library, you can select it from the Link drop-down menu in the Set Pop-up Menu Wizard.

WARNING

You cannot indent the first item of your menu.

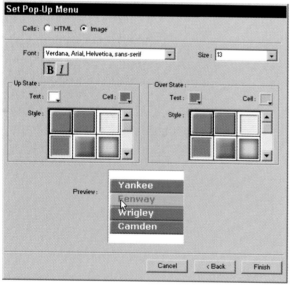

4.14

STEP 4 After you have entered all of the information for the menu item, click on the Add Menu button (a + sign) at the top of the wizard. Notice that your menu item name and the related hyperlink appear in the lower half of the Set Pop-up Menu Wizard. This is known as the Preview List. Continue the process by adding the rest of our pop-up menu items. The next items to add are

> Monument Park
> Stats
> > Capacity
> > Dimensions

Don't worry about assigning links to the remaining menu items for now.

STEP 5 As you may recall from our menu outline above, we decided that the Monument Park and Stats items are to be submenus of Yankee. To convert these items to submenus, select the menu item, in this case Monument Park, from the lower half of the Set Pop-up Menu Wizard, and then click the Indent Menu button. Repeat this for the Stats menu item.

We also decided that Capacity and Dimensions are going to be submenus of our first submenu. In order to accomplish this, you repeat the preceding steps, but this time you click the Indent Menu button twice. Finally, we are going to add the last menu item, called Fenway. Simply type **Fenway** into the Text field. Fenway is its own menu and does not need to be indented (4.14).

STEP 6 Now that you have all of the menu items in place, it's time to customize the appearance of your pop-up menu. So go ahead and click on the Next button, and we'll move to the second screen of the Set Pop-up Menu Wizard.

DEFINING THE APPEARANCE OF YOUR POP-UP MENU

This screen of the Set Pop-up Menu Wizard enables you to customize the appearance of the pop-up menu in many ways (4.15).

- Choose between plain HTML table cells or cells with a background image
- Define the font family for your menu items
- Define the size of your fonts
- Define the style for your fonts, such as plain, bold, or italic
- Define Upstate properties for the text and the cell
- Define Overstate properties for the text and the cell
- Format your table cells with images by choosing from 21 preset styles for both the Upstate and Overstate properties

STEP 1 With screen two of the Set Pop-up Menu Wizard open, select HTML for Cells.

STEP 2 Choose a font family. I have used Verdana, Arial, Helvetica, sans serif, bold. Try experimenting with other font families. Next, choose a font size by selecting a value from the drop-down menu or by typing it in the menu text Size box. During the entire process of customizing the appearance of your pop-up menu, the Set Pop-up Menu Wizard displays a preview of what your menu will look like with your current choices.

STEP 3 Finally, define the colors of the cells and the text in both the Up State and the Over State. Choosing colors is done in the same way as it is in any other processes in Fireworks. Simply click the color box and a color palette appears. Either select from the palette color with the built-in eye dropper tool, or type the Hexadecimal value directly into the text field at the top of the color palette.

For this tutorial, I have used the following colors:

- Up State Text: #FFFFFF
- Up State Cells: #666699
- Over State Text: #666699
- Over State Cells: #9999CC

Note that if we had chosen Image in step one, there would have been one additional step. We would have been presented with a dialog box that enabled us to select the style of the image for both the Up State and the Over State.

STEP 4 You have now defined all the necessary variables to customize the pop-up menu. Click on the Finish button to close the Set Pop-UP Menu wizard.

You'll notice that there is now an outline of your pop-up menu attached to the slice you added. The pop-up menu behavior is attached to a trigger slice or hotspot. When you close the Set pop-up Menu wizard, you see an outline (a wire frame, actually) of the pop-up menu attached to the slice or hotspot. You can use the Pointer tool to drag the outline of the menu and refine its position (4.16).

Before exporting the new pop-up menu to your Dreamweaver, you may want to preview it. Be aware that the pop-up menu behavior is the only behavior in Fireworks 4 that cannot be previewed in the internal Preview window and must be previewed in a browser. Use File➤Preview in Browser to view your new pop-up menu.

You may not be completely satisfied with all of your pop-up menu settings at this point. That's fine. It's very simple to reenter the Set Pop-up Menu Wizard

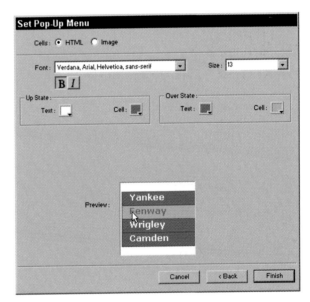

4.15

4.16

to edit them. Select the slice that has the pop-up menu behavior attached to it, open the Behaviors panel, and double-click on Show Pop-up Menu line. You can also open the wizard by double-clicking on the outline of the pop-up menu itself.

EXPORTING YOUR POP-UP MENU

Q. "How do I export a pop-up menu from Fireworks 4 to Dreamweaver?"

SCOTT K.

Exporting a pop-up menu from Fireworks is the same as exporting any other sliced object. Choose File➤Export. Make sure that the following options are checked in the Export dialog box: Save as Type: HTML and Images; HTML: Export HTML File; Slices: Export Slices; Include Areas without Slices. Click on the Save button.

If you check the directory that the pop-up menu was exported to, you'll notice that Fireworks has exported the HTML file, all of your images, and a JavaScript file named fw_menu.js. The JS file is the essence of the pop-up menu, and we'll explore it in the FAQ later in this section.

Q. "How do I use Dreamweaver to import a pop-up menu into my Web page?"

SCOTT K.

Using Dreamweaver to import a Fireworks pop-up menu into a Web page just like using Dreamweaver to import any other Fireworks-generated HTML.

On the CD-ROM in the back of the book, I have included a page that we are going to insert the pop-up menu into. The HTML file (layout.htm) is in the KevsBaseball directory. Open the file in Dreamweaver, and you will see a message Pop-Up Menu Will Go Here. Delete the message and keep your cursor positioned in that cell. From within the Dreamweaver document window, choose Insert➤ Interactive Images➤Fireworks HTML. Browse to the Fireworks-generated HTML and click OK. Dreamweaver will insert the entire menu as well as a reference to the JavaScript file fw_menu.js file that I mentioned earlier.

KEVIN'S POP-UP MENU FAQ

Although the Set Pop-Up Menu Wizard in Fireworks 4 provides several options to customize the appearance and functionality of pop-up menus, you may want to go beyond these limitations by creating your own styles for the buttons and customizing the fw_menu.js file. You do not have to be a master coder to make these customizations.

Q. "Is there a way I can use my own images for the button styles instead of the preset ones?"

You can easily add custom styles. Create a button style and save it by clicking on the arrow button at the top right of the Styles panel. Choose New Style from the menu that pops up, check the properties you want to preserve, and then click on OK. Scroll through the Styles palette until you find the Style you just created, then click on it to select it. Click on the arrow button again to reopen the Styles panel menu and choose Export. Export the style to the Fireworks Configuration/Nav Menu folder.

Q. "My pop-up menus do not appear in the correct location in the Web page. How do I fix this?"

Fireworks 4 pop-up menus are absolutely-positioned elements. They utilize X and Y coordinates based on the top, left corner of the canvas. Fireworks 4 assumes that the pixel locations of the pop-up menus in your Fireworks document will be at the exact same pixel location on your Web page. Obviously, this is not always the case. We have provided some work arounds that enable you to reposition the pop-up menu. The fw_menu.js file from the tutorial is available on the CD to help you walk through this procedure.

Load Dreamweaver and open the HTML page you created in the previous exercise. You'll notice that the pop-up menus do not appear in the proper location on the page. The first thing that we need to determine is the pixel coordinates from the upper-left-hand corner of the Web page. These coordinates are what determine the exact position of the pop-up menu elements.

To modify the absolute location of the pop-up select the image that triggers the pop-up menu. For this example, select the Photos button. Switch to code view in Dreamweaver by clicking on the Show Code View button. This feature is new in Dreamweaver 4, so if you haven't used it yet, you'll find the Show Code View button directly under the word File at the top left of the program window. The code relating to the image will be highlighted. In that line of code, find the following text:

```
window.FW_showMenu(window.fw_menu_0,147,20)
```

The last two numbers correspond to the absolute x, y coordinates of the pop-up menu from the top-left corner of the page. Change those numbers to reflect the desired absolute location. In this case, the location would be:

```
"window.FW_showMenu(window.fw_menu_0,147,145)"
```

Switch back to design view by clicking on the Show Design View button (third from the left of the Show Code View button). Select the Trivia button and the look at the highlighted code in the code view window. You should see the following:

```
"window.FW_showMenu(window.fw_menu_1,257,23)"
```

Change the x and y coordinates to read:

```
"window.FW_showMenu(window.fw_menu_1,257,145);"
```

Preview the page in your browser, and everything should look good. Finally, repeat the procedure for the Stadiums button. You're on your own with this one. Good luck!

Q. I've noticed that when I resize my browser window the pop-up menus do not reposition themselves as they should. Is there a work-around for this?"

GIOVANNI D.

E. Michael Brandt of *www.valleywebdesigns.com* has created a Dreamweaver command extension that every Fireworks and Dreamweaver user should grab.

It's called the *Popup Menu Motivator*. This command makes Fireworks' Popup Menus slide across the screen as the browser window is resized. Amazingly, it also compensates for different monitor resolutions. There are several options built into the extension that enable some control over the placement and tracking of the menus. You can download *Popup Menu Motivator* from the Dreamweaver Exchange, at *www. macromedia.com/exchange/dreamweaver/*.

Q. "The pop-up feature is only works properly if the page is justified top-left so the x-y coordinates for its location are static. My page needs to be center aligned. How can I do this?"

As an alternative, try using frames. Put the page that you want centered in the middle frame and let the outer ones expand to fill the gaps. Have a look at the index page of *http://extending-fireworks.com*. This is how Brian Baker got the menu to work centered in the browser. According to Brian, "If you create a frameset and set cols="*,600,*" then the center frame will stay at 600 pixels wide, and the other two will expand and contract, depending on the window size. The center one will also stay centered. So find the size of your page containing the pop-ups and make the width of the center frame the same.

"You will have slight problems with Netscape 4*x* browsers, because it they use a percentage method of working out frame sizes rather than pixels, though it will only be a few pixels out. (That's why I have the black border.) The pop-up menus will still work fine."

Q. "How do I modify the arrow image that appears in my pop-up menus that have submenus?"

The arrow is automatically exported from Fireworks to the same directory that you exported all of your other pop-up menu images to. Simply create a graphic that you want to replace the arrow with and export it to the same directory, renaming it arrows.gif to overwrite the existing file.

Q. "How do I change the time it takes for a menu to disappear once I mouse off of the menu?"

Again, the solution to this is found in the fw_menu.js file. Open the fw_menu.js file in a file editor and locate the following block of code:

```
function fwDoHide()
{
if (!fwDHFlag) return;
var elapsed = new Date() - fwStart;
if (elapsed < 1000) {
fwHideMenuTimer = setTimeout("fwDoHide()", 1100-elapsed);
return;
}
fwDHFlag = false;
hideActiveMenus();
window.ActiveMenuItem = 0;
}
```

The default values allow for one second after mouseOut before the menu will disappear. If you change the 1000 in the _if (elapsed..._ line to a lower number and change the 1100 to a lower number, the pop-up menu will only remain visible for half a second instead one second. For example:

```
Function fwDoHide()
{
if (!fwDHFlag) return;
```

```
var elapsed = new Date() - fwStart;
if (elapsed < 500) {
fwHideMenuTimer = setTimeout("fwDoHide()", 600-elapsed);
return;
}
fwDHFlag = false;
hideActiveMenus();
window.ActiveMenuItem = 0;
}
```

If you want to change any of the default settings permanently for all future Fireworks pop-up menus, you can edit the file \Macromedia\Fireworks 4\ Configuration\HTML Code\fw_menu.js so that all future pop-up menus have your custom settings. (Be sure to make a back-up copy of the original JavaScript file before you modify it!)

Q. "How do I eliminate the borders in the pop-up menus?"

Again, open up fw_menu.js and check lines 25 and 26 for the following code:

```
this.menuBorder = 1;
this.menuItemBorder = 1;
```

Change the 1 to the values that you desire. If you want to eliminate the borders completely, the modified code would look like this:

NAME:
Kevin French

COMPANY:
MM2K, Inc. PO Box 644
New Monmouth, NJ 07748
732-471-9100
Web Site: *www.MM2K.net*
E-mail: kfrench@mm2k.net

COMPUTERS:
Dell Dimension 8100 with 1.4 Ghz P4; Dell Inspiron 7500 Laptop with 450 Mhz P3.

CONNECTION TO THE INTERNET:
Cable.

PRIMARY APPS:
Macromedia Fireworks 4 (of course), Macromedia UltraDev 4, Macromedia Flash 5, Macromedia Freehand 9, Adobe Nothing.

PERIPHERALS:
HP ScanJet 5370C, HP DeskJet 880C, Wacom Intuos Graphics Tablet, Dazzle Digital Video Creator.

WORK HISTORY:
I was a bum my entire life until Linda asked me to contribute to this book. I expect fame, fortune, and exotic cars as a result. Seriously, I founded MM2K in 1997

while working toward my business degree. The degree hangs over my desk, and I've continued building MM2K. I'm having a great time as an Internet consultant.

FAVORITE PLEASURE:
I spend what little spare time I have with my beautiful and understanding girlfriend, Kathy. (I love you baby!) In addition, when I am not working, I like to hit the gym and go for drives to clear my mind and reduce stress.

```
this.menuBorder = 0;
this.menuItemBorder = 0;
```

Q. "How do I change the colors of the borders in my pop-up menus?"

Go to line 29 of the fw_menu.js file and look for the following:

```
this.menuBorderBgColor = "#777777";
```

Changing the hexadecimal value to the color that you prefer will change the border color of the menu. For example, if you wanted a black border, the resulting code would be:

```
this.menuBorderBgColor = "#000000";
```

Q. "Where can I find more information about Fireworks 4 pop-up menus?"

There are several resources on the Web. The following URLs deal specifically with Fireworks 4 pop-up menus.

www.macromedia.com/go/14181
www.macromedia.com/go/15007
www.macromedia.com/go/14995
www.macromedia.com/go/15001
www.macromedia.com/software/fireworks/-productinfo/demos/build_drop_down.html
news://forums.macromedia.com/macromedia.
fireworks
www.projectfireworks.com/classroom/class.asp?
lessonID=31

Thanks Kev. We should be seeing new fancy pop-up menus appearing on the Web very soon!

Some time ago, we were experimenting with ways to create rollovers with an image that couldn't be sliced into neat rectangles. The technique we eventually settled on was one suggested by Bob Haroche of On Point Solutions (*www.onpointsolutions.com*). Bob has handily mastered hotspot rollovers in Fireworks, as you'll see by his tutorial that follows.

HOTSPOTTING A LA HAROCHE

Creating irregularly shaped rollovers is a difficult task in Web design. JavaScript rollovers can only swap out rectangular images. The technique I'm about to describe is based on one from Joseph Lowery's *Fireworks Bible,* and it shows how to swap irregularly shaped objects, even if the area is within a slice, by first defining their shape with a hotspot.

I've done this as a practice technique using a ring divided into four equal segments, each one of which will be a hotspot rollover. Locate the hotspot_ring.png file on the book's CD-ROM and load it in Fireworks (4.17).

WORKING WITH FRAMES

Because all four shapes roll over, a total of five frames is necessary. The original static image (Frame 1); the original image with the first segment in the onMouseOver state (Frame 2); the original image with the second segment in the onMouseOver state (Frame 3); the original image with the third segment in the onMouseOver state (Frame 4); and the original image with the fourth segment in the onMouseOver state (Frame 5) (4.17).

CREATING THE HOTSPOTS

You can create the hotspots either with the Polygon hotspot tool or, if you want an entire vector object to be a hotspot, by simply selecting that object and choosing Insert➤Hotspot. The latter is a much faster, easier way to create hotspots than drawing them by hand.

4.17

The insert function also allows you to select multiple objects (Shift + select) and turn them into hotspots at the same time. Do this now with the ring segments in Frame 1. You'll be prompted to choose either one large hotspot or multiple hot spots. Choose multiple hotspots (4.18).

Now that you have your hotspots set, enter a URL for each segment in the Object panel. (If you don't add URLs, Fireworks simply inserts a null number so your rollover will work, but clicking won't take the viewer anywhere.)

CREATING THE ONMOUSEOVER STATES

STEP 1 Turn off the hotspots to see what you are doing by clicking on the Hide Slices button at the bottom left of the Tools panel.

Go to Frame 2 and edit the characteristics of just one of your segments. In my example, Frame 2 has the top-right ring segment highlighted by changing the base fill color from #990000 to #FF0000 (4.19). Everything else is the same as in static Frame 1. Next, go to Frame 3 and highlight the lower-right segment. In my example, Frame 3 has the lower-right ring segment beveled, and everything else is as it was in static Frame 1 (4.20). You get the idea.

> **TIP**
>
> The multiple selection/Insert Hotspot method works great if each of the areas to be hotspots is a vector object. However, if one of the objects consists of two pieces, join them together as one large object before inserting the hotspots.

STEP 2 Here's where things get interesting. Go back to Frame 1 and create a single, huge slice over your entire graphic. It is helpful at this point to use the Object panel and call this giant slice something descriptive like *ring*. Do that by unchecking the auto-name feature. Use lowercase letters with no spaces or funny characters. You're almost there.

STEP 3 You now want to select the hotspots and make each one swap out. How to do this when you have a giant slice overlaying them? There are two easy ways. The first is to use the Select Behind tool, which is the second flyout tool under the regular Selection tool in the Tools panel. Each time you click on the canvas with the Select Behind tool, the Object panel will show you what you're selecting — whether it's the grouped image, the slice layer, or the hotspot (4.21). When the Object panel shows that you've selected the hotspot, stop clicking. The other way is to open the Layers panel and click on the Hotspot icon.

ADDING THE BEHAVIORS

STEP 1 Select the hotspot over the top-right ring segment. When the drag-and-drop behavior handle appears (a small circle with crosshairs located in the center of the slice), click on the handle to

4.20

4.18

4.19

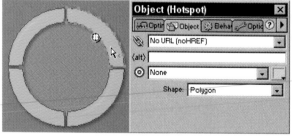

4.21

open the Behaviors menu. Choose Add Swap Image Behavior. The Swap Image dialog box opens, and you'll see a diagram at the top right that lets you choose which slice you want to swap. Because you have only one giant slice, choose that one. And now for the magic!

You also get to choose which frame you want swapped out. Because the top-right ring segment gets swapped out in Frame 2, choose Frame 2 in the Swap Image editor window.

STEP 2 Your first irregularly shaped hotspot has been set up to swap out to its mouseover state. At this point, I recommend choosing F12 to preview your work in a browser to make sure that the rollover does work right. If the rollover does work correctly, then go back and repeat selecting the hotspots and adding the swap behavior for the correct frame for each ring segment.

EXPORTING THE BEHAVIORS

To export, choose File➤Export. Choose a Filename. For Save as Type, use HTML and Images. For Slices, use Export Slices. Because there is only one slice, you can uncheck Include Areas without Slices. If you are storing your images in a different folder than the HTML page, check Put Images in Subfolder and

browse to the folder where you would like your images stored (4.22). It doesn't get any easier than that!

Thanks Bob. That was terrific!

TWIRLING KNOBS, WHIRLING DIALS

Q. *"I've seen a cool page selector on Derek Powazek's site at www.kvetch.com that looks like a radio or Hi-Fi control knob. Can I do something like that in Fireworks?"*

DEKE R.

Fireworks is an ideal platform for creating both the radio knob graphics and the associated code at the

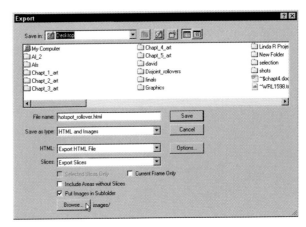

4.22

NAME: BOB HAROCHE

NAME AND ADDRESS OF ORGANIZATION:

OnPoint Solutions
P.O. Box 694
Occidental, CA 95465
707-874-1188 (phone and fax)
info@onpointsolutions.com

WHAT KIND OF COMPUTER(S) YOU WORK ON:

I develop on a Dell 400 MHz PII, 256 RAM, 16 Mb video card, 19" Optiquest monitor, running Windows 98. Test (and scratch my head while viewing) on an iMac, 350 MHz, 96 RAM, running OS 8.6.

YOUR CONNECTIVITY TO THE INTERNET:

56K dial-up (sigh). Formerly DSL until we moved to the country.

PRIMARY APPLICATIONS:

Fireworks, Photoshop, Dreamweaver, Top Style, Home Site.

PERIPHERALS:

Visioneer 5100b scanner, Iomega Jaz drive (1G), Iomega Zip drive (100MB).

WORK HISTORY:

After practicing trial law for eight years, I concluded there was more fun to be had in life than arguing for a living. I began donating my time building my first Web site for our local animal shelter. I was hooked. A few years later, and after many late nights slinging code, I'm happily working as an independent Web designer/Internet consultant specializing in small businesses and nonprofit organizations. I still like to argue though.

FAVORITE PLEASURE:

I love sea kayaking and wilderness exploration, but most recently my life's greatest pleasure has been tickling my baby's toes and blowing raspberries for him.

same time. The graphics we're going to work with are a knob image with a yellow indicator dot, a set of background détente dots, and an "LED" image to indicate an active détente dot. These images are available on the book's CD-ROM. (You can find instructions on how to create your own radio knob and LED image in Chapter 6 of this book.) The idea is to create the appearance of a knob that rotates as you move the cursor around the knob image. It's a remarkably effective illusion.

The technique for creating the rollovers is almost the same as the hotspot rollover technique you learned in the last exercise. The major difference between the two is that the second state of the hotspot rollovers, the On position of the radio knob and indicator light, needs to remain fixed onMouseOut.

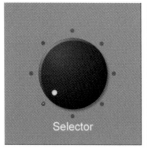

4.23

4.24

4.25

4.26

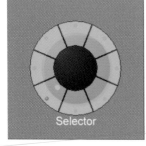

4.27

4.28

STEP 1 Locate the radioknob.png file on the CD-ROM and load it in Fireworks (4.23). Open the Frames panel and click through all eight frames to see how the image of the selector knob and lamp changes from frame to frame. Return to Frame 1 and, holding the Shift key down to constrain the shape, drag out a 166-x-166-pixel circle. Center it on the canvas over the knob and lamps (use Commands➢Document➢Center in Document). If the circle draws with a fill color, eliminate the color (in the Fill panel, select None, or click on the Fill color well on the Tools panel and select the white square with the red band through it) to make it easier to see what you are doing. Clone the circle and reduce the size of the clone to 80 × 80 pixels (Transform, choose Resize from the drop-down menu and enter 80 in the pixel size boxes). Center the clone inside the original circle. Select both circles and choose Modify➢Combine➢Punch. This leaves you with a ring, which will be divided further in the next step (4.24).

Double-click on the Polygon tool. Change the Polygon option to Star in the Object panel. Set the sides to 8 and the angle to 1. Place your cursor on the center of the ring created by the punched ellipses and then drag upward. You'll see an 8-pointed star with very narrow points. The tips of the star should extend a few pixels beyond the outer edge of the ring (4.25). Center the star in the document; then choose Modify➢Transform➢Numeric Transform➢Rotate -23°. Select the star and the ring; then punch the star through the ring (Modify➢Combine➢Punch). Choose Modify➢Split to separate the ring segments (4.26).

STEP 2 While the segments are still selected, Choose Insert➢Hotspot. When prompted to select single or multiple hotspots, select multiple. If the hotspots are not still selected, select the hotspots by holding down the Shift key and clicking on each of them (4.27). Choose Insert➢Slice. When you are prompted to choose between single or multiple slices, choose single. Click on the slice and send it backward (use Modify➢Arrange➢Send to Back). Because the slice will only move back one hotspot at a time, open the History panel and highlight your last step (Move) by clicking on it. Click the Replay button at the bottom of the

History panel until the slice has moved behind all of the segments (4.28).

STEP 1 To add the behaviors, click on the hotspot over the yellow indicator dot and LED image in Frame 1. Place your cursor over the drag-and-drop behavior button and drag a behavior line past the edge of the hotspot to the slice (4.29). Release your mouse button to release the behavior line. When the Swap Image dialog box opens, choose Frame 1 and click on the More Options button. Uncheck Restore Image onMouseOut in the next window and click OK.

Moving clockwise around the image, click on the next hotspot and drag and drop a behavior line to the slice. Choose Frame 2 in the Swap Image dialog box. Uncheck restore onMouseOut in the next window. Continue around the image, attaching the third hotspot to Frame 3, the fourth hotspot to Frame 4, and so on, until all eight hotspots have behaviors attached to them. Preview the mouseOver behaviors in your browser. Optimize the image and Export the image and the HTML

And there you have it, a working radio or Hi-Fi knob. To make the knob object a jump selector that you can use to swap images elsewhere on your Web page, you can add more behaviors to the Indicator Dot/LED hotspots to trigger the additional events.

ZOOMING IN

Q. *"I've seen a Java applet of a map on a science Web site that allows you to select a region of the map to zoom in on. I'm not too keen on Java in general. What's the potential for doing something like it with JavaScript in Fireworks?"*

JACOB H.

You can do a nice simulation of this kind of map in Fireworks. As our example, we'll use a map project that David intended for an as-yet-to be completed Web site on New Zealand ferns. The Web site consists of a small map that allows you to select an area of a bigger map to show close-up detail. The effect is achieved with a fascinating combination of Image Swaps and disjoint rollovers.

As usual, the first requirement is gathering the material from which to assemble the graphics. You want line maps that can be compressed efficiently as GIFs but are still large enough to show useful detail. A good source for this kind of map is the Xerox PARC map Web site at *http://mapweb.parc.xerox.com/map*. This remarkable site creates on-the-fly GIFs of maps of anywhere on the globe down to very fine detail. We've used some of these GIF maps to piece together a series of maps at two levels of detail: The first level is for a large-scale map with active areas, and the second level provides the detailed areas to be used as disjoint rollovers.

The large-scale map (4.30) with the North Island of New Zealand is covered by a red-outlined rollover

---

TIP

When you place a hotspot on top of a slice, the behavior is attached to the hotspot rather than to the slice. That allows you to make much more creative choices about the size, shape, and location for a trigger

---

4.29

4.30

4.31

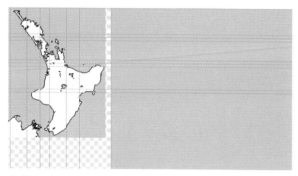

4.32

4.33

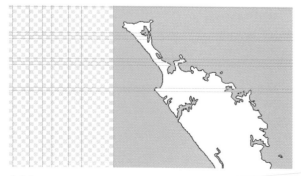

4.34

map. The red rectangles show the areas that will be enlarged on the disjoint rollover area.

To begin, we must delineate the slice areas that will trigger the disjoint rollovers. Note that the areas of the map outlined in red overlap each other, so it is also necessary to demarcate which hotspot is active where. To do this, we've dragged a series of guidelines over the image to mark out the edges of the red-outlined areas and also the boundaries between the adjacent slices. The color-shaded areas (4.31) represent the slice areas.

So much for the planning. It's time to get down to work.

STEP 1 Find the map_initial.png file on the book's CD-ROM and open it in Fireworks. The guidelines are already in place, so if you don't see them, choose View➤Rulers; then choose View ➤ Guides➤Show Guides. Next, enlarge the canvas to 300 × 550 (use Modify➤Canvas Size). Before closing the Canvas Size dialog box, click on the top-left anchor button to keep the original image at the top left of the new canvas. Copy the large blank map image (blank.gif) from the CD-ROM and paste it into the right-hand side of the working file (4.32). You now have the framework in which to do the rest of the job.

STEP 2 Open the Frames panel and add six frames: Frames 2, 3, and 4 for the red rectangle frames in the left rollover panel, and Frames 5, 6, and 7 for the large map disjoint rollovers.

Select Frame 2 in the Frames panel. From the CD-ROM, open the first rollover image file with the red rectangle (map1.gif). Cut and paste the rollover image file into Frame 2 (4.33). Do the same for the next two frames, pasting the second and third red rectangle images (map2.gif and map3.gif) into Frames 3 and 4.

STEP 3 Switch to Frame 5, From the CD-ROM, open the first large map (northland.gif), and cut and paste it into Frame 5, moving it to the extreme right (4.34). From the CD-ROM, do the same with the second (auckland.gif) and third (rotorua.gif) maps, copying them into Frames 6 and 7 respectively. We have now collected all the images and can set about creating the rollovers.

The assembled file is available on the CD-ROM as map1.png, in case you got confused with all that copying and pasting.

ADDING HOTSPOTS AND SLICES

STEP 1 The first step in constructing the rollovers is to create hotspots, using the guides that we dragged out at the start of the exercise to locate the hotspots. Switch to Frame 1 and select the first hotspot area with the Rectangular Marquee tool. When the selection is complete and you see the marching ants, choose Insert➤Hotspot (4.35). Create the next two hotspots, making sure that they don't overlap. The final one is slightly smaller than the first two because of the way the larger images fit into the main map. This overlap will not be noticeable. After the hotspots are created, they will show up as colored rectangles on the map (4.36). The hotspots also appear in the Layers panel.

Now we're getting into the interesting (and complex) part. Use the Slice tool to set a slice over the rollover map and over the blank blue area on the right (4.37). Notice that the slices appear in the Layers panel.

ADDING BEHAVIORS

STEP 1 To target the hotspot area that should trigger the first of the rollovers, use the Select Behind tool. Before proceeding, make sure that you deselect the right-hand slice by selecting the left-hand slice (important).

Click on the drag-and-drop behavior button to open the Behaviors menu. Choose Add Swap Image Behavior.

STEP 2 When the Swap Image editor opens, click on the left, smaller slice in the right window. It's a good idea to check the other settings in the Swap Image editor window before proceeding. The frame number should be set to 2. In this case, it is set at 2 by default. The Preload Images and Restore Image onMouseOut boxes should be checked. Click OK to accept the settings. The

newly set behavior shows up as a blue behavior line extending from the behavior control button in the middle of the hotspot.

STEP 3 The most interesting part of the exercise is next: adding the second rollover, this time a disjoint rollover, to the first hotspot. Our first rollover changed the image under the cursor. This next one will swap the image on the right.

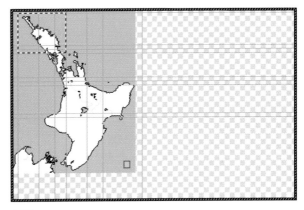

4.35

4.36

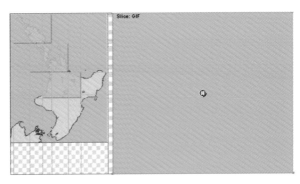

4.37

Click on the drag-and-drop behavior button in the hotspot again. Select Add Swap Image Behavior. Click on the larger, right-hand slice in the right window of the Swap Image editor. Set the frame number to 5 (which is where we added the first of the large maps) and deselect the Restore Image onMouseOut box to prevent the large image from swapping back to its original state after it is clicked.

A second behavior line is now looping from the hotspot to the right-hand image (4.38).

STEP 4 But wait; there's more. . . . The default event of an added behavior is onMouseOver. We need to change the default to onClick so that when the viewer mousse over the first hotspot (on the left), the image under it will change to a red rectangle, but nothing will happen to the large map image on the right until he clicks inside the red rectangle.

To edit the behavior, open the Behaviors panel and select the second of the two lines. Click on the Event menu button and choose onClick from the drop-down list (4.39).

The rest is all downhill. Repeat the same procedure with the second hotspot, this time selecting Frame 3 for the source of the direct rollover and Frame 6 for the disjoint rollover (with the Restore Image onMouseOut box unchecked). For the third hotspot, it's Frame 4 and Frame 7, respectively.

The only thing to watch out for is that you have the correct hotspot selected before you start to attach behaviors. Otherwise, you'll get a tangle of blue behavior lines going in all directions! When properly selected, the hotspot should show a blue outline, and the drag-and-drop behavior button (which sits in the exact center of the hotspot) should pop up.

And now you have the completed PNG, ready for export (4.40).

The final step in Fireworks is to export the images, slices, and HTML. Choose File➤Export. Ensure that the Save as Type box is set to HTML and Images, the HTML box is set to Export HTML File, and the Slices box is set to Export Slices.

The only remaining work involves importing HTML into your Web page, adding a few flourishes (such as a caption under the left image), adding ALT tags, and so on.

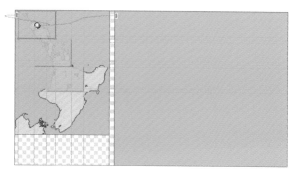

4.38

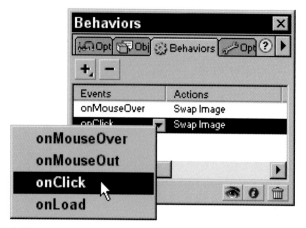

4.39

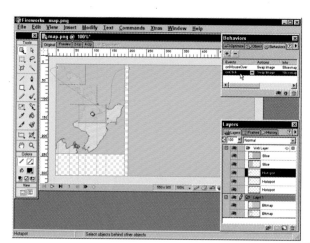

4.40

As an exercise, think about adding a small *x* in a square box in the lower-right of the left-hand map with a behavior that clears the main map display back to blank. Hint: The Frame number is 1.

SHOWING AND HIDING IN VERSION 3x (+) BROWSERS

Q. *"How do I add links to my disjoint rollovers and prevent the layers from restoring to their original state before I can click on the links? How do I add hotspot links to my disjoint rollovers without them being active on all layers? Can I show/hide layers in Fireworks?"*

LEGIONS!

If you've read through (and hopefully, performed) the previous exercises, you are aware by now that you need to uncheck the restore function in the Swap Image editor to prevent a rollover from restoring onMouseOut.

You cannot add hotspots to rollovers without the hotspots being active on all layers, but if you are clever about placing these hotspots, no one will notice.

Finally, you can use slices and hotspots in Fireworks to emulate Dreamweaver Show-Hide layers. While not practical for large areas of a Web page, you may find these useful for small, interactive elements like menus. One bonus is that, unlike real Dreamweaver Show-Hide layers, older browsers support this type of "now you see it, now you don't" object

STEP 1 Open the thomson.png file on the CD-ROM in Fireworks (4.41). All necessary frames are supplied in a finished state. Click on the Preview tab to see what the element will look like when you are finished; then delete all the slices and hotspots. We've put the buttons close to the disjoint rollover area in this example. The buttons can be as far apart as opposite ends of the canvas, with a large area between them that will be exported as text.

Select all three of the buttons on Frame 1 and insert hotspots. When prompted to choose between single or multiple hotspots, choose multiple. Open the Frames panel and advance to Frame 2 (4.42).

The button on the left of Frame 2 is the button the viewer will use to return the index image on the first frame. Because the button does not exist on Frame 1, it would be necessary to use the Select Behind tool or click on its icon in the Layers panel to select it before inserting a hotspot. As long as you are already working in the Frames panel, you can improve your workflow by taking advantage of the fact that hotspots and slices are shared across all frames. Select both buttons on Frame 2 and insert hotspots. On Frames 3 and 4, insert hotspots on the buttons that don't already have them. Return to Frame 1.

STEP 2 Drag a slice guide over the top part of the canvas. The guide should reach just past the top edge of the white area at the bottom of the image. Open the Object panel and uncheck Auto-Name Slices. Type **upper**.

4.41

4.42

Add a second slice to cover the lower part of the canvas. Name the slice **lower**. Though not absolutely necessary, our preference is to color-code the slices and hotspots (4.43).

ADDING BEHAVIORS

STEP 1 Open the Layers panel and click on the hotspot layers in the Web Layer folder (4.44). Watch the canvas so that you can see when the hotspot over the *home* button becomes selected. When the *home* button is selected, return your cursor to the canvas and click on the drag-and-drop behavior button in the hotspot. Choose Swap Image from the pop-up menu that appears. In the right window of the Swap Image editor, editor (which appears when you have selected Swap Image), click on the "lower" slice and change the frame number to 1. Allow preloading but uncheck the Restore Image onMouseOut box. In the Behaviors panel, change the Event from onMouseOver to onClick.

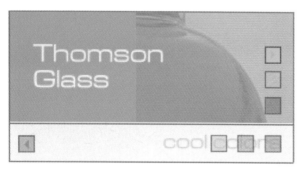

4·43

4·44

Select the drag-and-drop behavior button a second time and choose Swap Image from the menu. This time, click on the "upper" slice, change the frame number to 1, and uncheck the restore box. Change the event to onClick.

STEP 2 Still using the Select Behind tool, select the drag-and-drop behavior button in the teal hotspot at the lower right (or the hotspot over the teal button if you haven't used color coding). Chose Swap Image from the menu that appears. Swap the "upper" slice. Choose Frame 2 and uncheck the Restore Image onMouseOut box. Change the event to onClick. Repeat for the lower slice.

Repeat the sequence with the orange and hot pink buttons, choosing Frames 3 and 4 respectively, swapping both upper and lower slices, unchecking Restore Image onMouseOut, and changing the event to onClick.

ADDING URLS

STEP 1 Select the teal hotspot in the upper slice (see, we told you that it was a good idea to color-code them) and open the Object panel. Highlight the text in the Link box and type in the URL for the "cool color" pages of our fictional glass company: *www.thomson_glass.com/cool.html*. Select the orange hotspot in the upper slice and attach the URL for the Thomson "warm color" pages: *www.thomson_glass.com/warm.html*. Attach the URL for the "wild color" pages to the hot pink hotspot: *www.thomson_glass.com/wild.html*.

STEP 2 Test the links in your browser. Optimize the images and export the images and HTML.

TABBING AN INTERFACE

Q. "I am trying to make tabs to use for the navigation bar on my site. Does anyone know of a site with premade GIFs that look like folder tabs or the information on making folder-style tabs?"

DEMITRIS C.

Making folder tabs is simple and fun to do yourself. We'll show you how.

STEP 1 Drag out a rectangle appropriate to the size of your tabs; then open the Object panel. Use the Roundness slider to shape the corners if you like. Use the Skew tool to widen the base so that your rectangle forms a roughly trapezoidal shape. To widen just one side, use the Distort tool (4.45). Clone the tab to create two or three additional tabs. Use the arrow keys to organize the tabs horizontally. Drag out a large rectangle. (The rectangle represents the folder the tabs attach to.) Move the top edge of the rectangle just over the bottom edges of the tabs (4.46).

STEP 2 Open the Frames panel and click on the Panel menu button. Choose Duplicate Frame. Enter the number, minus one, of your tabs. In Frame 1, move the leftmost tab to the front (choose Modify➤Arrange➤Bring to Front). Select both the tab and the rectangle and choose Modify➤Combine➤Union. In Frame 2, move the second tab to the front, select the tab, and select the rectangle; choose Modify➤Combine➤Union to join them. In Frame 3, align the third tab to the front and join it with the rectangle. Continue in this fashion until all of the tabs are appropriately joined to the rectangles.

To add the behaviors, follow these steps:

STEP 1 Zoom to 200% and use the Polygon Hotspot tool to draw a hotspot over the first tab in Frame 1 (4.47). Because each of the tabs on Frame 1 will need hotspots and because it is really time-consuming to draw them, clone the first hotspot and use your arrow keys to move the clone to the second tab. Repeat for each tab. After each of the tabs has its own hotspot, drag a slice guide over the whole interface: tabs and rectangle.

STEP 2 Use the Select Behind tool to select the hotspot over tab 1. Click on the drag-and-drop behavior button and choose Swap Image from the pop-up menu. Highlight the slice in the right pane of the Swap Image editor. Set the swap frame to Frame 1. Check the Preload Images box but uncheck Restore Image onMouseOut. In the Behaviors panel, change the event from onMouseOut to onClick. The remainder of the tabs follow in sequence. Tab 2 swaps Frame 2; tab 3 swaps Frame 3; tab 4 swaps Frame 4; and so on. Uncheck the Restore Image onMouseOut box in

each case and change the event to onClick (4.48). Optimize the images and Export the images and HTML. Simple, wasn't it?

> **TIP**
>
> If you'd like to give your tabbed elements more visual depth, lighten the color of the forward tab on each frame. A subtle drop shadow will enhance the illusion.

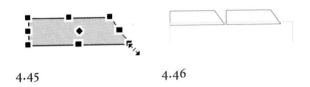

4.45   4.46

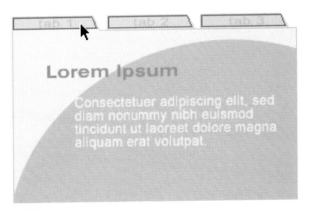

4.47

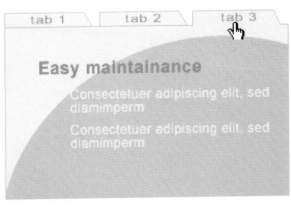

4.48

SLICING IT RIGHT

Q. *"I am looking for some help with slicing images in Fireworks. I am trying to create a navigational interface from an image. It is a large open case, and I want the inside to act as a separate frame . . . I think a good place to start would be a basic tutorial on slicing images . . ."*

DAVE C.

One of the reasons for slicing images is to allow for the possibility of adding an interactive element. Other important reasons are that slicing permits you to compress different parts of an image by varying amounts, to export parts of images as different file types, to take advantage of the fact that most browsers are able to download and decompress more than one part at a time. The latter reason only makes the image appear to download faster. In truth, downloading multiple image slices takes just as long and may even take longer. Why?

Under some circumstances, where there are too many slices resulting in an overly complex table, slicing can slow the loading of a page due to the increased demands on the server. Taking all of these factors into account during the planning stages is a good idea. Simplifying the layout also helps you to avoid the bane of many a Web designer's existence — the exploding table.

One common cause of exploding tables is arranging buttons asymmetrically and then attempting to slice the image around them. Whenever possible, design the table so the image can be sliced into neat rows and columns.

A circle intersected by button shapes is an interesting example to experiment with. It's more difficult to slice the intersected circle in a way that it makes the center of the circle useful. If you would like to follow along in Fireworks, locate the slicing_demo.png file on this book's CD-ROM and open it in Fireworks (4.49).

STEP 1 To see how you can set up button shapes to intersect a circle effectively, begin by opening the View menu and enabling Rulers. Under View➤ Guides, check Show Guides and Snap to Guides. Pull guidelines into the center of the image to mark off the cutout. Add more guidelines to define the button slices (4.50). That result looks like a lot of slices, doesn't it? (Twenty-four button slices, to be exact, plus shims.) The actual file size of the compressed image is 4KB. Adding shims to support the table will almost double the file size. The next step illustrates how to eliminate the shims safely and reduce the number of slices by twelve.

STEP 2 To prevent the shims from being created, choose File➤HTML Setup. Click on the Table tab and choose Single Table — No Spacer.

Activate the Slice tool and, working from the top-left corner down, begin dragging your cursor against the guidelines to create a slicing template. As you can see by the red lines of the slicing template (4.51), we've dropped slices over each row of the first column and created one large slice for the cutout. Try it. Move slowly, and you will find that the slices snap nicely to the guidelines. No more warnings about overlapping slices!

To reduce the total number of slices, create a second large slice out of the middle rows of the

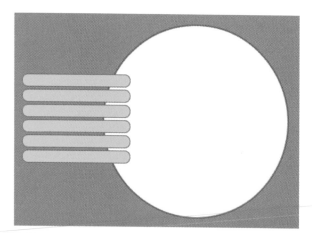

4.49

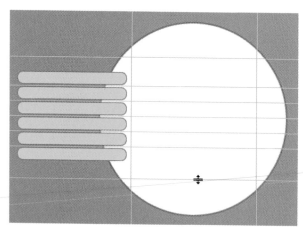

4.50

right column. Finish by adding slices to the top and bottom rows of columns two and three. The right-hand column and the top and bottom rows act as shims for the table.

Numbering any slices that have behaviors attached to them is a good idea. To number the slices with behaviors, open the Object panel; uncheck Auto-Name Slices; and for each button slice, type the word **button**, then an underscore, and then the number (button_1, button_2, button_3, and so on). Click on the large slice in the middle of the circle and type in the word **cutout**.

STEP 3 Turn off the slices and hotspots view. Duplicate Frame 1 six times. Add an image to the large slice in the center of the circle on Frame 2. We've used a Dingfont called Sports Figures to create ours. When the Duplicate Frame dialog box appears, type **5** and tick the At the end radio button (4.52). Add images to the center of the circles on Frames 3 through 7. Hint: Your images need to be approximately 180 × 180 pixels.

To add the behaviors, follow these steps:

STEP 1 Click on the Show Slices and Hotspots button to display the slice overlay again. Right-click on each of the button slices and choose Add Simple Rollover Behavior from the pop-up menu that appears.

Right-click on the top button and choose Add Swap Image Behavior from the right-click pop-up menu. When the Swap Image editor window opens, click on the word *cutout* in the left pane. The cutout slice will turn black. Frame 2 should be selected by default. Frame 2 is the frame you want. Leave the Preload Images and Restore Images onMouseOut boxes checked and click on OK. When the Swap Image editor window closes, click on the Hide Slices and Hotspots button. Click on the preview tab at the top of the canvas window and mouse over the buttons to make sure that they roll over and that the first button swaps the image on Frame 2 into the cutout area. To double-check, preview this in your browser.

Right-click on the slice over the second button and choose Add Swap Image Behavior from the right-click pop-up menu. In the Swap Image Editor, click on the large slice in the center of the

right window. Change the frame number to 3, leave the Preload Images and Restore Images onMouseOut boxes checked. Repeat with button slices 3, 4, 5, and 6. Button 3 should swap Frame 4, button 4 should swap Frame 5, button 5 should swap Frame 6, and button 6 should swap Frame 7. In all cases, leave the Preload Images and Restore Images onMouseOut boxes checked.

Preview your work in your browser (4.53). If all has gone well, optimize the images and export the images and HTML.

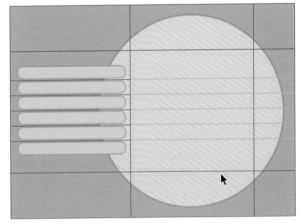

4.51

4.52

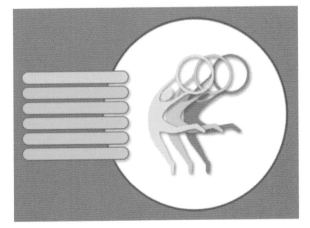

4.53

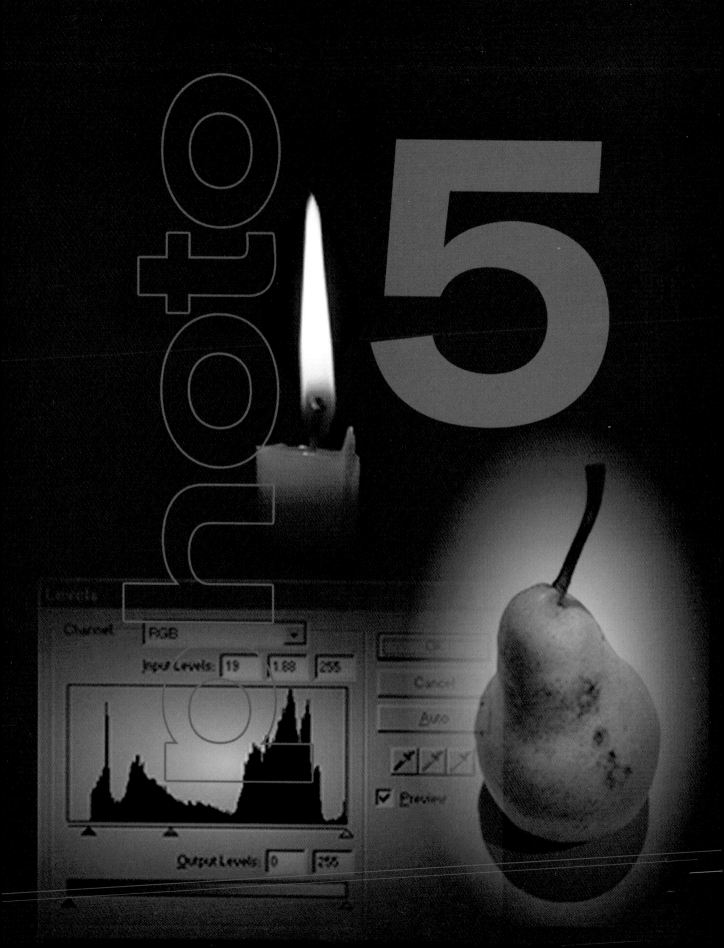

CHAPTER 5
PROCESSING AND KNEADING PHOTOGRAPHIC IMAGES

We've all seen Web sites that take a long time to load — especially when a huge photograph is embedded in the page. A large image file may be acceptable if it is a feature of the page and shows something important. But when several large photographs are used just for decoration, that's another thing altogether. Making a Web page that loads quickly for the viewer has everything to do with the dimensions of the image, how well it is compressed, and the sort of photograph you choose in the first place. That's what this chapter is about — how to choose, manipulate, and manage photographs as JPEG files in Fireworks.

The JPEG file format is described as a lossy format. *Lossy* means that the file format discards some of the picture information in order to reduce the file size. The JPEG file structure also splits the picture data into two parts: monochrome information and color information. The monochrome information is what delineates the objects in the picture — it provides the detail, brightness, and darkness. This is the most important part as far as the human eye is concerned. The eye is less sensitive to variations in color, so color information can be compressed more than the monochrome information without too much degradation of the image.

The JPEG format is very good at reproducing parts of an image where the detail varies in small stages. An example of an image that can be compressed efficiently and with good fidelity to the original would be a blue sky, where the brightness and color of the sky gradually changes across the picture. Where JPEGs

"Break any of these rules rather than write something outright barbarous."
GEORGE ORWELL, *POLITICS AND THE ENGLISH LANGUAGE*

have most problems is in parts of a picture where the detail changes rapidly — for example in the branches of a tree, where there are sharp edges between the dark branches and a bright sky. An over compressed JPEG file with this sort of detail shows "wiggly" artifacts next to the edges. The only way to avoid them is to reduce the amount of compression at the expense of a larger, slower-loading image file. Or you can use an image that doesn't have too many sharp edges.

CHOOSING IMAGES THE SMART WAY

Q. "How do I tell whether an image will work well on the Web? What should I look for?"

JASON T.

There are three aspects to choosing an image that will work well on the Web. The first is finding a photograph that illustrates what you want. The second aspect is to make sure the photograph is composed in a way that lends itself to efficient compression. The third aspect is cropping the image to show just the bits you need. Other considerations (such as choice of color combinations, composition, and the like) are artistic ones.

Here are some rules to follow when selecting images:

- **Rule 1:** Don't create a graphic for the Web with screen dimensions any larger than necessary. The more pixels, the bigger the file, the slower the load. According to current statistics, the average users are running their screens at 800 × 600 pixels, set to 16-bit color, and browsing with Internet Explorer 5. This means that the largest image they can possibly see all of is around 770 × 450 pixels. There's no sense in creating a graphic that can't fit on the screen. Prudent, conservative design suggests around 50KB as a good maximum size for a Web page, including text and graphics. How many Web site developers follow that? Moral: Keep the images as small as you can manage.

- **Rule 2:** Don't follow Rule 1 so slavishly that the image is too small and you can't see the details. A lot of Web designers seem to think that, by squishing up the graphics, they can fit a lot of

images on the page. The result is cluttered Web pages with images that are too small to make a statement of any kind.

- **Rule 3:** If you have a photograph with a lot of detail in it destined for the Web, see what you can do to reduce the detail, particularly in the background and other elements not important to the image's message.

You can reduce the detail of a photograph in three ways: blur the image, reduce its color range and brightness variation, or delete the detail altogether. (We explore these techniques later in this chapter.)

- **Rule 4:** Use the correct file format. GIF's are not for photographs; JPEG's are not for blocks of single colors.

When it comes to designing pleasing graphics for Web pages, we get into the realm of aesthetics and artistic taste. Two elements need to be considered: color and composition.

It's worth remembering that warmer colors have a different effect than cooler ones, color photographs look more intense against a dark background, and good contrast in a photograph is more pleasing than a low-contrast, flat image. As for composition, that's where the technology leaves off and the artist takes over.

Finally, PC users should remember that images usually look paler on a Mac and vice versa. Mac designers should perhaps lighten their images a bit, and PC designers might like to darken theirs. Just a thought. But you knew all that already, didn't you?

Q. "Our agency has finally purchased a digital camera, and someone (not me) will be taking pictures of staff to go on the Web site I'm creating. What resolution (other settings?) do I tell them to use? I plan on bringing them into Fireworks for editing before ending up in Dreamweaver. They won't be used for print at all. I know the 72-pixels-per-inch limitation for Web stuff; so do I, therefore, go with the lowest resolution to start with or start with the best quality picture and cut it down in FW?"

ALISON M.

Although Web images only require 72-pixels-per-inch resolution, it is a very good idea to do your graphics processing at a much higher resolution and only resize the image and reduce the resolution for the final Web graphic. This way, you lose the minimum amount of picture quality. So you should set your camera to the highest resolution that it can manage and — if it only allows you to store the images as JPEG files — at the lowest JPEG compression. Some cameras can store images in TIFF format. If your camera does this, use this setting. The two limitations of current digital cameras, compared to film cameras, are the limited resolution of the image chips (in budget cameras) and the limited space available on the storage media. Technology is advancing at a great rate, so in a few years time, these limitations are not likely to be a problem.

ACQUIRING IMAGES IN FIREWORKS

Q. "How do I get an image from a photo or slide into Fireworks?"

MIKE T.

To paraphrase Mrs. Beeton, "first catch your image." If you've been playing with Fireworks a bit, you will have noticed the Scan option under the Files menu. This opens a dialog window that allows you to Select a Twain source or Acquire the image from the Twain source already selected (5.1). *Twain software* allows

> **NOTE**
>
> Mrs. Beeton is the author of a Victorian era best-selling cookbook. Her recipe for Jugged Hare begins with "First catch your hare."

your graphics program to access your scanner and tell it what to do.

Every scanner has its own software interface, and if you've used your scanner before, you will recognize the interface when you accept the twain source. Fireworks merely calls the scanning software when you do this.

After you have opened the scanning software, scan the image (photograph, negative, or slide) the way you normally do, using any preprocessing image management the scanner interface offers. When you are happy with the result, accept the image, and the scanner goes off and scans the image as you have instructed it. After this process is complete, the scanned image opens as a bitmap in Fireworks. (You may need to close the scanner interface software before proceeding.)

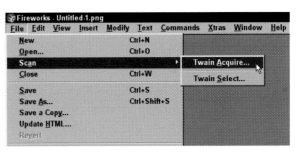

5.1

> **TIP**
>
> If you have more than one scanner — for example, a flatbed scanner and a negative or slide scanner — you need to choose which one you want to use before calling the scanner by using the Twain Select option, or you may open the wrong one.

The end result is an image file that is ready for further manipulation in Fireworks. Saving a copy as soon as you have scanned a satisfactory image is a good idea. You can save this in the native PNG file format used by Fireworks, or if you want to save a bit if disk space, you can export it as a 24-bit TIFF file.

To export a file, for example in TIFF 24-bit color format, select TIFF24 from the drop-down box in the Optimize panel; then choose File ➢ Export and proceed as normal.

Q. "I Just installed a new scanner, and I'm trying to use it with the scan option in Fireworks. I go to options and select the twain; I then select the scanner. I'm a little unsure what to do next. When I go back to scan, the same options are still there. What am I missing?"

TOMO L.

When you select File ➢ Scan, you have two options, Twain Acquire and Twain Select (5.1). If you have more than one scanner installed — for example a flatbed and a negative scanner — you need to choose the one you want by using Twain Select; then you invoke the scanning by using Twain Acquire. You should see the scanner software window open at this point. If not, something is most likely wrong with the scanner installation.

5.2

Q. "My scanner allows me to choose BMP, TIF, or JPG format. Which is the best for Web work?"

DHAL G.

Normally, you scan directly into Fireworks by using the Twain interface, so choice of file type is handled in Fireworks. However, if you are scanning directly to file from the scanner (for example, if Fireworks is not installed on the machine the scanner is attached to), choose a nonlossy format, such as TIFF or BMP. Select at least 24-bit color depth if the scanning software allows this.

SELECTING WITH MARQUEE TOOLS

Q. "There are lots of sites which use an image which looks like it has been cut out from a photo. How is it done? Do I have to draw around the image to be removed with the lasso? How can I get the edge so perfect?"

BRENT C.

Q. "Is there a way to easily remove background from scanned photos with FW? For example, I have a picture of a person standing in front of a brick wall. I want to remove the brick wall and add a solid background."

JIM W.

Q. "If I wanted to remove a person from the photo and add an elephant to the background, how would I do this in Fireworks?"

CHRISTOPHER R.

These questions all ask much the same thing: How do you remove the background (or some feature) from a photographic image and/or change it?

The Marquee tools are the basis of nearly all selective image manipulation in Fireworks. They behave in much the same way as similar tools in other graphics software, so they may be familiar to you already.

There are two main ways to use the tools: selecting and cutting the background from the original bitmap image or creating a mask to hide (and remove) the background. Both of these topics are covered in detail later in this chapter; but because they're such important skills, it's worth going over them more than once.

We'll use as an example a photograph of a butterfly (a Monarch, we think) sitting on a daisy. The original photograph has this set among many other flowers, and we want to extract the butterfly and its particular flower from the rest of the image (5.2).

You can extract the target in several ways, and all require careful drawing around the part you want to extract. Precision is necessary to avoid messy edges around the selected area. In this exercise, we treat the process entirely as a bitmap. Later in the chapter, we do exactly the same thing by using a vector mask.

STEP 1 Double-click on the image to switch to bitmap mode. Activate the Polygon Lasso tool. This tool allows you to "stitch" a marquee along any path you choose. To make things easier to see, zoom the image to 200%. Set the Edge for the tool to Anti-Alias in the Options panel and start drawing the marquee around the target, clicking every few pixels to place the polygon points (5.3). Marquee-marking is a slow and tedious process, but care is repaid in not having to do much tweaking of the marquee boundary later on.

After you have worked your way around the entire target, the Polygon Lasso tool will display a small square next to the drawing tip to indicate that the path is ready to be closed. One more click and the path is complete. A quick inspection of the marquee boundary is a good idea, using the (normal) Lasso tool to make any minor changes to the boundary (5.4).

STEP 2 The next step is to invert the selected area: Use Modify ➢ Marquee ➢ Invert so that you can cut the background. Before cutting, however, just to soften things a little more, feather the edge by 1 pixel: Use Modify ➢ Marquee ➢ Feather. Then choose Edit ➢ Cut to cut the background out, and there's the butterfly and its flower (5.5). To add a color to the background, choose Modify ➢ Canvas Color. Now you're ready to optimize and export the image.

5.4

5.3

5.5

5.6

5.7

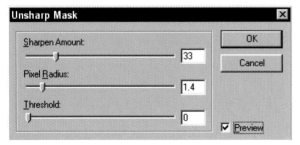

5.8

We almost forgot the elephant! If you want to add an elephant (or something more appropriate) to the picture, create a new layer (use the Insert ➢ Layer command), drag it below the butterfly layer in the Layers panel, and cut and paste your pachyderm.

MANIPULATING PHOTOGRAPHIC IMAGES

Q. *"Is there is any way that I can take part of the photo (like the background scene) and de-focus it; and then take the other part (for example, me) and leave it focused. I have seen it before on the Web and on TV, and I think this would be a neat effect."*

MIKE B.

Selectively blurring the background is a very good way to emphasize the main subject of a photograph by focusing the viewer's attention on the foreground. A side benefit is that it reduces the file size of a JPEG. We use a photograph of a fern for this demonstration (5.6). The background contains so many details that it competes with the details of the fronds. You'll find a copy of the photo on this book's CD-ROM, a copy that you can open in Fireworks and practice on.

STEP 1 Locate the fern.tif image on the CD-ROM and open it in Fireworks. Double-click on the Magic Wand tool and set the tolerance to 90 in the Options panel. Use the Magic Wand to select the main parts of the fern in the foreground. You'll need to do this in several selections, holding down the Shift key to add each selection to the preceding one. Increase the magnification to 200% and exchange the Magic Wand tool for the Lasso tool. Hold down the Alt key and use the Lasso tool to surround and deselect stray bits of background that you don't want to include (5.7).

STEP 2 Sharpen the selected details by using the Unsharp Mask option: Xtras ➢ Sharpen ➢ Unsharp Mask. Set the controls (5.8).

Using the Unsharp Mask option adds a little extra edge to the fern fronds that will compensate for a loss of detail when the image is later compressed for the Web.

STEP 3 The next step is to de-emphasize the background. First select the inverse of the current selection: use Modify ➢ Marquee ➢ Select Inverse. It's a good idea to feather the selection a little so no obvious sharp edges appear between different parts of the image (use Modify ➢ Marquee ➢ Feather, with 2 pixels of feathering). Now the background is ready for manipulation.

STEP 4 There are three things you'll want to do to the background: make it darker, reduce the contrast, and blur it. These steps reduce its impact and also reduce the amount of detail that JPEG compression has to deal with later on.

Add a Gaussian blur first: Use Xtras ➢ Blur ➢ Gaussian Blur (5.9). Then, using the Brightness/Contrast tools, dim the background. Use Xtras ➢ Adjust Color ➢ Brightness/Contrast (5.10). You've now achieved your goal (5.11). As you can see, the fern fronds stand out much more clearly from the background.

Without doing any tweaking or resizing of the original 535-×-451-pixel image, and accepting the 80% default quality setting for JPEG export, the unmodified file exports as a 108KB JPEG. The modified version weighs in at 74KB — a worthwhile saving.

Q. *"That was a cool trick! Is there something more I can do to reduce the file size of JPEG's?"*

MIKE B.

Absolutely! Fireworks has a new trick of its own, called Selective JPEG compression. We've asked Macromedia Evangelist, Brian Baker to explain it to us.

SELECTING BITS FOR EXTRA COMPRESSION

In these days of faster and faster connection to the Internet, it is easy to forget that vast numbers of people still connect with slow modems, and many hosts, especially outside the U.S., charge their customers extra if their bandwidth use goes over a certain limit.

To help keep those files sizes as lean as possible, Fireworks 4 has a new feature called Selective JPEG compression, which enables you to set the important features of your image at one level of compression and the rest of the image at another. Grab yourself an image and get to it:

STEP 1 To set a different level of compression, you need to create a mask. Do this by using the Marquee tools to create a selection and then converting the selection to a Selective Compression Mask. Depending on the distribution of the parts of the image you want left at higher quality, it may be easier to select the areas you want compressed more and then invert the selection by using Modify ➢ Marquee ➢ Select Inverse. Getting the selection exact is not essential; make sure, though, not to include any of the area you want at the higher compression. Having some of the less-important background at a higher quality level is better than having part of the main subject at a lower quality.

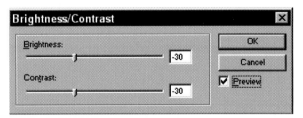

5.9

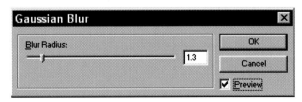

5.10

Gaussian Blur

5.11

To decide which tool you use to create the selection, check this list.

- **Marquee tool, Oval Marquee tool:** Useful if the areas to be selected are regular in shape.
- **Lasso tool:** Use for irregular shapes that can be drawn around comfortably. Usually works best with a tablet rather than a mouse.
- **Polygon Lasso tool:** Works well for irregular shapes, especially complex ones or when using a mouse.
- **Magic Wand tool:** Best used when there is a reasonable difference in colors between the main subject and the rest of the image. Setting a suitable Tolerance level (Options panel) can help.

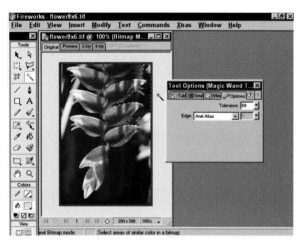

5.12

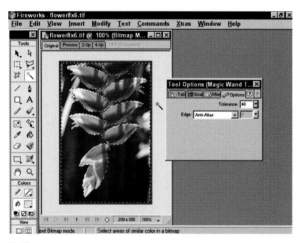

5.13

STEP 2 After you have created the selection, convert it by using Modify ➢ Selective JPEG ➢ Save Selection as JPEG Mask. A translucent overlay should appear over the selected area to show that the selected area is a JPEG Mask. If the selection needs altering at a later time, use Modify ➢ Selective JPEG ➢ Restore JPEG Mask as Selection, make the necessary changes, and reconvert it.

Two more entries appear in the Selective JPEG menu. The first is Settings, which opens the dialog box where the parameters for the compression can be entered. The other entry on the menu is Remove JPEG Mask, which, as you would expect, deletes the mask.

STEP 3 After you have created the mask, open the Optimize panel and switch to the Preview window to see the effect. Make sure that the Export File Format is set to JPEG. If the box beside the Selective Quality is grayed out, click on the Edit Selective Quality Options icon to the right of the box. This action opens the Settings dialog box where you should check the Enable Selective Quality option.

You will now be able to enter the settings you want for both the Quality and Selective Quality options in the Optimize panel. The figures should be in the range 1 to 100 (inclusive). Anything outside that range will be adjusted to the closest allowable figure. Start by setting the Quality to an appropriate level for the main subject. After you have done this, adjust the Selective Quality to as low a figure as is acceptable for the rest of the image. You can keep a check on the image quality and file size in the Preview window.

Note that, for simple bitmap images, you can use the mask area to set either the higher or lower quality parts of the image. The mask merely distinguishes between the two areas of the image. The Selective Quality and Quality settings in the Optimize panel determine what the image qualities (and compression ratios) will be.

When the image includes vector objects, you would normally use the masked area to select areas of the image for lower quality (higher compression), because, using the menu options listed below, you can preserve the image quality of text or buttons included within the mask.

There are three other options in the Settings dialog box:

- **Overlay Color:** This option allows you to change the color of the mask, which can be useful if the starting color is similar to the subject.
- **Preserve Text Quality:** If you have any text objects within the mask area, checking this option will keep the compression of that text at the level set for the main subject rather than reducing it to the level of the masked section. This will not work on any bitmap text.
- **Preserve Button Quality:** Works the same as the text option for any buttons within the masked area. As with text, these buttons need to be vector objects, not bitmaps, to have their quality preserved.

CASE STUDY 1

I had a picture of a flower that was 600 × 900 pixels in size, saved in TIFF format. From that, I wanted to export a JPEG sized at 200 × 300 pixels. After resizing the image. I decided that, because the background was a different color from the subject, the Magic Wand tool might be suitable.

My first attempt resulted in part of the flower also being selected (5.12), which meant that the tool tolerance was set too high.

I used Edit ➢ Deselect to deselect the current selection, reset the tolerance to a lower level, and tried again. This second try was more successful, so I moved around the image, adding to the selection by holding down the Shift key while using the Magic Wand tool (5.13). There was one small area (in the upper right of the image) that I did not add because this area was too similar in color to the flower for the tolerance setting I was using. I decided that the reduction in file size that could be gained by adding that small piece was not worth the time in starting again.

The next step was to convert the selection to a Selective JPEG Mask; I chose Modify ➢ Selective JPEG ➢ Save Selection as JPEG Mask and exit bitmap mode by clicking the red and white cross at

the bottom of the image window. This left the background showing the mask color (5.14).

I switched the image to the Preview window and opened the Optimize panel. I was now able to adjust the Quality and Selective Quality settings to reach an acceptable output (5.15). The resulting file size had been reduced from 15.93K using the default JPEG settings to 13.35K with the selective compression.

CASE STUDY 2

In this example I started with a picture of a pelican also in TIFF format, 600 × 900 pixels in size. The image is available on the CD-ROM as pelican.tif. I again wanted to export a JPEG sized at 200 × 300

5.14

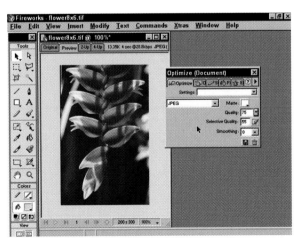

5.15

5.16

5.17

5.18

5.19

pixels. As well as the bird itself, I also wanted to retain detail in the reflection. After resizing it, I tried the Magic Wand tool and found that the tolerance had to be set so low that it was impractical. I decided to use the Polygon Lasso tool instead (5.16).

After the selection was complete, I inverted it to select the background (5.17), converted it the selection to create the mask (5.18) and exit bitmap mode by clicking the red and white cross at the bottom of the image window.

I then opened the Optimize panel and adjusted the settings for the Quality and the Selective Quality until I reached the lowest settings that still produced an acceptable image (5.19). This resulted in a reduction in file size from 19.27K to 13.50K.

Thanks, Brian, for explaining Fireworks' excellent Selective JPEG compression tool.

REMOVING RED EYES FROM PHOTOGRAPHS

Q. "I'm brand-new to Fireworks. Can anyone tell me a fast, easy way to remove red eyes from scanned photographs?"

FRANK G.

Red eyes in photographs are the bane of many a photo album. The effect is caused by the illumination from the flash reflecting off the retinas of the eyes. Correcting them in Fireworks is very straightforward.

We've appropriated a photograph from Bob Haroche, one of our contributing authors, to use as our example. The dreaded red-eye effect is quite evident in this image of Bob's son Liev (5.20).

STEP 1 Open your image in Fireworks and magnify it 200% to reveal the extent of the problem (5.21).

You want to select the red areas in the iris and change their hue, saturation, and lightness. The quickest way to select the area is with the Magic Wand tool. Set the Edge type to Anti-Alias and the Tolerance to around 30. Touch the wand to a red spot in the eye: It should select just the red part. If it selects too much, reduce the Tolerance setting; if not enough, increase the Tolerance setting. Add adjacent red areas that have not already been selected. A close-up of the selected area is shown (5.22).

STEP 2 Next, adjust the color of the red spots. The easiest way to do this is by using the Hue/Saturation control (choose Xtras ➢ Adjust Color ➢ Hue/Saturation (5.23).

The values you use for the Hue, Saturation, and Lightness controls will depend on the particular image, but the control window (5.24) shows some initial values that might be a good starting point. Experiment and see what effects the controls have. (Make sure that the Preview box is checked.) You can

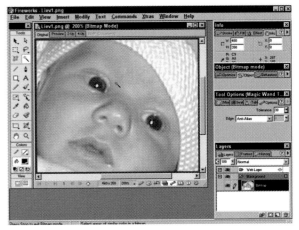

5.21

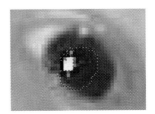

5.22

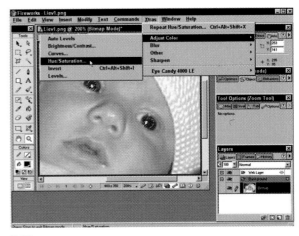

5.23

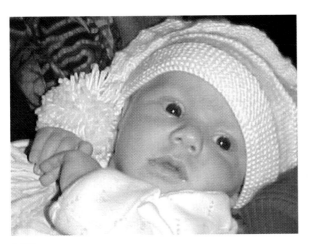

5.20

5.24

also get some weird *X-Files* effects if you adjust the Hue control instead of the lightness and saturation controls: luminous green eyes (5.25)!

Q. *"There are 4 methods of resampling an image in Fireworks: bicubic, near neighbor, soft, and bilinear. What the are differences; which is better or more accurate for what?"*

JEFF P.

When a bitmap image is resampled during resizing an image, pixels are added or removed from the original to permit the change in image size. These pixels can be selected from the original colors or created as an average of two or more nearby pixels, depending on the resampling method chosen:

5.25

> **TIP**
>
> You may find it easier to adjust the color of the selected areas with the marquees hidden. Hide the selection marquees by using the F9 key, but remember to turn them on again if you plan to do more processing, or you may forget that you still have the areas selected.

■ **Nearest Neighbor:** This method creates new pixels in the expanded or reduced image that carry the color of one of the adjacent pixels in the original canvas. For example, if the original canvas had only two colors, black and white, then the new canvas will also only have black or white pixels — no intermediate gray ones. You wouldn't normally use this method to enlarge or reduce a photograph because it could result in jagged edges and sharp contrasts with no smoothing. However, it is entirely appropriate for a GIF image because it adds no new colors. You can also turn resampling off when resizing a GIF; the choice depends on which method gives the better results.

■ **Soft interpolation:** This method gives a soft blur and eliminates sharp details. It is useful when other methods of scaling produce unwanted artifacts.

■ **Bilinear interpolation:** This method gives sharper results than soft interpolation but not as sharp as bicubic.

■ **Bicubic interpolation:** This method gives the sharpest and best quality results most of the time, and it is the default scaling method for Fireworks. This is the method you would normally use when resizing a continuous tone image, such as a photograph, but you would not normally use it when resizing a GIF. You may wish to compare it with the other interpolation methods to see whether they give better results.

Q. *"What in the world is an Unsharp mask and what do I do with it?"*

BRIAN H.

Unsharp masks were first used in conventional photography to sharpen the detail in a printed photographic image. In particular, astronomers use the technique to sharpen images of star fields. The physical process involves creating a blurred copy of the original negative and printing the final photograph though it. In other words you use the original to create a mask through which to print the final photograph. Appying an unsharp mask is vastly easier to do digitally than physically.

The unsharp mask filter is the preferred method of digital sharpening because it gives a great deal of control over how much an image is sharpened. It works by adjusting the contrast of the image edges. To access the tool in Fireworks, choose Xtras ➤ Sharpen ➤ Unsharp Mask or chose the Effect panel ➤ Sharpen ➤ Unsharp Mask. The Unsharp Mask is handy for sharpening a slightly blurred photograph or for pre-sharpening an image that will be converted to a JPEG, compensating for the slight blurring that results from the compression.

EMULATING DARKROOM TRICKS

Q. "Does Fireworks allow photo editing capabilities, such as freehand touchups like blend, smear, lighten, darken, soften?"

TOM M.

Q. "Does FW have the ability to dodge and burn?"

JASON B.

Fireworks doesn't have specific dodge and burn tools, but we've found that these are a bit overrated. In fact, you can achieve the result more easily (no matter what graphics program you use) by using the appropriate Marquee tool to select areas of an image that require attention, feather the selections, and darken, lighten, or blur as required.

STEP 1 If you are working on an area with a dominant color or areas of uniform brightness, the Magic Wand tool is very handy. Use this tool first; then clean up with the Lasso Tool to add or remove bits as appropriate. Feather the selection so that any changes to the area blend in gently with the surroundings. The amount of feathering will depend on how big the image is, but somewhere between 5 and 25 pixels is usually a good choice.

STEP 2 When you have selected the appropriate areas, choose Xtras ➤ Adjust Color ➤ Brightness/Contrast. To burn the selection, adjust the contrast slider. To dodge the selection, adjust the brightness slider. A combination of both contrast and brightness is versatile and effective. If you want to try something fancier, use the Levels control in the Xtras ➤ Adjust Color menu tree (5.26).

Blend and smear can be done in small areas with the Rubber Stamp tool. Move the edge softness slider all the way to the top and change the stamp size to a small one. Practice is the best teacher, and practice is time well spent.

If you want to blur (or soften) an area, the best choice is the Gaussian blur (choose Xtras ➤ Blur ➤ Gaussian Blur). This kind of blur allows a great deal of control over the final result. You can change the broadcast area of the blur by adjusting with the edge settings of the selection. You'll find the Edge settings menu for the Marquee tools in the Options panel. Note that you will need to set these *before* your make the selection. Lighten and darken are available in Fireworks both as Live Effects and as Xtras. Check under the Adjust Color menu in the Effect panel or under Xtras menu: Xtras ➤ Adjust Color ➤ Brightness/Contrast. Note that any changes made through the Xtras menu are not editable except by undoing them, whereas you can edit the Live Effects at any time.

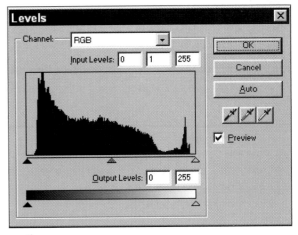

5.26

Q. "Some software allows you to do an automatic white balance. You select a spot that is supposed to be white or gray, and it adjusts the color balance of the entire picture. All three colors are adjusted simultaneously. This is especially useful in removing the complex colorcast of color photographs taken under fluorescent lighting or near dawn or dusk. It is also very good for removing the slightly 'off' color of some commercially processed photos. Is this possible in Fireworks?"

FRANK M.

The simple way to adjust the color balance is to use the Select highlight color eyedropper in the Levels control, either via the Xtras menu (Xtras ➤ Adjust Color ➤ Levels) or following a similar path in the Effect panel. Access the Select highlight color eyedropper (the right-most of the three eyedroppers in the Levels box) and sample an area in the photograph that you want to appear full white. Of course, if there's no part of the photographic image that should be full white, you don't get the result you want. We'll explore another way in just such a photograph.

The Levels and Curves tools in the Xtras (choose Xtras ➤ Adjust Color ➤ Levels, or Curves) and Effect panel menus (choose Adjust Color ➤ Levels, Curves) are powerful tools to adjust the color balance of an image. Each of these tools can be used on the overall picture or on the red, blue, and green levels individually. Either tool gives you tremendous control over the final result.

The Curves tool equates to the gamma curves of photographic papers, so the photographers among you may well find this an intuitive method to use. The Levels command provides more data on the picture. It uses a histogram (a bar graph) to show where, in the brightness scale, the image information is present. There are three eyedropper controls in the Levels box that enable you to set the shadow, midtone, and highlight brightness and colors. They require some practice to get right but are worth experimenting with.

The right-hand photograph (5.27) illustrates the use of the Levels control sliders in Fireworks on a photograph that has a strong red cast. Fireworks power goes beyond being able to correct the red tones, but also brings up some of the shadow detail.

The left image is the original as scanned from the negative and is close in color to the commercial print. The other is the result of adjusting the Levels controls and took only thirty seconds, using the skin tones as a guide. The reddish cast from the setting sun has been much reduced. The image would not have lent itself to a simple white balance control, because no white or gray object appears anywhere in the image.

Q. "If I scan B&W images, they all have a grayish background. Trying to change that into pure white causes other items to change lighter gray. So what I mean is that I don't seem to be able to replicate this nice B&W image in FW."

KALEVI K.

The first approach to resolving a problem with a grayed background is checking to make sure that your scanner is correctly calibrated. It may be that the scanner software is not set up correctly or that you need to update the drivers for the scanner. Avoiding

5.27

the problem at its source is better than trying to compensate for it later.

If this doesn't solve the problem, the alternative is to correct for it in the image. The best place to try is the Levels control (5.28)(choose Xtras ➢ Adjust Color ➢ Levels). You can also access this control as a Live Effect via the Effect panel. Because you are dealing with a monochrome image, you only need to adjust in the RGB option, not the individual colors.

The key to the Levels control, and why we think it easier to use than the Curves tool for normal image adjustments (as distinct from special effects!), lies in the histogram box that shows where the brightness information is distributed.

In this histogram, notice that there are gaps at both ends of the spectrum, meaning that no image information is at those brightness levels. These gaps indicate that the image information is compressed into a lower contrast range than the medium permits. If you move the left and right Input Level Slider arrows up and down to the points where the data is nonzero, so that it occupies the full spectrum available, you'll see that the image contrast increases. This technique makes use of the full dynamic range of the screen, and it's a good idea to make this change unless you are after a special reduced-contrast effect. The middle Input Level Slider arrow sets the *effective brightness,* or the part of the image that is in the middle of the brightness range. Adjust the middle slider arrow as required.

In the question at hand, however, the problem is that the highlights are gray. You can cure this problem by reducing the level of the upper Input Level Slider. This adjustment sets the point in the image that corresponds to full white. Adjust the slider until the gray highlights have turned white.

A quicker method is to select the right-most of the three eyedropper tools (the Select highlight color eyedropper) in the Levels box, and sample the image at a point where you want it to be full white. The whole image immediately adjusts as required. However, this is a bit "sudden death" as a control, and the Levels sliders allow more adjustment.

The techniques are well explained in the Fireworks Help files. Choose Help ➢ Using Fireworks. In the Index, look under Levels Xtra.

Q. *"I have a scan of some hand-drawn calligraphy — black ink on white. I simply want to select the black characters, change them to white, and drop them on a red background. I know this is simple, but I can't seem to get a good selection using the Magic Wand. Also, how can I ensure that the characters 'matte' well on their new background?"*

RICHARD H.

If you can't get the Magic Wand tool to select all of the black areas, it may be because the scan has converted the apparently black characters to a range of dark grays. You can get around this by adjusting the Tolerance setting for the Magic Wand in the Options panel. But even with this set optimally, selecting and converting the black characters without also carrying over some gray fringes onto the red background is a problem. Fortunately, Fireworks provides a much simpler way to do it, using the Levels Control, which doesn't even involve cutting and pasting.

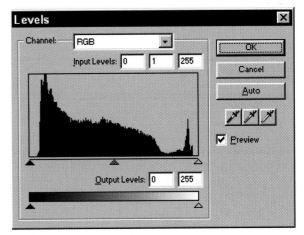

5.28

We'll start with an original scanned grayscale image with a grayscale (5.29). Locate the calligraphy.tif file on the CD-ROM this book's CD-ROM and open this file in Fireworks.

STEP 1 First, remove the gray tints in the background. Choose Xtras ➢ Adjust Color ➢ Levels or Adjust Color ➢ Levels from the Effect panel, select Adjust Color ➢ Levels from the Effect panel menu. With the Channel set to its default RGB, reduce the upper Input Level Slider to the point where all the pale grays in the background drop out to white, without losing any of the edge detail on the black characters. The gray background is replaced with white (5.30).

STEP 2 Next, select the Red Channel in the Channel pop-up menu and move the upper Output Level Slider fully to the left so that it sits over the left slider and click OK. The image is now black characters on a Cyan background (5.31).

STEP 3 The Final step is to invert the colors: Choose Xtras ➢ Adjust Color ➢ Invert or Effect ➢ Adjust Color ➢ Invert, or, from the Effect panel menu, select Adjust Color ➢ Invert. Voilà! White characters on a red background, with the edge subtlety retained. The black has become white, and the cyan, red (5.32). If you don't like the tone of red (in this case #FF0000), you can modify it by using the Adjust Color ➢ Hue/Saturation controls.

5.29

5.30

5.31

5.32

5.33

FADING PHOTO EDGES

Q: "How do I fade the edges of photographs? I need to use the image on multiple pages, so I want to use some kind of vector technique that remains editable."

GARY L.

Fading photo edges is easily done in Fireworks, and there's more than one way to do it. We've asked well-known Fireworks expert and author, Sandee Cohen, to describe these fading techniques.

USING MASKS TO FADE PHOTO EDGES

If I had to join one ecology group, it would have to be "Save the Pixels." The goal of this group is to keep people from deleting or destroying poor innocent

pixels in order to mask part of images. Fortunately, Fireworks 4 offers a wealth of techniques to mask images. The easiest technique is as simple as adding feathered edges around a photograph.

STEP 1 Open the photo you wish to work on (5.33). Make sure that you are not in bitmap mode by clicking with the Selection tool outside the image area. Activate the Ellipse tool and create an oval filled with black. Position it over the area of the image that you want to see (5.34). Choose Edit ➢ Cut to cut the oval to the Clipboard. Then select the image and choose Edit ➢ Paste as Mask. The oval now acts as a mask, revealing only the parts of the image that are inside the oval (5.35). The oval shape is still selected. However, if it

5·34

5·35

5.36

5.37

becomes deselected, you can easily select it again by clicking the mask icon in the Layers panel (5.36).

STEP 2 With the oval mask selected, use the Feather settings in the Fill panel to add the desired amount of feathering around the edge of the image (5.37). The image and the mask are now grouped so that they move together. You can move just the image within the mask by selecting the image and then dragging the diamond-shaped controller inside the image (5.38). If you want to move just the mask, leaving the image in place, you need to click the link icon to hide it in the Layers panel. This unlinks the image and the mask from each other.

A variation on this technique is to use the Pen tool to create a polygon shape (5.39). This technique is

5.38

5.39

extremely helpful in masking out the odd background or just giving the image a more interesting shape (5.40).

Fireworks 4 has added a terrific feature that lets you turn the selection on a bitmap image into a mask. This feature makes it possible to use the Magic Wand or Lasso tools to create the mask shape.

STEP 1   Start by using the Magic Wand to make the selection. In many cases, selecting the background of an image will be easier than selecting the main subject, as I have done (5.41). That's not the part we want to keep, but don't worry. We will fix that later by inverting the selection.

STEP 2   With the selection indicated by the marching ants, click the Add Mask icon at the bottom of the Layers panel (5.42). Because the background

5.41

5.42

5.40

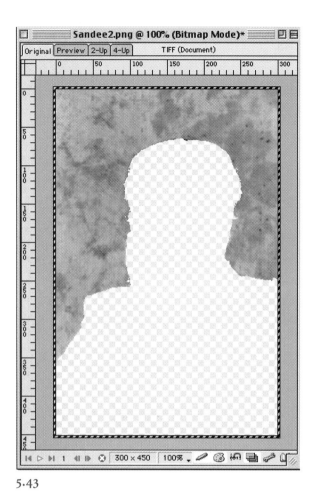

5.43

was selected, the image itself is hidden — the inverse of the area that you actually want to see (5.43) (5.44). What has actually been created is a grayscale image that has been set to act as a mask. This grayscale image is currently selected as indicated by the yellow line around the mask thumbnail in the Layers panel. Because the image is already selected, simply choose Xtras ➢ Adjust Color ➢ Invert. This action changes the grayscale image so that the white areas are black and the black areas are white. This action also corrects the mask so that the selected area is no longer visible (5.45) (5.46).

STEP 3 Finally, you can use any of the bitmap drawing tools, such as the Paintbrush, to touch up any errant edges on the mask. A black stroke color for the Paintbrush erases more of the background. A white stroke enables you to add back more of the image (5.47).

5.44

● **ARTIST AND ORGANIZATION:**
Hah! No organization, my life is too chaotic. (And I work for myself.)
  Sandee Cohen
  33 Fifth Avenue
  New York, NY
  212 677-7763

SYSTEM:
A new Macintosh G4 with 450 MHz dual processor. And a Macintosh Powerbook G3 (Wall Street) model.

CONNECTIVITY:
Now that I've got my Cable Modem connection I feel like Super-Downloader!

PRIMARY APPLICATIONS:
QuarkXPress, Illustrator, Photoshop, for print. Fireworks, Flash, Dreamweaver for web.

PERIPHERALS:
Wacom Tablet and a CD Burner. No scanner, though. I have to walk three blocks to the school where I teach to scan things.

WORK HISTORY:
I started out 25 years ago in advertising. Clients such as American Express and Lever Bros. 12 years ago started teaching and training computer graphics. Am the Graphics Coordinator for New School Computer Instruction Center in New York City. Author of the Visual Quickstart Guides for Fireworks, FreeHand, InDesign, and KPT. Co-author of Real World Adobe Illustrator and Non-Designer's Scan and Print Book. Speaker for Seybold Seminars, MacWorld, and Thunder Lizard Conferences.

FAVORITE PLEASURE:
I don't know that she's a pleasure, since she's nasty and bites, but I must mention Pixel, my cat who watches me work.

TIPS FOR WORKING WITH MASKS

- You can select either the image or the mask by clicking the appropriate thumbnail in the Layers panel.
- The small Pen icon in the mask thumbnail indicates that the mask is a vector object.
- A yellow and black stripe around the image indicates that you are working in the bitmap mode on the bitmap mask image.
- Use the Disable Mask command in the Layers panel to temporarily turn off the effects of the mask.
- To delete the Mask, drag the mask thumbnail onto the Delete (Trash Can) icon. A dialog box will ask you if you want to apply the mask or discard it. Choose Apply if you want to permanently delete the pixels that were being masked. Choose Discard to delete the mask without affecting the image.

5.46

5.47

5.45

5.48

Q. "How can I fade the edges of photographs to get the 'vignette' effect like on old photos? I've been using the FW Marquee tool, but I can't seem to get it to work right."

PETE H.

The vignette is an old photographic darkroom technique that was popular in the late 1800s. As you have seen, this can be done with vectors. The technique is also easy to accomplish in Fireworks with the Marquee tool.

Let's start with a vintage photograph to set the scene. The photograph of David's great-grandfather (5.48) dates from around 1910. No doubt you can track down images of your own ancestors to practice on.

STEP 1 Enlarge the canvas by 40 pixels in both directions to give yourself a bit of room to process the image. Select an elliptical area within the photograph's borders by using the elliptical Marquee tool (5.49).

5.49

STEP 2 Choose Modify ➢ Marquee ➢ Select Inverse to invert the selection. Feather the result by 16 pixels (more if you want a deeper fade). (Choose Modify ➢ Marquee ➢ Feather to feather the result.) Press the Delete key three or four times: The vignetting cuts in a step at a time.

An appropriate color treatment for this image would be to change it from monochrome to sepia by using one of the Firework program's Creative tools (5.50) (use Commands ➢ Creative ➢ Convert to Sepia Tone).

ARTISTIC PHOTO EDGES

Q. *"How can I create artistic photo or image edges in Fireworks without resorting to special filters?"*

TAI O.

We've experimented with a number of ways to create interesting edge effects without filters. One way is to

draw a black rectangle over the image, add a textured stroke in white, and then create a mask group of the whole thing. It works well enough except that, with many strokes, the edge of the finished image doesn't blend into the background as smoothly as it should. The better way seems to be as follows:

STEP 1 Open the image you wish to add the edge effect to and enlarge the canvas height and width by a minimum of 20 pixels to create enough space to add a border to. Change the Canvas color to the same one you will be placing the finished image against. Drag guidelines to the edges of the image. Make sure to choose View ➢ Guides ➢ Snap to Guides to be sure that Snap to Guidelines is turned on (5.51).

STEP 2 Drag out a rectangle that covers the whole canvas. Its fill color should be the same as the color you changed the Canvas to. Place your cursor where the guidelines cross at the upper left of the canvas and drag diagonally to where the guidelines cross at the lower right. You should now have a second rectangle that is exactly the same size as the image hidden by the first rectangle. Select both

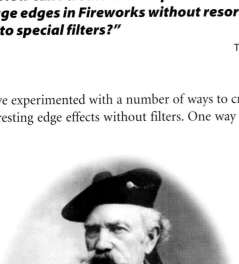

5.50

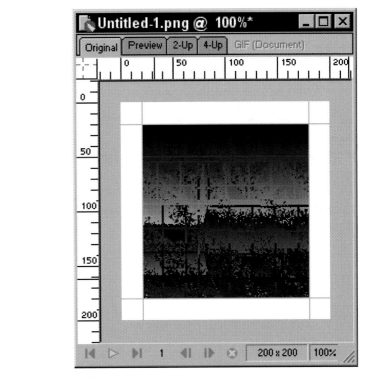

5.51

rectangles and choose Modify ➤ Combine ➤ Punch. Remove the guidelines by pulling them back into the rulers or by choosing View ➤ Guides ➤ Edit Guides ➤ Clear All.

STEP 3 Any Fireworks live effects, such as textures, strokes, and bevels that have been added to a shape, are added to the edge of a hole you punch through the shape as well. You'll now use this property of the hole to decorate the edges of your image with a combination of stroke and texture.

Stroke placement is important in this case. To make sure that the edge strokes you add will fall inside the punched area, depress the rightmost of the three stroke placement control buttons on the Object panel.

If the punched rectangle isn't still selected, click on it to ensure that it is (5.52). Open the Stroke panel and choose Unnatural ➤ Toothpaste. The Tip size should be 6. Move the edge softness slider to the middle position. The color of the stroke should be the same as the color of your Web page.

Choose the Onyx texture and set the amount of texture to 80%. Deselect the rectangle (5.53).

Fireworks has eleven main stroke types with subtypes for each. Add to this the list of built-in textures, and the number of potential artistic edge types grows exponentially. Happy Edging!

Q. "Does anybody have an idea how to accomplish that look that photos used to have in the sixties, with a white border around it and with jaggedy edges?"

MARION K.

Creating a jagged photo edge look requires a steady hand and a bit of trial and error, but it's easy to accomplish.

> **TIP**
>
> In case you haven't seen the "Easter Egg" yet, select Help ➤ About Fireworks. Hold down the Ctrl key, and then click the Macromedia logo. I know what 26-hour days can do to you, but …

5.52

5.53

We'll use the photograph of the pelican again, but this time a smaller version, 240 × 360 pixels.

STEP 1   Locate the file named pelican_small.tif on this book's CD-ROM and open it in Fireworks. Enlarge the canvas (choose Modify ➢ Canvas Size) to 300 × 420 pixels. Center the image (choose Commands ➢ Document ➢ Center in Document). Set the Canvas color to black (5.54).

STEP 2   Click on the Pencil tool. In the Stroke panel, set the color of the stroke to white, the stroke type to 1-Pixel Hard, and the texture to 0%. Next (and very important!), get out of bitmap mode (use the Esc key) to ensure that the Drawing tool operates in vector mode. Draw a jagged edge around the image in the black area that surrounds it. This may take a little practice. You'll need to develop a "controlled wobble" in your drawing stroke to make the results look right.

Follow the picture all the way around. As you get close to closing the loop, a small square box

appears next to the cursor tip. The appearance of this box means that you can lift your finger off the mouse button, and the path will close (5.55).

STEP 3   Add a white fill. This immediately fills the vector path and (temporarily) hides the picture.

Click on Layer 2 in the Layers panel (5.56) and drag it below the lowest part of Layer 1 (just below the box named Bitmap). When a double black line appears, release the mouse button. You should

5.55

5.56

5.54

immediately see the picture emerge from behind the solid white frame (5.57).

If you deselect the Path box below Layer 2 in the Layers panel, you'll see the completed jagged border. While we're at it, why not add a few extra touches? Why not add a drop shadow and choose a better background color?

STEP 4   First, change the Canvas Color to whatever color pleases you (choose Modify ➤ Canvas Color). We've chosen #CC9933 to go with the pelican's eye color.

For the drop shadow, we could use the Drop Shadow option from the Effect panel drop-down box. But as an exercise, let's do it manually, if for no other reason than to point out how useful the Live Effect is.

While the Layer 2 path is still selected (if it isn't, reselect it by clicking on the path thumbnail in the Layers panel), clone the path (choose Edit ➤ Clone). A duplicate path thumbnail is created second from the bottom of the Layers panel. Select the bottommost path thumbnail. Change the Fill color to black. Then convert the vector path to a bitmap (choose Modify ➤ Convert to Bitmap). Blur the newly created bitmap (choose Xtras ➤ Blur ➤ Gaussian Blur) with around 4 pixels of Blur Radius (5.58). Reduce the opacity of

the blurred image to 50%, and then drag it slightly down and to the right (5.59).

MASKING MAGIC

Thanks to Kleanthis E. for a useful tutorial on Masks, from which much of this material is drawn.

Q. *"Can someone tell me what masks are, do, and how to use them in Fireworks?"*

TERRY M.

Masking is a tool used to isolate parts of a bitmap or vector object (or groups of objects). The mask itself can be either a vector or a bitmap object. Parts of the mask are opaque, and you use it to show or hide parts of what lies beneath it. Masks allow us to change things later, with minimal wasted effort. Using masks is also a powerful way to create special visual effects.

5·57

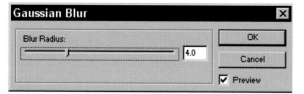

5·58

5·59

This example shows a straightforward way to use a mask to crop a photograph. We looked at this process earlier this chapter, when hiding the background and isolating the butterfly and its flower. Let's try the same example, this time by using a mask. Locate the file named butterfly.tif on this book's CD-ROM and open it in Fireworks (5.60).

STEP 1   Begin by pressing the Escape key to exit bitmap mode.

Activate the Pen tool and begin tracing around the part of the image you wish to retain. This time, instead of creating numerous anchor points, just create them by clicking at the vertices of the flower — its tips and indentations — and a few along the main points of the butterfly's wing. As you near the end of the path and get back to the starting point again, a small square appears next to the cursor to tell you that the next click will complete the path (5.61).

It's obvious that we haven't finished yet because the path is only a crude outline of the target. Activate the Subselection tool and click on one of the Bézier points to display the control handles for each of the anchor points. Use the handles to make the curve fit the target (5.62). When the path is complete and fits the parts of the image you want to keep, you are ready to apply the mask.

STEP 2   The masking method you'll use is Paste as Mask. Make sure that the vector path is highlighted (5.63).

5.61

5.62

5.60

5.63

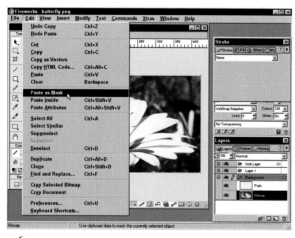

5.64

5.65

5.66

The name Paste as Mask implies that we need something to paste. In fact it is the vector path that you'll be pasting, so choose Edit ➤ Copy to copy it, select the bitmap image by clicking on it so that the vector path is no longer highlighted (important), and choose Edit ➤ Paste as Mask (5.64). The mask immediately appears. Its color is whatever the canvas color is set to (5.65).

The Link icon between the two objects in the Layers panel (next to the arrow cursor, lower right) indicates that the objects are linked and that any movement of the group will affect image and mask together. If you deselect the link, you can select just the mask or just the image and move either around. Give it a try.

We can change the canvas color simply enough through the Modify menu. Let's do this to complete the image (5.66). (Choose Modify ➤ Canvas Color and either choose white (the default) or Custom, and select the color by clicking on the color well and selecting from the palette.)

You can save the file in PNG format for editing later, and/or export it (as a JPEG).

You can use masks in many ways. This example has been but one simple illustration. To learn how to use masks effectively, you need to spend some time experimenting and playing with the options. As you start to understand masks, you'll find that you use them more and more.

Thanks, Kleanthis, for making masks less of a trap for new players.

Q. "You won't believe this one! I have a client who wants a word embedded in a photo. Not drawn on top of it, but so it looks like it was part of the original image, with pieces parts of foreground in front of it. Please don't tell me it's impossible!"

OZZI L.

It's not impossible. That word can be embedded in the image with a mask. To follow along with us as we demonstrate how it's done, locate the file named histiopteris.tif on the CD-ROM and open it in

Fireworks. (*Histiopteris incisa* is the type of fern in the image, in case you were wondering about the file name. It's more commonly known as Bat's wing fern).

STEP 1   Click on the canvas outside the image to exit bitmap mode. Type the text you want to use. The color for the text must be similar to the main color of the image to be most effective. Too much contrast with the image will allow the colors of the text to bleed through the mask. Add a drop shadow if you like. A good setting for the shadow is a distance of 7, 80% opacity, and a softness level of 10 (5.67).

STEP 2   Click on the photo and clone it (choose Edit ➤ Clone), then cut the clone to the clipboard by selecting it and pressing Ctrl X, or choosing Edit ➤ Cut). Select the text and choose Edit ➤ Paste as mask. Some enhancement with the Unsharp mask is all that's needed (5.68). Then you can save as a PNG or export as a JPEG.

5.67

5.68

BLENDING MODE WITCHERY

Q. *"I've been looking at those 'Blending Modes' options for a while and wondering what to do with them. What are they for and how do you use them?"*

JONATHAN B.

Den Laurent from the U.K. is another talented designer. We've asked her to explore blending modes for us.

Blending modes enable you to take two or more overlapping images and blend them together in various ways to get some interesting effects. Blending (or *compositing* as it is sometimes called) affects the color, tonality, and transparency of the images it's applied to.

For example, I want to match the tint of a photograph to the same color of a Web page on which it will appear (5.69). You'll find a copy of my photograph on the CD-ROM; the file is named autumn.tif. I know of three blending modes that will give me good, but slightly different, results. We'll give all three a try and see which one does the best job.

5.69

USING COLOR FILL TO BLEND

STEP 1 Open autumn.tif in Fireworks; then open the Effect panel. From the Adjust Color menu, choose Color Fill (5.70). The image will suddenly turn bright red. Click in the color well to open the palette; locate color #6699CC in the palette and click on the swatch with the Color. The red overlay will turn Wedgwood Blue. For Blending Mode type, select Color. The image becomes rather like a black-and-white photograph tinted with blue. It looks lovely, the highlights are softened (especially around her face), and there is a slight flattening of the image, as if we were looking at it through a plate of blue glass. This is a nice effect, but I need to keep more of the tonal range in the photograph.

STEP 2 Let's try Hue and see what that does. Reopen the Color Fill edit window by clicking the Info button, (the small, blue circle with the "I" in its middle) in the Effect panel. Select Hue from the Blending mode list. The range of tones in the photograph comes through very well. The highlights have a little more contrast than the original image, and areas with strong yellows and reds (like the leaves around her head) have become very blue. Areas that were already a little blue in color, like her dress, have become a warm gray. The result of using Hue as the blend mode is much more interesting than the result of using the Color blend, but it's a little too much for this image (5.71).

STEP 3 We'll try Luminosity but apply it in a different way. Deselect the Hue blend mode in the Effect panel by choosing Normal. Drag a rectangle over the canvas. The fill color of the rectangle should be #6699CC. Move the rectangle behind the image by choosing Modify ➤ Arrange ➤ Send to Back (or by dragging the rectangle under the image layer in the Layers panel). Select the image layer and make sure that you are working in vector mode by pressing Escape. Select Luminosity from the Blend Modes drop down menu on the Layers panel (5.72).

The tonal range of the photograph is excellent. The end result is not as soft as using Color as blend mode and not as hard as using Hue. The balance in the skin tones is just right, and this is the one I'll use (5.73).

5.70

5.71

When you work with blend modes in layers, you are blending one layer into another and you are working in vector mode. However, you can also use Blending Modes with tools when you work in bitmap mode.

Here I have a photo of a Somali cat with gorgeous amber eyes (5.74). Unfortunately, the brief for this image calls for a cat with green eyes. Think that this is too difficult? No way! This isn't a problem because we can change the color of her eyes by using blend modes and the Paintbrush tool.

STEP 1 Locate the muffin.tif file on the CD-ROM and open it in Fireworks. It opens in bitmap mode because it's a raster image. Select the Paintbrush tool and, in the Stroke panel, choose Basic from the Stroke drop down menu, and Soft Rounded from the Stroke Name menu. Adjust the tip to make it very soft and choose a size for the brush from the size slider.

STEP 2 Click on the Swatches panel tab to access its features and choose a color for the brush with the eyedropper. I've used #99CC33. Open the Layers panel and choose Blend Mode ➢ Color. Change the opacity to 50% and brush over the cat's eyes. The amber eye color is changed to

5.73

5.74

5.72

5.75

5.76

green, but all the texture, shadows, and highlights in the eyes are preserved (5.75).

Choosing the right color and blend mode to use can take a bit of trial and error. You may need to try several different colors and blend modes before you find the one that produces the color you want. Both Color and Hue work well. If the effect of the blend mode is too strong, adjust the opacity and try it again.

Of course, you could give her any color eyes by using this method, even blue (5.76)!

Thanks, Den, for explaining the mysteries of blending modes in such a practical manner and for sharing the photo of Muffin the cat.

As you've seen from the variety of tasks we and our contributing authors have illustrated in this chapter, you can do a great deal of your photo manipulation in Fireworks. Once you master these techniques, there's very little you're likely to want to do with photographic images for the Web that you won't find a solution for here.

reizen

6

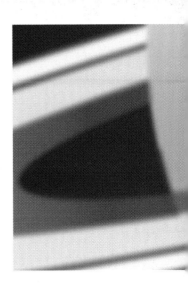

CHAPTER 6
A LITTLE RAZZLE DAZZLE

Depending how long ago you started out in Web design, you may have thought "Wow, what a boring medium! Bloated Roman text, gray backgrounds, and little GIF images stuck everywhere." As people explored the technology, Web pages started to look a little more sophisticated when compared to printed publications. What was lacking was really sophisticated graphics. Even if you could find an image that looked nice, it was usually a photograph and far too large to use on a Web page without reducing its quality too much. Guess what? The future is now.

This chapter is where we show you some of the really dazzling visual effects you can achieve in Fireworks. Anything from translucent wineglasses, beads, gem and optical effects, through bronze jewelry and deep space images. The following exercises are the result of many hours of experimentation with masks, Live Effects, and a plug-in filter or two. We've taken the backtracking out of this collection for you, and, though still fiddly, these effects are all great fun. Let the play begin!

"Dazzle mine eyes, or do I see three suns?"
WILLIAM SHAKESPEARE, *KING HENRY VI,* ACT II, SCENE I

DAZZLING GLASSWORKS

Q. *"I am a newbie at graphics and at Fireworks. My boss really liked the 'Aqua' button at the Apple Web site. (That's what I get for showing it to him.) Can something like it be done in Fireworks?"*

DIANE I.

One group of images that caused a lot of excited comment in Web graphics forums — not the least the Fireworks forums — was the translucent graphics that appeared last year on the Apple Web site. The most beautiful of these is probably the "Aqua" button that appears on the Apple OS X page.

Let's take a look at our quarry. You can find it at *www.apple.com/macosx/technologies/aqua.html*. The button is capsular in shape and has a reflection on the upper half; a subsurface glow under the lower half and a bit below the button; a soft internal glow around the edge; a drop shadow from the main button body; some "embedded" text; and a soft drop shadow from that text.

There are at least three tutorials for them on the Web. We think this one, based in part on Japi Honoo's Fireworks 3 version (but with a good deal of subsequent experimentation), wins the Kewpie doll.

STEP 1 Start by opening a new canvas, 420 × 220 pixels. A pale gray color is useful initially, though you may wish to change it to white from time to time to see the results of some of the steps. Set up a framework of guidelines: horizontal ones at 50, 56, 100, and 150, and vertical ones at 40, 65, 355, and 380. Make sure that Snap to Guides is turned on (View ➤ Guides ➤ Snap to Guides) (6.1). For

> **NOTE**
>
> Kewpie dolls, based on an illustration by Rose O'Neill for the 1909 Christmas issue of *Ladies' Home Journal* magazine, became an international craze. They were available in every price range, from the finest bisque to cheap celluloid versions that served as carnival giveaways.

now, use the sizes we suggest. If you need a larger or smaller button, you can always resize it later by grouping all the objects on the canvas (Modify ➤ Group) and using Numeric Transform.

STEP 2 Starting with the cursor exactly on the spot where the top and leftmost guidelines cross, while holding down the Shift key, use the Ellipse tool to drag out a 100-pixel-diameter circle. It is a good idea to open the Info panel so that you can keep watch on the size as you draw. Set the stroke to none and the fill to white. Clone the circle (Edit ➤ Clone) and use your arrow keys to move the clone down to the other end of the guidelines so that it touches the rightmost line and is located between the upper and lower lines.

STEP 3 Zoom to 200% and select both circles. Switch from the Ellipse tool to the Rectangle tool and, starting from the top Bézier point of the left-hand circle, drag out a rectangle that fills the space between and overlaps the inner halves of the two circles.

Select all three objects, the two circles and the rectangle, and choose Modify ➤ Combine ➤ Union. You now have a single vector object the shape of your button-to-be (6.2). You'll need five copies of this object, so clone it four times and hide the copies until you need them by clicking on the eye icons for each of the clones in the Layers panel.

STEP 4 After selecting the rounded button, set the fill color of the button to #283C78 by typing the numbers into the color value box. Press the Enter key to accept the value and close the palette. Your

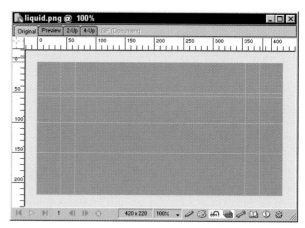

6.1

button shape should now be a rich, ultramarine blue. Click the eye for the shape in the Layers panel to make it invisible.

STEP 5 To build the upper reflection, select (and make visible) one of the button clones. Click the Scale tool to activate it and drag the top of the button down to the second guideline (at the 56-pixel mark). Drag the bottom of the button up to the middle guideline (at the 100 mark); drag the left end in to the inner left guide (65), and drag the right end in to the inner-right guide (355). Set the fill color to white (6.3). This is the bulk of the reflection, but we want to fade it into the rest of the button. You'll do this with a mask.

STEP 6 Draw a rectangle that sits exactly over top of the squashed button. Make sure that the stroke is set to None and set the fill to Linear. The fill colors should default to black and white, but if they don't, select the black/white option from the Fill panel drop-down box (6.4). The result will look like Figure 6.4.

Click on the rectangle with the Pointer tool to display the fill rotation bar. Rotate the gradient so that the black part of the fill is at the top. The square handle of the fill rotation bar should be centered at about the 89-pixel mark and the round one at 56. Keep the handle line vertical.

Select both the gradient-filled rectangle and the squashed button shape by using the Select Behind tool (6.5) or just use the Layers panel. You'll use the rectangle to mask the squashed button. Choose Modify ➤ Mask ➤ Group as Mask. The

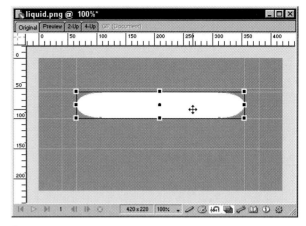

6.3

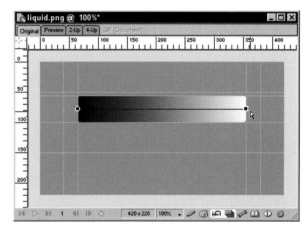

6.4

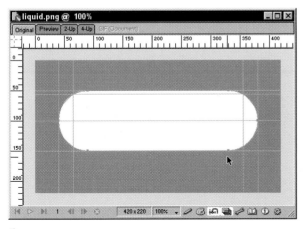

6.2

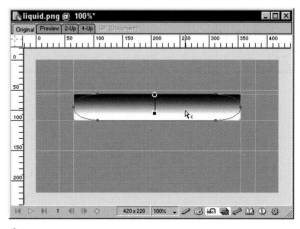

6.5

squashed button adopts the gradient of its mask. If you move the dark blue, full-size button beneath the mask group, you see the beginnings of the finished button (6.6). While the blue button image is selected, reduce its opacity to 80%.

STEP 7 Add a Drop Shadow to the blue button shape (Effect panel ➢ Shadow and Glow ➢ Drop Shadow). Set the shadow Distance offset to 36, the Opacity to 50%, the color to the same dark blue as the button, the Softness to 15, and the angle to 270. Change the background to white and temporarily hide the guides to see the effect (6.7). Show the guides again and you're ready to add a background.

STEP 8 Create a background for the button by using the Rectangle tool to drag a rectangle over the entire canvas. In the Stroke panel, set the Stroke to None; in the Fill panel, set the Fill to Solid black. Select the Line-Horiz 4 Texture from the Texture drop-down menu and move the amount slider to 100%. Drag the rectangle layer beneath both the mask group and the blue button and set its opacity to 30%.

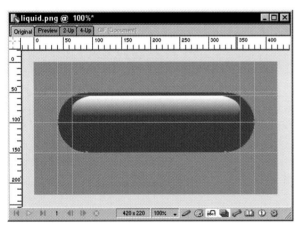

6.6

6.7

STEP 9 Add the text layer and set the text in the middle of the blue button outline. In the Layers panel, move the text beneath the mask group but above the blue button. We've used Bauhaus Medium at 72, Smooth Anti-Alias, and black, but a variety of other choices would work nicely. Add a Drop Shadow to the text. Set the Distance to 10, the Color to black, the Opacity to 28%, the Softness to 10, and the Angle to 270. This effect will only become obvious right at the end, but it is very important (6.8).

STEP 10 To add the soft edge glow, hide the work you've done so far. Select (and display) the third (and only the third) of the five button shapes. Set the Canvas color to gray again. Set the Fill to None and set the Stroke to Airbrush Basic, the Tip Softness slider to maximum, the Color to white, and the Tip size to 30. The result will be a glowing white edge (6.9). In the Layers panel, reduce the Opacity of the white edge to 40% and drag it immediately above the blue button image.

STEP 11 For the inner, luminous glow, move the last two button shapes, one above the other. Unhide them and hide all the other images. Make sure that the opacity of both button shapes is set to 100%. You're going to transform these two shapes differently, fill them with appropriate colors, group and blur, and then tweak the Brightness and Contrast. Start with the upper of the two. Select it and transform it via Modify ➢ Transform ➢ Numeric Transform ➢ Scale. Uncheck both the

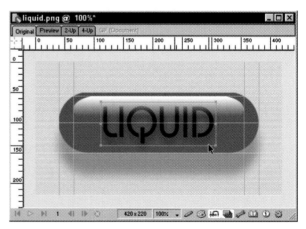

6.8

Scale attributes and Constrain proportions boxes and set the width to 94% and the height to 34%. In the Fill panel, set the fill to Solid and the color to #CCFFFF. Set the Stroke to None.

Select the second (lower) of the two button shapes and follow the same process as before, but set the Numeric Transform width to 100% and height to 50%. Fill with color #373782 (6.10).

STEP 12 Group the two shapes (Modify ➢ Group); then from the Effect panel, add a Gaussian blur of 18 pixels. In the Effect panel drop-down menu, choose Adjust Color ➢ Brightness/Contrast. Set the Contrast to +14 and the Brightness to +24. In the Layers panel, tweak the Opacity to 98% (6.11).

STEP 13 Select the group you've just been working on and move it down the canvas so that it sits between the lower two of the horizontal guides. In the Layers panel, drag it above the inner edge of the glow and blue button shape but below the text. The sequence of images in the Layers panel, with their opacities, should be, top to bottom, the upper reflection mask group (100%), the text (100%), the inner luminous glow (98%), the edge glow (40%), the main blue button body (80%), and the rectangle with line-fill (30%). Finally, the moment you've been waiting for: Set the Canvas color to white, hide the guides, turn on the visibility of all the images, deselect the images, and, as Japi says, "Voilà, the button" (6.12).

If you want to compare this with the original Apple version, change the text to *AQUA* and use Lucida Sans as the font. The result is quite close.

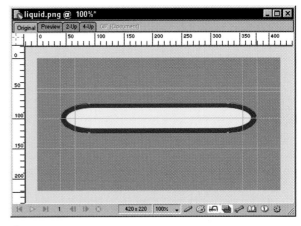

6.10

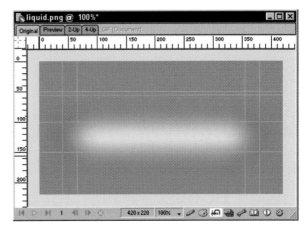

6.11

6.12

6.9

CREATING A WINE GLASS

Q. *"I'm trying to create an image of a glass of white wine. I thought this would be quite a common tutorial topic, but I can't find any information anywhere on how to do something like this in Fireworks."*

ANDY C.

Creating an image of a glass of wine isn't simple — nothing worthwhile is — but doing so should give you a feeling for how to explore Fireworks capabilities for yourself. Our example is done in a "commercial" style you might see in a glossy magazine. (Many thanks to Xara Xone's Gary Priester for the inspiration). It uses four layers and many objects, making it quite complex. However, no one step is difficult in itself. If you have worked through the preceding aqua button tutorial, you already learned the techniques necessary for creating your glass of wine.

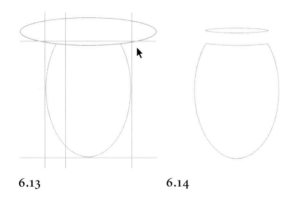

6.13   6.14

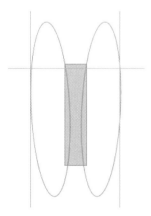

6.15

THE BOWL OF THE WINE GLASS

STEP 1 Open a 200×400 pixel white canvas. Add horizontal guidelines to positions 17, 40, 204, and 336. Add vertical guidelines to positions 36 and 163. Insert a new layer (Insert ➢ Layer) and name it Bowl. Click on the Ellipse tool to activate it. Beginning at the corner where the horizontal guideline at 336 meets the vertical guideline at 163, drag upward and to the left until you reach the corner where the topmost horizontal guideline meets the leftmost vertical one. That should have created a long oval, approximately 162 pixels wide and 187 pixels high. Remove the top guideline.

STEP 2 Create a second ellipse, starting at the top-left corner of the canvas. Drag diagonally to the point where the horizontal guideline at position 40 meets the right edge of the canvas (6.13). Open the Info panel, and (watching the Y coordinate update as you move the ellipse) use your down-arrow key to move the ellipse to the Y 6 position. Select both ellipses and choose Modify ➢ Combine ➢ Punch. Make two clones of the bowl shape.

Drag out a 94-×-8-pixel ellipse across the top of the bowl. It should just fit the curve you punched in Step 2 (6.14). Clone it and move the clone up and out of your way for now.

THE STEM AND FOOT OF THE WINE GLASS

STEP 1 Insert a new layer and name it Stem. Click the Rectangle tool to activate it and drag out a 33-pixel-wide by 140-pixel-high rectangle. Use the Ellipse tool to drag out a 54-×-238-pixel oval. Choose Modify ➢ Transform ➢ Numeric Transform ➢ Rotate. Rotate the oval by 5°. Clone the transformed oval and flip the clone horizontally (Modify ➢ Transform ➢ Flip Horizontal). Arrange the ovals over the rectangle (6.15). Select the right-hand oval and punch (Modify ➢ Combine ➢ Punch) it through the right side of the rectangle. Punch the left-hand oval through the left side of the rectangle. This shape is the foundation for the stem of the wineglass.

STEP 2 Drag out a 34-×-6-pixel ellipse. Arrange the ellipse so that its bottom half covers the top edge of the stem. Punch the ellipse through the stem to create a shallow concavity where the stem joins the bowl. Drag out a 22-×-8-pixel ellipse. Arrange it so that its top half covers the bottom edge of the stem. Choose Modify ➢ Combine ➢ Union to create a shallow convexity at the bottom of the stem. Use your up arrow key to move the top of the stem shape to where it is just touching the bottom of the shapes that form the bowl of the glass.

STEP 3 To create the foot of the glass, drag out a 129-×-28 ellipse and align it so that the bulb at the bottom of the stem sits in its exact center (6.16). Clone the ellipse and move the clone down out of your way.

6.16

THE LIQUID

Create a new layer and label it Wine. Drag one of the clones of the bowl shape into the new layer. Activate the Scale tool and (working from the top-right corner) drag diagonally toward the bottom left. Watch the size update in the Info panel as you drag. When the width is reduced to about 118 pixels, stop. Center the shape inside the outer bowl (6.17).

Drag out a 174-×-45-pixel ellipse. Align it so that its top Bézier point lines up with the top-center Bézier point of the outer bowl (6.18). Shift + select the ellipse and the scaled bowl shape and choose Modify ➢ Combine ➢ Punch. This new shape will be the liquid inside the glass.

The liquid needs a top surface, too. To create one, draw a 118-×-8-pixel ellipse. It should fit snugly into the curve at the top of the liquid shape. If it appears off by a pixel or two, adjust the width or height by changing the values in the Info panel.

6.17

6.18

HIGHLIGHTING

STEP 1 Create a new layer and label it Highlight. Drag a new vertical guideline to the 66-pixel position. Drag a new horizontal guideline to the 176-pixel position. Activate the Pen tool and click on the new vertical guideline about even with the lowest part of the curve that makes up the rim of the glass. Drag straight toward the left. When you reach the first vertical guideline (position 36), lift your finger off the mouse button; move your cursor down to where the two new guidelines intersect and click (6.19). Switch to the Subselection tool and drag the Bézier handle at the top of the

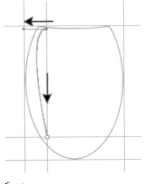

6.19

pen line down and to the left until the curve of
your line mirrors the curve of the bowl (6.20).
STEP 2 Choose Modify ➢ Alter Path ➢ Expand
Stroke and expand it by 15 pixels. Use the square
corner, a miter limit of 10, and the square end cap

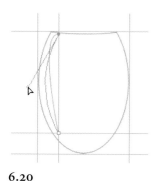

6.20

6.21

6.22

6.23

style (first button). Zoom in and use the
Subselection tool to pull the Bézier point at the
top-left corner of the highlight shape even with
the one at the top right.

Hide all layers except for the Bowl layer.

That completes the wire frame of your image (6.21).
Now for the fun part: adding color!

ADDING COLOR TO THE BOWL

STEP 1 Select the first of the two bowl shapes,
and if it doesn't have a fill, add a white fill and a
Basic, Soft Rounded stroke. The stroke color
should be pale gray (#E5E5E5), and the stroke
width should be 1. Open the Effect panel and
choose Inner Shadow. Set the color to black, the
distance to 8, the opacity to 65%, the softness to 4,
and the angle to 90°. Add a black fill color to the
second bowl shape.

In the Layers panel, Shift + select the bowl with
the shadow and the bowl with the black fill and
choose Modify ➢ Mask ➢ Group as Mask (6.22).
STEP 2 To form the rim of the glass, move the
first of the two ellipses in the Bowl layer to the top
of edge of the bowl shape. Add a Basic, Soft
Rounded stroke: color #999999 and width 1.
To create the rim highlight, add a 2-pixel, white,
Basic, Soft Rounded stroke to the second ellipse.
Drag a rectangle over it and give the rectangle a
black/white linear fill. Select both the ellipse and
the rectangle and choose Modify ➢ Mask ➢
Group as Mask. Move the mask group on top of
the first ellipse. Hide the Bowl layer (6.23).

CREATING THE STEM

STEP 1 Unhide the Stem layer. To create the inner
highlight of the stem, clone one of the stem
shapes, open the Effect panel, and apply an Inner
Glow (Effect panel ➢ Shadow and Glow ➢ Inner
Glow). Set the color to #CCCCCC, the width to 8,
the opacity to 100%, and the softness to 3.
STEP 2 Remove any fill from one of the other
stem shapes and add a Basic, Soft Rounded stroke.

The width should be 1 pixel and the color, #999999. Move it to the front of the stem shape with the glow to give it a soft outline.

STEP 3 To add the shadow to the top of the stem, change the fill of the remaining stem shape to black. Drag a rectangle over the black stem shape and change the fill type of the rectangle to a black-white linear fill. Rotate the fill so the black part is at the top. Select both the black stem shape and the rectangle and choose Modify ➢ Mask ➢ Group as Mask. Reduce the opacity of the mask group to 90%. Click on the Path icon of the mask group and use the gradient adjustment bar to move the colored part of the mask to approximately one-third of the way from the top (6.24).

ARRANGING THE FOOT

STEP 1 Clone one of the ellipses you created for the foot of the glass and add an Elliptical fill. Set the dark color to #333333 and the highlight color to white. Move the pivot point of the fill rotation bars to the bottom-center Bézier point of the ellipse. Stretch the short handle to the same length as the long one and rotate them so the square handles are at the bottom (6.25). Copy the filled ellipse; then select the second ellipse. Choose Edit ➢ Paste Attributes. Stretch the short arm of the gradient and rotate it in the in the same way you did for the first ellipse, but move the pivot point to the top-center Bézier point of the ellipse. Cover the second ellipse with the first and choose Modify ➢ Mask ➢ Group as Mask.

STEP 2 To create the highlight on the rim of the foot, add a 2-pixel, white, Soft Rounded stroke to the remaining ellipse and remove any fill. Drag out a rectangle. Add a black-white linear fill to the rectangle and position it over the ellipse with the stroke. Select both the rectangle and the fill and choose Modify ➢ Mask ➢ Paste as Mask. The part of the ellipse covered by the white of the gradient disappears. Move the remaining half of the ellipse on top of the grouped foot images to create the rim highlight (6.26). Shift + select the group-highlight and grouped foot images and choose Modify ➢ Arrange ➢ Send to Back. While they

are still selected, use your arrow keys to align them so the base of the stem falls directly in their center. Hide the Stem layer.

ADDING THE WINE

STEP 1 Unhide the Wine layer. Select the bowl shape you created for the liquid and add a Radial fill. The colors are #E2C56E and white. Grab the round handle of the gradient with your cursor and move it diagonally from the center, halfway to the 5:00 position.

STEP 2 Select the ellipse that forms the top of the liquid and add a linear fill. Use the same colors you used for the body of the liquid. Move the round handle of the gradient to around the 62-pixel position and pull the square handle about 10 pixels past the right edge of the canvas. Hide the Wine layer (6.27).

ADDING THE HIGHLIGHT

STEP 1 Drag a rectangle over the highlight and give the rectangle a black-white gradient. Rotate the gradient so the black part is at the top. Move the

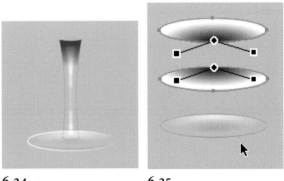

6.24   6.25

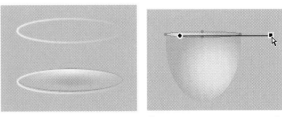

6.26   6.27

6.28

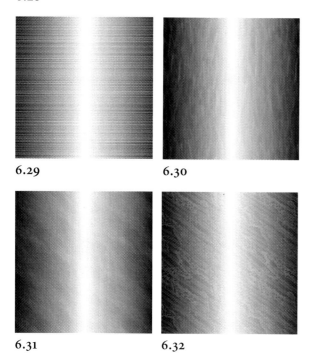

6.29　　　　**6.30**

6.31　　　　**6.32**

NOTE

Live Effects are editable elements that you can come back to and change later on, even though you may have done a lot of other stuff since first creating the effect. This is Fireworks' greatest single trick and we love it.

square handle so that it is over the bottom-right corner of the highlight shape. Select both the gradient rectangle and the highlight shape and choose Modify ➤ Mask ➤ Paste as Mask.

STEP 2 Unhide all the layers. We've added both a shadow and a small violet for some color and texture contrast (6.28).

TEXTURING METALS

Q. *"How would you go about creating a brushed-metal texture. In Photoshop you use noise and a motion blur. How about Fireworks?"*

FRED W.

Rather than applying filters to create a brushed-metal effect in Fireworks, you apply a texture to a metallic gradient (6.29). Because Textures are applied as Live Effects and remain editable until they are exported, you can experiment with different textures and variations on the amount of texture, plus add some color effects until the effects are exported. The Fireworks Grass texture (6.30), the Parchment texture (6.31), and the Onyx texture (6.32) are illustrated.

Q. *"I am trying to get the look of a machined finish you would see on the end of a piece of metal that has been turned in a lathe. Any help would be appreciated."*

DENNIS R.

In this case, a prefab texture won't work the magic. Instead, generate the texture live by converting the shape to a Symbol; then tween between the original and an Instance of the Symbol. You'll need to load the Metal Gradient Styles from the CD-ROM at the back of the book before starting this exercise.

STEP 1 Open a 150-×-150-pixel canvas. Click the Ellipse tool and drag out a 132-×-132-pixel circle. Center it on the canvas (Commands ➤ Center in Document). While the circle is still selected, add the Silver style and a Basic, Soft Rounded stroke. The Stroke color is #999999, and the width is 1 pixel stroke (6.33).

STEP 2 Select Insert ➢ Convert to Symbol. When prompted to select a Symbol type, click the Graphic radio button. Open the Library panel and drag an Instance of the new Symbol onto the canvas. Click the Scale tool; reduce the Instance to a 39-×-39-pixel circle and center it on the canvas (6.34). Select the Instance; then select the original Symbol and choose Modify ➢ Symbol ➢ Tween Instances. Enter a number between 8 and 12 in the Steps box (we used 8) and click OK (6.35).

This last step, although unnecessary, does add a nice finish to the outer edge.

STEP 3 Choose Edit ➢ Select All; then choose Modify ➢ Group. Select the group and convert it to a bitmap. Double-click on the bitmap to put the image in Bitmap Edit Mode. Click the Elliptical Marquee tool and open the Options panel. For Style, choose Fixed Size; for size, choose 125 × 125; for edge, choose Anti-Alias. Click on the bitmap and carefully center the marquee (6.36). Choose Modify ➢ Marquee ➢ Select Inverse. Choose Xtras ➢

Blur ➢ Gaussian Blur. Set the blur radius to 0.6. Exit Bitmap Edit mode, and there you have it (6.37)!

Q. "I can do the basics in Fireworks and can create nice functional designs for sites. I, however, want to do some fancy stuff. What I want to achieve is to get a worn, rusted, scratched effect on some metal. I can't really figure a good way of doing it."

OWEN P.

If you can imagine the use, exposure to chemicals, and weathering that the surface of the metal has been subjected to as being layered on, you are most of the way toward creating this kind of effect.

STEP 1 Open a 150-×-150-pixel canvas and drag out a rectangle to cover it. Add the Steel style and a 25% Scratch texture (6.38). Click on the Pencil tool and scribble a couple of loops over the rectangle. Add an Airbrush stroke to the pencil scribble. Set the color to black, the Tip Size to 72, and

---

TIP

Tweening is a traditional animation term that describes the process in which a lead animator draws the key frames, while assistants draw the frames in between. In Fireworks, tweening blends two or more instances of the same symbol and is useful for movement of an object across the canvas.

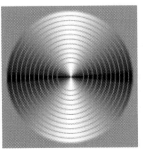

6.35

6.36

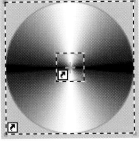

6.33

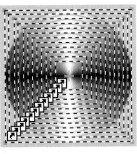

6.34

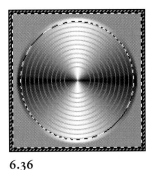

6.37

6.38

move the softness slider all the way to the top (6.39). Reduce the opacity of the scribble to 45%.

STEP 2 Make a second pencil scribble, somewhat smaller than the first, and add a black, Unnatural, Fluid Splatter stroke. Set the Tip Size to 13. Reduce the opacity to 55% and change the Blend Mode from Normal to Tint (6.40).

STEP 3 Add another pencil scribble by setting the Stroke style to Airbrush ➤ Textured, the Tip Size to 60, and the color to #574931 (6.41). Clone the scribble and move it a few pixels down and to the right of the original. Change the color of the clone to #FF6600 and reduce its opacity to 40%. Add a drop shadow to the clone by using the default shadow settings. Repeat this step over another area of the rectangle.

STEP 4 Choose Edit ➤ Select All; then choose Modify ➤ Convert to Bitmap. Open the Effect panel and choose Adjust Color ➤ Levels. Change the numbers in the three Input Level boxes to 30, 1, and 230. Click OK. Still in the Effect panel, choose Sharpen ➤ Sharpen (6.42).

PEARLIZING A BUTTON

Fireworks forum regular Japi Honoo has a particular talent for creating realistic-looking objects in Fireworks. When we decided to include a tutorial on pearl finishes in the book, we knew that she was the right person to consult with. You'll have to look very carefully to convince yourself the final image is not a photograph. Here is the way Japi creates a pearl:

STEP 1 Open a 150-×-150-pixel canvas. I've used #999999 as a canvas color. Drag out a 90-×-90-pixel circle and give it a radial fill. Make the base color #B19E72 and the highlight color #EDEDD5 (6.43). Add a 30% Ripple texture (6.44).

STEP 2 Pull a guideline to the left edge of the shape. Click on the Pen tool to activate it and click down at the 5:00 position. Drag straight across to the guideline, release the mouse button, and click at about the 3:00 position (6.45). Add an Airbrush stroke to the pen line. The settings are Color — white; the Tip Size is 72. Move the Edge softness slider all the way to the top. Cut the new pen line to the Clipboard, select the circle and choose Edit ➤ Paste Inside (6.46).

6.39

6.40

6.41

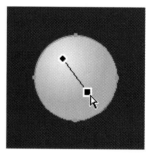

6.43

6.44

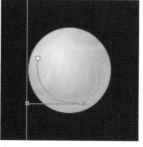

6.45

6.46

STEP 3 Choose Modify ➤ Deselect; then set the stroke color well in the Tools palette to white. Click on the Pencil tool; then click on the pearl shape at the 3:00 position. That action should have put a white dot on top of the image. While the image is still selected, turn it into a soft highlight by changing the stroke to Airbrush ➤ Basic, Tip Size 39. Clone the highlight and leave the clone in place. Repeat at the 12:00 position (6.47).

6.47

Not Bad! Now to really smarten it up, add a third-party plug-in effect. If you have Alien Skin's EyeCandy 4000 installed (if not, a demonstration version of Alien Skin's EyeCandy 4000 is included on the CD-ROM located at the back of this book), choose Edit ➤ Select All; then choose Modify ➤ Group; finally, choose Modify ➤ Convert to Bitmap.

Select the bitmap and choose the EyeCandy Glass filter from the Effect menu. Here are the settings:

Basic
Bevel width = 46.04, Smoothness = 38, Bevel Placement = Inside Marquee, Edge Darkening = 7, Gradient Shading = 16, Refraction = 89, Opacity = 75, Tinting = 83, and Color = R-237, G-236, and B-217.

Lighting
Direction = 80, Inclination = 48, Highlight Brightness = 100%, Highlight Size = 86, Highlight Color = white, Ripple Thickness = 36, Ripple Width = 210.22, and Random Seed = 1.

Bevel Profile
Bevel Profile = Subtle Button.

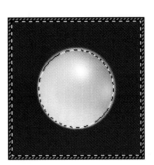

6.48

6.49

Adding the Glass filter as a live effect allows you to adjust and readjust the settings until they please you. After you are satisfied with the effect it is necessary to embed it in the image by converting the image to a bitmap a second time, Choose Modify ➤ Convert to Bitmap.

To soften the outer edge, click the Elliptical Marquee tool to activate it and choose Options ➤ Fixed Size. Set the height and width to 85; then click on the image to drop the marquee. If necessary, use your arrow keys to align it. Choose Modify ➤ Marquee ➤ Invert (6.48). Choose Xtras ➤ Blur ➤ Gaussian Blur. Set blur between 0.6 and 0.8. And here is the realistic result (6.49)!

Japi, that was super. Thanks!

MOTHER-OF-PEARL

As long as we are on the subject of pearls, we'd be remiss in not including a brief overview of how to create a mother-of-pearl finish. The lovely colors and iridescence of this material are easily simulated by a gradient (6.50). The colors we've used, from left to right, are #FFFFFF, #E1E1FF, #DFD8CA, #CCFFFF, and #A8A480.

The button (6.51) was created by first dragging out a rectangle and applying a shiny gold gradient — then topping it with a rectangle to which we applied the mother-of-pearl gradient. The gradient style was changed from Linear to Ripples. Next the gradient was rotated and stretched by pulling out the handles of the fill rotation bar. (Make sure the Pointer tool is selected so you can see the fill handles.) Grouping the two rectangles and adding a drop shadow finished it.

6.50

6.51

WATER DROPS

This exercise began one night when DN noticed the lighting effects on a droplet of water sitting on a plastic ice cream container. As scientists will do (DN's degree is in physics), he pulled out a magnifying glass to study it. He then posted his observations to LR. Synchronicity! That very morning, LR had been asked how to create a water drop by one of the visitors to the Fireworks forum. The result (in case you were curious about how co-authors living on different continents do these things) was an exchange of e-mailed PNG files, with each author's version building upon the previous one. It ended in a phone conversation wherein DN's final version was declared the winner.

The thing to do before trying to construct a water droplet in Fireworks is to observe how water drops actually look in nature. They have subtleties that, if you miss them, make the image look somehow wrong. So take a close-up look at a water drop with a magnifying glass. Notice the way the light hitting the droplet is internally refracted to set a gradient in intensity across the backdrop of the droplet and how, under some lighting conditions, there is both a shadow beyond the droplet and, right next to it, a slight glow. The most obvious and difficult thing to capture is the reflection on the surface of the droplet. The backdrop gradient, shadow and inner glow are the elements we'll try to re-create.

NAME:
Japi Honoo

UM, YOUR REAL NAME:
Paola Baffetti

HA-HAH! YOU READ IT HERE FIRST, FOLKS!

COMPANY:
I work as a freelance graphics designer and Web consultant. My location and contact number is:
Via Nazionale 12 Bis, 30032
Fiesso D'Artico (VENEZIA), Italia,
+39 049 502 806.

COMPUTER:
Pentium III, 500Mhz, 128RAM, 18G.

CONNECTION TO THE INTERNET:
56K modem; but by the time this book is printed, I'll be on ISDN.

PRIMARY APPS:
Fireworks and Dreamweaver.

PERIPHERALS:
IomegaZIP250 USB and a Wacom Tablet. For printing and scanning, I use machines from the company I collaborate with. I have a little, little home.

WORK HISTORY:
I started sniffing around computers in 1984 with a Commodore 64. I learned to program in BASIC on it. In 1990, I built my first PC (an 80286 Jurassic PC). In 1998, I built a Pentium 133 with 32MB RAM. It was on that machine that I did my first professional work. I buy my machines now.

Before taking the plunge into Web design, I worked as bookkeeper. A job in a software house allowed me to free my creativity, and it has been onward and upward since.

We're going to work in monochrome, using a mid-gray canvas color as background. We'll draw a large droplet and then reduce it in size. This takes advantage of the slight smoothing effect that image resizing has.

STEP 1 Open a new image with a canvas size of 400 × 400 pixels and with a mid-gray canvas color (#999999). Select the Ellipse tool. In the Fill panel, set the Fill to Solid, Edge Anti-Alias, the Fill Color to white, and the Layer Opacity to 100%. In the Stroke panel, set the stroke to None.

Using the Ellipse tool with the shift key held down to restrain the ellipse to a circle, draw the circle with a diameter of 200 pixels. Select the Info panel to keep track, or turn Rulers on (View ➣ Rulers) and watch the setting as you drag out the circle. Then center the circle in the window (Commands ➣ Document ➣ Center in Document).

STEP 2 Draw a second circle with a diameter of 192 pixels, with the same settings as before, except for the Edge, which should be set to Feather, 8 pixels. Center this circle also; then use the arrow keys to move it down and to the right across the Canvas by 6 pixels in each direction. The result is shown with centered guides to show the offset (6.52). Drag this circle down to the bottom of the Layers panel and reduce its Opacity to 75%. This object provides the refracted glow inside the ordinary shadow. Hide it for the moment (click the "eye" next to it in the Layers panel).

STEP 3 Still in the Layers panel, select the 200-pixel-diameter circle. In the Effect panel, set the Fill to Ellipse and the Edge to Anti-Alias. Edit the Fill as shown (6.53). The right color chip is white, and the left one is #4B4B4B. To get the gradient correct, the left color chip is dragged in from the left margin as shown.

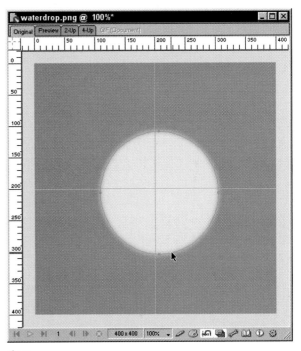

6.52

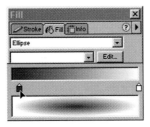

6.53

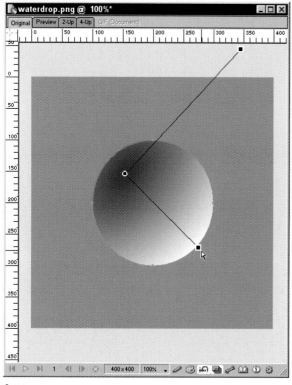

6.54

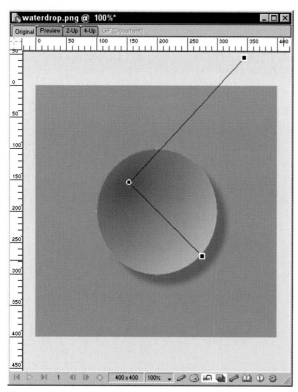

6.55

After accepting these settings, the fill handles appear on the circle. Drag, extend, and rotate these handles until they appear as shown (6.54). You will probably need to extend the window to give yourself room. The angles of the handles should be about 45° left and right of the vertical.

STEP 4 Add a drop shadow from the Effect panel, with the following settings: Offset Distance 25, Color black, shadow Opacity 60%, and Softness 8; leave the angle at its default, 315. After you have done this (the sequence is important), choose Effect panel ➢ Adjust Color and adjust the Brightness/Contrast: Brightness unchanged; Contrast set to 48 (6.55). The Opacity of the object should be 100%, as initially set. This object will be the body of the droplet. For the moment, hide it also.

STEP 5 Draw a new circle above the one we were just dealing with (diameter 13 pixels). Set the Fill to white and set the Edge to Feather, 8 pixels. Set the stroke to Airbrush Basic, the color to white, the Tip to maximum softness, and the Tip Size to its maximum, 72. The object Opacity should be 100%. Move the object so that it is centered at x =170, y =170. The new highlight appears as a small fuzzy blob (6.56).

STEP 6 The final part: With the small circle at the top (opacity 100%), the 200-pixel circle next (also with opacity 100%), and the 192-pixels circle lowest in the Layers panel (opacity 75%), make them all visible and deselect them all. The final effect is achieved (6.57).

You may like to experiment with different highlights if you want to retain the current size of the droplet. The droplet appears a little diffuse at this size. If you reduce the droplet in size to 100 × 100 pixels or less, the illusion improves. Before you resize, select all objects in the Layers panel and then convert the image to a bitmap (Modify ➢ Convert to Bitmap). Resizing it as a bitmap gives a slightly better result in this situation.

CARVING JADE

Q. *"I'm doing a Web site for an importer of fine nephrite and soapstone carvings. The client would like the header text to look like it is carved out of nephrite or jade. Do I need to use a 3-D rendering program for something like this, or can I do it in Fireworks?"*

DAN S.

Boy, we love a challenge! While it may be more common to do something like your carved text with a 3-D program, we think that doing so is a lot more interesting in Fireworks. We'll use one of Fireworks built-in patterns for this, some subtle stroking and shadowing, plus a sneaky displacement of an object that has been pasted inside another.

NOTE

For the really daring: If you want a texture beneath the droplet, you should take a careful look at how a real droplet magnifies and distorts the texture. Among other things, the size of the droplet affects the amount of magnification and distortion. Creating one of these digitally is not for the faint-hearted!

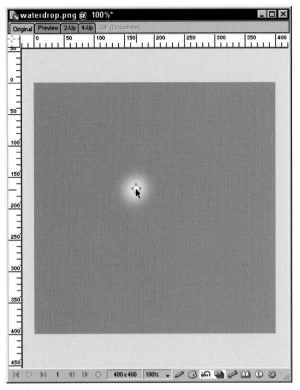

6.56

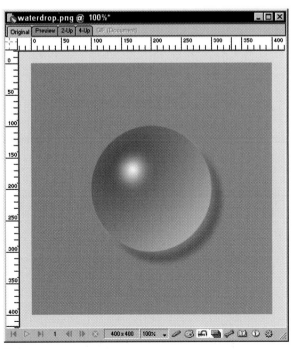

6.57

STEP 1 Type your header text and fill it with the Blue-Green pattern. Add a 2-pixel, #669999, Basic, Soft Rounded stroke (6.58). Clone the text, remove the stroke from the clone, but add an Inner Bevel. Use the default Flat Bevel Edge shape. Set the bevel width to 10, the Contrast to 100%, the softness to 4, and the angle to 157 (6.59). Cut the beveled text to the Clipboard. Select the original text and choose Edit ➢ Paste Inside to mask it with the beveled clone.

6.58

6.59

6.60

6.61

STEP 2 Open the Layers panel and click on the link icon between the objects of the mask group to unlink them. One of the two objects in the Layers panel is a grayscale rendering of the original text with a pen icon next to it. The other is in color and represents the pasted, beveled text. Click on the beveled text thumbnail. A small, star-shaped mask handle appears over the mask group on the canvas. Click on the mask handle to select it and use your right-arrow key to shift the pasted object about 7 pixels to the right and 1 or 2 pixels down. Click between the two thumbnails in the Layers panel to restore the link (6.60).

STEP 3 While everything is still selected, choose Modify ➢ Group. Then choose Effect panel ➢ Sharpen ➢ Unsharp Mask. Set the Sharpen Amount to 114, the Pixel Radius to 0.5, and the Threshold to 0. Add a drop shadow. Set the Distance to 20, the Color to #003333, the Opacity to 50%, the Softness to 15, and the Angle to 185 (6.61).

IN THE BAROQUE MANNER

ba·roque : adj
"Of, relating to, or characteristic of a style in art and architecture developed in Europe from about 1550 to 1700, emphasizing dramatic, verging on excessive ornamentation typified by bold forms and overall balance of disparate parts" — Merriam Webster OnLine.

What the dictionary doesn't mention is how much fun it is to play with Baroque design in Fireworks. You'll need a decorative Dingfont, such as Woodtype Ornaments or Fleurons, to create the ornamental details for this project. Check out *www.dingbatpages.com/florals/florals.html* for more information about Dingfonts.

STEP 1 Open a new canvas in a dark color. We've used #333333. Drag out a 226-×-74-pixel rectangle and center it on the canvas. Clone the rectangle; then reduce the dimensions by 6 pixels. Center the clone; then select both rectangles and choose Modify ➢ Combine ➢ Punch to create a frame. Add the Bright Gold gradient to the frame and rotate the gradient so the highlight falls across its top (6.62).

STEP 2 To simulate a tortoiseshell background for your piece, drag out a 224-×-72-pixel rectangle and choose Fill ➤ Pattern ➤ Flames. Add an Inner Glow to the patterned rectangle. (Effect ➤ Shadow and Glow ➤ Inner Glow. Set the Glow width to 3, the Color to black, the Opacity to 65%, and the Softness to 4 (6.63).

STEP 3 Draw a 194-×-44-pixel rectangle and center it inside the punched out area. (This rectangle will be the base of a carnelian baguette.) Fill it with red #993300 and add an Inner Glow. The settings for the Glow are Width= 3, Color= #660000, Opacity= 40%, and Softness= 6.

Click the Line tool to activate it and, while holding down the Shift key, draw a short 45° angle line from the top-left corner of the baguette toward its center. Switch to the Rectangle tool and draw a 6-×-186-pixel rectangle, 4 pixels down and 4 pixels from the top-left corner of the baguette. The top-left corner of the rectangle should touch the diagonal line (6.64).

Click the Skew tool to activate it. Zoom in to 200% and (using the 45° angle line as a guide) use the Skew tool to decrease the width of the bottom of the rectangle (6.65). Delete the 45° angle line and add a fill color to the rectangle. We've used #AD1012E.

Remove the stroke and add an Inner Glow. The Glow color is white. Set the Width to 2, the Opacity to 100%, and the Softness to 3. Add a 1-pixel, Soft, white pencil stroke to the top and bottom edges of the highlight (6.66).

STEP 4 Choose a Dingfont ornament to use as a filigree mount for the baguette. The style should be roughly triangular and wider than it is deep. Add a gold gradient to it and convert it to paths (Text ➤ Convert to Paths). Clone the Dingfont

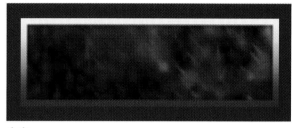

6.63

6.64

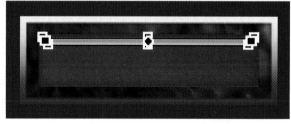

6.65

6.62

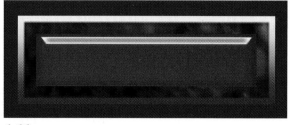

6.66

ornament three times and arrange the clones at the ends, top and bottom of the outer frame. The ornaments should be just large enough to touch the edges of the stone.

You may wish to save a copy of your art at this point because you'll be converting it to a bitmap file in the next step.

STEP 5 Select the gold frame and bring it to the front (Modify ➢ Arrange ➢ Bring to Front). Add a 3-pixel Drop Shadow. The color we've used is #660000. The Opacity is 90%, the Softness is 4, and the Angle is 272. Group all objects.

Draw a 236-×-83-pixel rectangle and fill it with the gold gradient. Move it to the back (Modify ➢ Arrange ➢ Send to Back) and center the image group in front of it.

Choose Edit ➢ Select All; then choose Modify ➢ Group; finally, choose Modify ➢ Convert to Bitmap. Just to add drama, we've added a Drop Shadow, a small Lens Flare to the middle of the top mount, and a background gradient (6.67).

LEADED GLASS

Q. *"I've been asked to contribute some graphics to the Web site of a local church. I'm more than happy to do the work, but they want something that looks like a stained glass window. Where do I start?"*

DALE K.

Japi Honoo has developed a terrific technique for creating images that look just like real leaded glass. We'll let her describe it for you.

STEP 1 I've used a beautiful Dingfont called Botarosa for the Tudor-style rose in this pattern.

6.67

Botarosa was generated in Macromedia Fontographer by artist-botanist Ivan Louette of Belgium. It can be found in the Florals section at *www.dingbatpages.com*.

Add the rose (or whichever pattern you would like to use) to the center of your canvas. Drag out two rectangles and align them to create a frame around the rose. Add some "lead" lines to divide the image into segments. These segments, plus the shapes that make up the rose, will become your glass pieces. Choose Edit ➢ Select All; then choose Modify ➢ Group. Convert the group to a bitmap (6.68).

STEP 2 Double-click the Magic Wand tool to activate it. In the Options panel, set the Tolerance to 10 and the Edge to Anti-Alias. While holding down the Shift key, carefully select each segment of your pattern (6.69). When all are selected, delete them. You should now see the gray and white checkerboard of a transparent canvas behind your pattern.

> **TIP**
>
> If you haven't already done so, install Ilya Razmanov's wonderful AmphiSoft filter package in the Fireworks Xtras folder. You'll find the installer on the CD-ROM at the back of this book.

6.68

It may seem unnecessary, but, once again, convert the image to a bitmap (6.70).

COLORING THE WINDOW

Now for the best part. Let's add the glass pieces.

STEP 1 Drag out a circle the same size as the rose in the center of your window and add a Radial Fill. The fill colors are #FF6600 on the outside and white for the center. Add a 40% Ripple Texture. Move the filled circle to the back (Modify ➤ Arrange ➤ Send to Back) (6.71). Double-click on the image to enter Bitmap Edit Mode.

STEP 2 Click the Magic Wand tool and select all the outer frame segments. In the Fill panel, choose Pattern ➤ Goo Blue. Use the Ripple Texture set to 40%. Click inside each of the segments with the Paint Bucket tool.

STEP 3 For the inner frame pieces, double-click the Magic Wand tool and change the Edge setting to Feather, 1 pixel. Select all four inner frame pieces. Choose Modify ➤ Marquee ➤ Expand Stroke. Expand the stroke by 1. Change the Fill pattern to Blue Wave with no texture. Click inside each of the segments with the Paint Bucket tool.

STEP 4 To color the leaves, change the Fill type to Linear. The colors are #336600 and #99CC00. The texture is Ripple at 40%. Select the leaves with the Magic Wand tool (you'll notice that the Magic Wand tool is blind to the vector object behind the leaves) and then expand the marquee by 1 pixel. Use the Paint Bucket tool to fill the leaves.

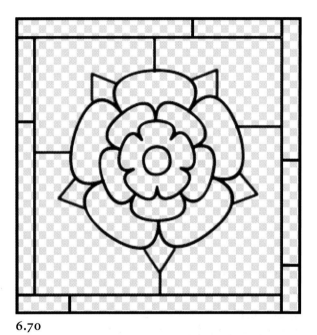

6.70

6.69

6.71

STEP 5 To fuse the gradient behind the rose with the rest of the window, choose Edit ➢ Select All; then choose Modify ➢ Convert to Bitmap. Change the canvas color to #003399 (6.72).

Hmm. It looks good but something is missing. Ah, yes . . .

LET THERE BE LIGHT

What's a stained glass window without the glow produced by sunlight?

STEP 1 First, let's deepen the colors and increase the contrast. Open the Effect panel and choose Adjust Color ➢ Brightness-Contrast. Decrease the Brightness to around -30. Increase the Contrast by about 40. Though fiddling with the effects produced by lens flare filters might add some glitter, I've found that the subtle, dappled glow produced by the AmphiSoft Convolution Shaman filter is ideal for this project.

STEP 2 Select the window image and choose Xtras ➢ AmphiSoft ➢ Convolution Shaman. Set the Kernal Radius to 8 and check the Square box. Choose Sharpen Light Edges from the Function drop-down list for Apply Mode, choose Normal; under Special, adjust the intensity slider to 20 (6.73).

LIGHTING EFFECTS

Q. *"How do I make lens flare in Fireworks?"*

J. H.

Many excellent filter packages for creating flare and lighting effects are available. They're expensive for one-trick ponies that don't get called on to perform very often. If you are willing to do some work, you can create your own flare and lighting effects in Fireworks and save the file as an editable PNG that can be used over and over again. These homemade lighting effects are exceptional because they can be used on both vector and raster images.

STEP 1 Start by dragging a black rectangle across your canvas to cover it. Next, add a 20-×-20-pixel white circle. With the circle selected, choose Effect panel ➢ Shadow and Glow ➢ Glow. The settings for the Glow are Color #FFFFFF, Width 6, Opacity 100%, and Softness 23. Drag out a second circle somewhat larger than the first. Set the Fill to none, the Stroke to Basic, Soft Rounded, the Stroke Width to 1 pixel, the Color to #FF0066, and the Opacity to 31%. This circle is barely discernible but becomes important in the next step.

STEP 2 While the second circle is still selected, clone it. Change the stroke properties of the clone to Airbrush, Basic style, Tip 8x, Width 200,

6.72

6.73

Opacity 77%, and Color #CC0066. Use your arrow keys to move the clone slightly down from its parent and to the right. The parent circle is now quite visible as a red ring (6.74).

STEP 3 Click on the Pencil tool to activate it and begin drawing some lines across the canvas, lines that intersect the middle of the 20-×-20-pixel circle. These will be the spectral lines that appear to radiate from the brightest spot in the flare. Set the Stroke to Basic, soft line, the Width to 2 pixels, the Color to white, and the Opacity to 5%. You'll need to draw at least twenty lines. To draw the other lines very quickly, make a clone of the line you just drew and use the Numeric Transform command to rotate (Modify ➤ Transform ➤ Numeric Transform ➤ Rotate). Shift + select the clone and transform steps in the History panel and click on the Repeat button. Continue using the Repeat button until you are satisfied with the way the spectral lines look (6.75).

STEP 4 We'll add some other shapes to create a compound flare. First, beginning from the top-right and dragging to the bottom-right, draw a 45°-angle line that intersects the center of the flare. Use the line as a guide for placing the other elements.

Drag out a small circle midway between the center flare and the top-left corner. The Fill is Radial, with the #000000 on the outside and #CC9900 in the center. The Opacity is reduced to 52%. The lower group consists of an unfilled half-ellipse and two ellipses with linear fills.

To create the half circle, draw a full circle; then click the Knife tool to activate it. Hold the Shift key down to restrain the angle to 45° and drag the knife cursor from the top-right of the circle to the bottom-left. Click on the path of the circle to separate the two halves. Delete the lower half and select the upper one. Choose Modify ➤ Alter Path ➤ Expand Stroke. In the Expand Stroke dialog box, choose 2 for Width, a rounded corner (the middle button), a Mitre Limit of 10, and the straight End Cap (the first button). The fill for the expanded, half-circle path is Linear, #6633CC to black. Rotate the gradient so the blue color is at the leading edge of the half circle and the ends

fade into the black color of the canvas. Reduce the opacity to 95%.

Drag out two more small circles. Place them along the diagonal line just behind the half circle. Both are filled with linear gradients. The colors of the first one are #FF00FF and #000000; the opacity

6.74

6.75

6.76

6.77

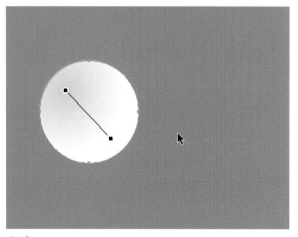

6.78

is 20%. The bottom ellipse is filled with #0066FF and #000000, and its opacity is 52%. Rotate the gradients for both circles in the same way you did for the half circle (6.76).

At this point, you'll want to save an editable copy of your design. Choose Edit ➤ Select All; then choose Modify ➤ Group. Make sure that your group includes the black rectangle you covered the canvas with at the beginning. Choose Save as from the File menu and browse to the folder where you would like to store your lens flare PNG. If you would like to be able to access your lens flare directly through the program interface, create a folder on your computer called Libraries 2.

Convert your lens flare to a graphic symbol and save it to the Libraries 2 folder. To transfer the lens flare to a photo, choose Insert ➤ Libraries ➤ Other and browse to the lens flare symbol in the Libraries 2 folder. In the Import Symbols dialog box, select the lens flare PNG and click on the Import button.

We'll guess that you might be thinking, "Well what good is it? It completely obscures the image." A little Blending Mode magic fixes that. Open the Layers panel and choose "Lighten" from the Blending Mode drop down list. The black background disappears but leaves the effect in place (6.77). Unlike the same thing created by a plug-in filter, you can move the lens flare around on the photo, change the lens flare opacity, scale it, transform it as well as insert multiple copies and experiment with the other blend modes for special effects.

Other possibilities include using the same techniques to create plasma, spotlight and floodlight effects, film scratches, and the like.

Have fun with the idea and leave a note on the Contact page of the Playing with Fire Web site *www. playingwithfire.com* to let us know what you come up with. We'll publish examples of the best ones on the site.

MAGNIFYING GLASS

Q. *"Is there a lens effect available in the straight-from-the-box version of FW4? I'm interested in modifying a circular part of an image to make it look like it would through a magnifying glass."*

MATT H.

FW4 doesn't have a built-in magnifying glass effect, but if you work through the following tutorial prepared by Brian Baker, you'll see how easily it can be done in Fireworks without any special gadgets. The effect is done in two parts: creating the magnifying glass and distorting the text beneath it.

STEP 1 Open a new canvas in a mid-tone color so that you can see the lighter colored pieces you'll be creating more easily. You can reset the canvas to a lighter color when you have finished.

Drag out a circle the size that you want for the glass. Set the fill to Solid and the color to a very pale blue, such as #EAFFFF. Clone the circle so that it remains over the original (Edit ➢ Clone) and change the fill type of the cloned circle to Radial. Edit the gradient so that the left color is a light grey (#CCCCCC) and the right is a lighter gray-white (#EFEFEF). Use the Fill rotation bars to move the fill highlight to the top left. Rotate the square end of the fill rotation bar to the bottom right (6.78).

Select both of the circles, either by using the Pointer tool to drag a rectangle over them or by using the Select Behind tool with the Shift key; choose Modify ➢ Mask ➢ Group as Mask (6.79).

STEP 2 The next stage is creating the crescent-shaped highlight, which is made by punching one circle through another. The first circle should be slightly smaller than the glass, with a Solid fill set to white. The second should be about the same size as the glass with a different color fill. Using a different color for the fill of the second circle makes it more visible, and, therefore, easier to position.

Lay the second circle over the first so that you can see a crescent shape (6.80). Then select both circles and choose Modify ➢ Combine ➢ Punch. Change the opacity of the crescent to around 40% and move it into position (6.81).

STEP 3 To make the metallic rim, you need two more circles. The first should have a diameter of about 10 pixels more than the glass, and the second should be the same size as the glass. Center the second circle over the first (select both; then Ctrl + Alt + 2, Ctrl + Alt + 5). While they are both still selected, punch out the center by choosing Modify ➢ Combine ➢ Punch. Set the Fill to Linear and edit the gradient so

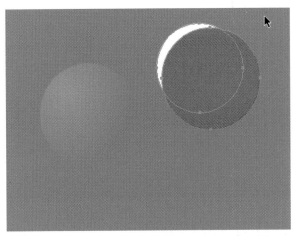

6.80

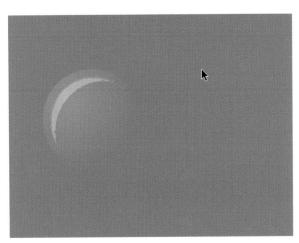

6.79

6.81

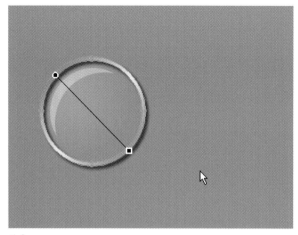

6.82

6.83

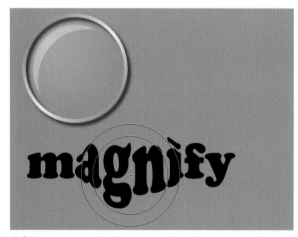

6.84

that it is mid-gray (#999999) at both ends and light gray (#EEEEEE) in the center. Adjust the handles of the gradient so that it is at a 45° angle to the horizontal. To complete the effect, add a drop shadow to the rim (6.82).

Position the rim around the glass; then finally select all the objects and group them (Modify ➢ Group). This will make moving the magnifying glass to different positions easier.

ADDING AND DISTORTING THE TEXT

STEP 1 Add the text to the document. Chunky fonts give the best effect, but experiment to see which font is best. I've used Cooper Black, size 70 (6.83). So that the text can be distorted, it first needs to be converted to paths. Choose Text ➢ Convert to Paths. To make the text easier to work with, use the Subselection tool to drag a rectangle around the text so that all the letters are selected; then join them (Modify ➢ Join).

STEP 2 The next tool to use is the Reshape Area tool; to find it, hold down the mouse button over the Freeform tool. In the Options panel, set the Size to the size of your glass and the Strength to 60%. Make sure the Preview box in the Tool Options panel is selected so you can see the effect you are creating. If the text isn't selected, you now need to select it.

Position the Reshape Area tool over the area of the text you want to reshape, hold down the mouse button, and move the mouse in small up and down movements. It's better to make lots of small movements than a few large ones because this gives you more control over the effect (6.84). If you are not happy with the result, use Edit ➢ Undo and try again.

FINISHING OFF

All you need to do now is move the glass and the text to where you want them. If you have followed these instructions in order, you should find that the text appears to be over the magnifying glass. To arrange the text so that it appears to be beneath the magnifying glass, select the glass and choose Modify ➢ Arrange ➢ Bring to Front (6.85).

RADIO KNOB

Finally, having exhausted the translucent and optical effects, we come to the piece on how to create the rotating knob metaphor that we used in Chapter 4. Simple but elegant, it shows a structural approach you can take to creating realistic images of everyday objects.

The first thing we'll do is create a framework in which to line everything up:

STEP 1 Open a 400-×-400-pixel mid-gray canvas. The color we've used is #999999. In the Fill panel, set the Fill to None and the Layer Opacity to 100%. In the Stroke panel, set the stroke to Pencil, 1-Pixel, Hard, black.

Click the Ellipse tool to activate it. While holding the Shift key down to restrain the ellipse to a circle, draw a 240-pixel-diameter circle. Center the circle in the window (Commands ➤ Document ➤ Center in Document). Draw a second circle, this time 50 pixels in diameter. Center the second circle.

While holding down the Shift key, draw a vertical straight line down the middle of the canvas; then center the line. Follow this with a horizontal line and two diagonals between opposing corners, centering these as you complete them. Shift + select all the elements in the Layers panel and group them to create a kind of spider web (6.86).

STEP 2 To construct the gray détente markers around the outside of the knob, draw a 12-pixel-diameter circle. Set the Fill to #999999 and the

Stroke to none. Clone it to create a second circle. Move these circles so that they overlay the left and upper-left junctions of the straight lines and outer circle in the spider web. These small circular "dots" will become the détente markers for the knob. Select both dots and join them (Modify ➤ Join) (6.87).

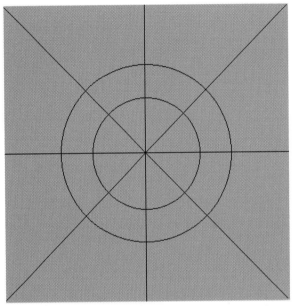

6.86

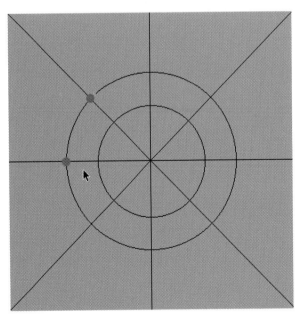

6.87

6.85

We will use the first pair of dots to create the remaining ones. Clone the dot pair; then rotate the cloned group through 90° clockwise (Modify ➢ Transform ➢ Rotate 90° CW). Shift the newly rotated dot groups so that they overlay the lower left and bottom intersections of the straight lines and outer circle in the spider web. Clone the dot pairs and rotate 90° clockwise again. Shift the cloned dot group to the next position around the spider web. Repeat this process once more to fill the remaining intersections. Select all the dot groups and Group them together (6.88).

Keep the spider web for later, but for now, turn off its visibility by deselecting the appropriate "Eye icon" in the Layers panel.

We still have to draw the knob itself, an indicator dot to go on the radio knob, and an LED image that sits over top of the gray détente dots during the "rotation" of the selector onMouseOver. (See "Twirling Knobs, Whirling Dials" in Chapter 4.)

STEP 3 Drag out a 200-pixel-diameter circle. Set the Stroke to None, the Fill to Solid, the Edge style to Anti-Alias, and the Fill color to black. Center the circle on the canvas. This is the base of the knob body, to which you'll add the bevel, shadow, and slanted illumination.

First add an illumination effect to make the knob look slightly convex. With the knob body still selected, add a Radial fill. Edit the gradient so the left color chip is dark gray (#505050 or thereabouts) and the right color chip is black. After the Fill has been added, a gradient rotation bar appears over top of the knob image.

Relocate and lengthen the bar so that the brightest spot of the radial fill is at the top left area of the knob, as shown (6.89). This completes the convex surface effect.

STEP 4 Next, you'll add a drop shadow. With the knob selected, choose Effect ➢ Shadow and Glow ➢ Drop Shadow (6.90). Onward to the bevel.

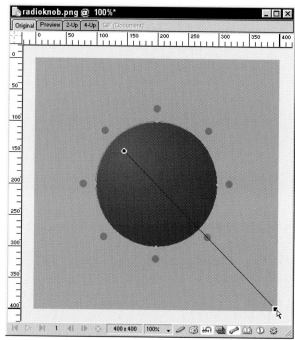

6.89

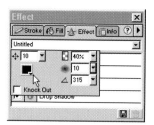

6.90

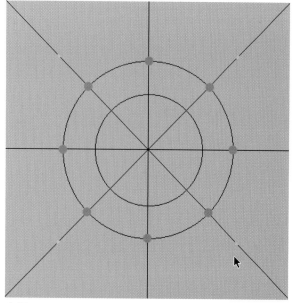

6.88

STEP 5 You have at least three ways to add a bevel. You can use the Inner Bevel Live Effect or the EyeCandy Bevel Boss filter. Although these are easy ways to create a bevel, we'll take the slow route and create one from scratch. It looks better than the auto-generated ones too.

To start, hide all the existing elements by deselecting the "eyes" in the Layers panel. Draw a new circle with a diameter of 200 pixels and center it in the document. The Fill should be Solid, black, the Edge style Anti-Alias, and the Stroke set to none. Draw another circle with a diameter of 186 pixels and process it in the same way. Select both circles and use Modify ➤ Combine ➤ Punch to cut a hole in the center of the large circle with the smaller one. This leaves us with a black ring (6.91).

In the Fill panel, change the Fill from Solid to Ellipse, set the Edge to Feather at 1-pixel, and edit the colors so that the left color chip is #CCCCCC and the right one is #2E2E2E. You'll see the control handles for the ellipse fill appear at the 12- and 3-o'clock positions. We want to shift them so that the light appears to be coming from top left, so you'll need to drag, rotate, and lengthen the handles. Locate the round fill handle at the 10:30 position, rotate the handles and adjust the arm lengths so they look like handles (6.92).

Now all you need to do is to create the LED image and knob marker, as follows:

STEP 6 The LED is a 12-pixel-diameter circle with solid red fill and no stroke. To create a spectacular highlight reflection on the LED, use the EyeCandy Bevel Boss filter. The settings are as follows: Under the Basic tab, set the Bevel Width to 3.00, the Bevel Height to 12, the Smoothness to 1, the Bevel Placement inside the marquee, 0 darkening, and interior shading unchecked.

Under the Lighting tab, set the Direction to 135, the Inclination to 50, the Highlight Brightness to 100%, the Highlight Size to 77, the Highlight color to white, and the Shadow color to #FF0000. Leave the Bevel Profile settings at the default. (It would probably be easier to hand paint a bit of white on top of the red circle!)

The indicator dot on the knob is a 16-pixel-diameter yellow circle with a slight inner shadow. Choose Effect panel ➤ Shadow and Glow ➤ Inner Shadow. The settings are an Offset of 2, 65% Opacity, and a Softness of 4. The Angle and Color are both left at the default settings.

STEP 7 Now we're ready to move the LED and indicator marker into place. Hide the knob body and reveal our old friend, the spider web. Move the LED and marker into place (6.93). The LED

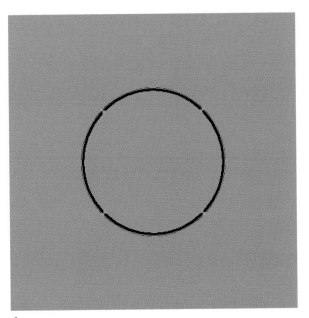

6.91

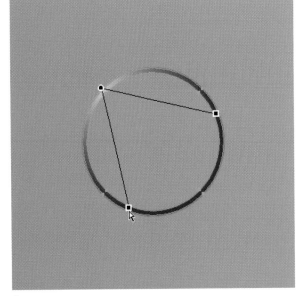

6.92

and indicator markers drawn here show the effect in a static example. Chapter 4 shows how to use them in a dynamic rollover.

Finally, hide the spider web and reveal the knob to show the finished image (6.94).

Save the PNG file and export the knob as a JPEG — Quality 80 or greater — (minus the indicator marker, which is handled separately in the rollover exercise) and you are done!

BY JUPITER!

Since the 1970s, NASA has been providing stunning images of the major planets Jupiter, Saturn, and so forth. Starting with the two Voyagers and continuing with the current Galileo spacecraft, images of Jupiter have been especially spectacular. Jupiter's complex surface clouds and cloud belts have become almost as easily identified in the public mind as Saturn's rings. But how do you draw an image of something so complex in a regular graphics program like Fireworks? In the movie *2010*, film producers used Cray and Silicon Graphics machines to simulate the fluid dynamics of the clouds. But how we do simulate the clouds in Fireworks? Well, we'll have to cheat a bit, but the result is pretty good.

Time for a mini science lesson to get some background on what you are creating.

Jupiter rotates very rapidly, so it's oblate (flattened at the poles), not spherical, and its cross section is elliptical instead of circular. Its disk is crossed by a several semi-regular cloud belts. Within and between these belts are complex vortex patterns, swirls, and loops. The colors vary between near white and deep red ochre due to the methane and ammonia atmospheric chemistry. The planet's terminator (day/night edge) is soft due to scattered sunlight in the atmosphere, and the disk itself has a soft edge, also due to the atmosphere. Images of Jupiter often show one or more of its four large Galilean moons, and frequently the moons create shadows on the surface of the planet. Recreating all these features is important to a realistic result.

Okay, school's out. Let's crank up Fireworks.

STEP 1 Start with a black 400-×-400-pixel canvas. Click the Ellipse tool to activate it; and with Stroke set to none and Fill to Solid white, draw a 200-×-187-pixel ellipse. This allows for Jupiter's oblateness factor of 1/15.4.

STEP 2 We're going to use both a patterned fill and a texture in this disk. The Fill will create the "bands" across the disk, and the texture will provide the details of the cloud patterns.

Set the Fill style to Bars and choose Copper from the gradient presets. The fill appears with

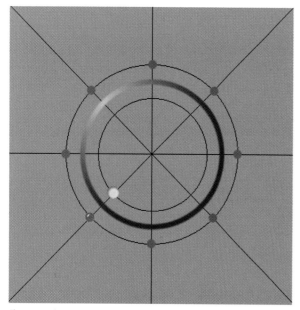

6.93

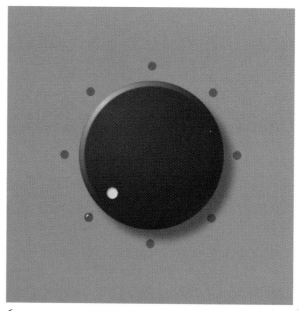

6.94

vertical banding. Rotate the gradient until the square handle of the gradient rotation bar sits over the top Bézier point of the ellipse (6.95).

A more-complex band structure is needed — more than the basic Bars/Copper combination provides — so edit the gradient and add more color chips. The exact arrangement isn't vital as long as it is somewhat random (6.96).

The settings we have used, from left to right along the 200-pixel-wide gradient Editor window, are: 0 = #FBD8C5, 26 = #97461A, 36 = #6C2E16, 53 = #783517, 80 = #FBD8C5, 104 = #783517, 132 = #EFDBCD, 156 = #6C2E16, 179 = #FBD8C5, and 199 = #FFFFFF.

STEP 3 The next step is to rotate the disk before we add the texture. We need to do this because the texture we are going to use, Swish, repeats itself; and by tilting the disk, we avoid obvious pattern repeats along the bands. Choose Modify ➢ Transform ➢ Numeric Transform ➢ Rotate. Set the angle to 342.

Return to the Fill panel, select the Swish texture box, and set the texture amount to 100%. This is an ideal texture for the job because it contains semi-random fluid-like swirls very similar to the cloud structure you are trying to emulate (6.97).

STEP 4 We'll use a mask to make our planet look like it is lit by the distant Sun. Drag out a rectangle that exactly covers the ellipse. Change the rectangle's fill to Elliptical and the Gradient to

TIP

Screen Ruler, by Jesse Carneiro of MicroFox Software, is our tool of choice to measure an object on our monitor screen. It floats above all open windows and can be set up to measure pixels, inches, picas, centimeters, and percentage of length. You'll find a trial version of Screen Ruler on the CD-ROM at the back of the book.

6.96

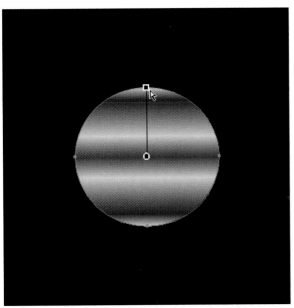

6.95

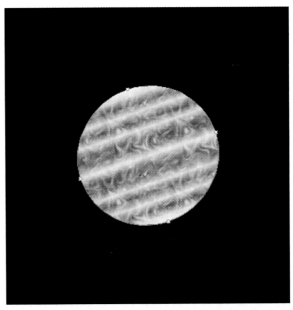

6.97

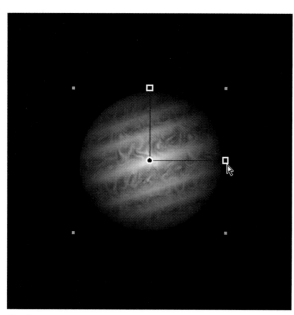

6.98

6.99

Black-White. To apply the mask, Shift + select both and choose Modify ➤ Mask ➤ Group as Mask. Now it's starting to look interesting (6.98)!

In the Layers panel, click on the grayscale path thumbnail of the mask group. When the gradient rotation handles pop up, drag the circular handle to location 140, 213, the upper square handle to 203, 91, and the lower square handle to 269, 284. These needn't be exact, but we're assuming that you haven't shifted the ellipse away from the center of the document window (6.99).

Finally, for the planet itself, feather the edge of the disk: Select the disk object (the left-hand object in the Mask Group in the Layers panel), and in the Fill panel, set the Edge to Feather at 2 pixels.

STEP 5 Adding one Galilean moon and its shadow is the final step. Draw an 8-pixel-diameter circle. Clone it (Shift+Ctrl+D). Select one of the small circles and set the Fill to Solid white, the Edge to Anti-Alias, and the Texture amount to 0%. Drag it to position 40, 290, below and to the left of the planet disk.

To add a shadow to the moon, change the Fill to Linear, Black-White. Click the moon with the Zoom tool (magnifying glass); then rotate the gradient so the white side of the moon is to the bottom left.

Select the second small circle and change its Fill to Solid black. Drag it to position 180, 250 on the planet. Add a Gaussian blur of 0.7.

Shift + select all three objects in the Layers panel and shift them to the right to center the image (6.100).

The final image is spectacular and not too bad a facsimile of Jupiter, considering the fact that we have only used the standard Fireworks tools. Save the file as a PNG or export it as a JPEG, resizing as you wish.

You may like to tackle Saturn, too. It is much easier than Jupiter as Saturn's disk has far less features. The chapter introduction page illustration shows how you might do this in Fireworks.

6.100

animate

7

CHAPTER 7
ANIMATING TECHNIQUES

Although computer-generated animation may seem quite modern to us, the basic technique hasn't changed much since the flipbook, which predates it by over 100 years. In case you've never seen one, a flipbook is a small booklet that has pages made from stiff paper or card printed with line drawings. The drawing on each page is largely the same as on the previous page but with some minor changes made to represent movement in the image. The changes in the image accumulate slowly through the sequence of pages. If you hold the book and rapidly flip the pages, you see what looks like a moving image. The eye sees each image separately but, because each page flies by very quickly during the flip process, the eye blends consecutive images into a more or less smoothly moving animation.

Computer animation exploits the same physiological property of the eye used by television and movies, namely persistence of vision — the inclination for the eye not to notice flicker in images that change faster than about 24 frames per second.

In Fireworks, the drawings are rendered on *frames* (a term borrowed from film) that are stacked one on top of the other, just like the pages of a flipbook. The images can be drawn frame by frame or done as *keyframe animations,* where the user specifies the key frames, and the program generates the in-betweens.

"If you can dream it, you can do it. Always remember this whole thing was started by a mouse."

WALT DISNEY

FLIPPING PAGES

Q. *"How can I create picture buttons that animate onMouseOver like the ones at www.kaliber1000.net? I've tried to create a Web page within Fireworks consisting of rollover images that had animated states, and I can't get it to work."*

JEZ A.

We've found that the best way to do an animation triggered by an onMouseOver event is by creating the animation as a separate element and importing the file into the Fireworks HTML page. Let's focus on the animation first. We will use a kind of flipbook technique in this example.

Because file sizes for Web animations need to be kept very lean, striking a balance between larger file size (more frames) and realism in the movement is necessary. Our example is intended to look like a series of stills taken from a strip of film. We've used the face of a girl as the subject of our animation. To emphasize the changes of expression on her face, we'll use a limited number of frames and loop the frames at a slow speed. That limited number of frames, plus the use of only two colors in addition to black ensures a minimum file size for the final output.

THE ANIMATION

STEP 1 Open a new canvas to serve as a storyboard for your images. Arrange the images (these can be photos or drawings) into an interesting sequence. The face of the girl we have used is from a Dingfont called Ann's Guest Stars, by designer Ann Stretton of *www.dingbatcave.com* (7.1). The images are scaled to 96 pixels wide and have been converted to paths. You'll find copies of the images we used in the Chapter 7 files on the CD-ROM at the back of the book.

7.1

STEP 2 Open a second canvas approximately twice the width of the images. Add your text. We placed a horizontal guideline across the eyes of the first image to help line up all the other images (7.2). Click on the menu button at the top right of the Frames panel and choose Add Frames from the drop-down list. In the Add Frames dialog box, enter the number six and select the After Current Frame radio button. Then close the dialog box.

Return to Frame 1 and select the text. We want the text to appear on each frame of the animation, so select the text and reopen the Frames menu. Choose Copy to Frames. The Copy to Frames dialog box appears. Select the All Frames option (7.3).

Different camera angles are used to inspire specific emotional responses in film. The technique, called a *truck shot,* moves the camera along with

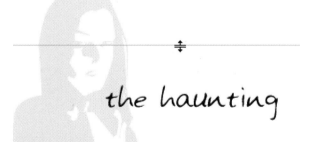

7.2

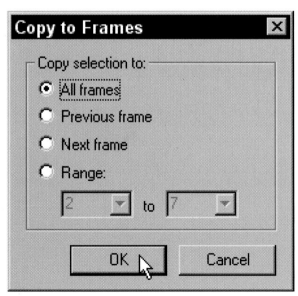

7.3

the subject so that the background appears to be moving instead of the subject. Truck shots combined with quick cuts to different camera angles were used to great effect in films directed by Alfred Hitchcock. We'll emulate his technique by shifting the placement of the girl in our animation from left to right in subsequent frames.

STEP 3 Open the Onion Skinning menu (the first button at the bottom left of the Frames panel) and choose the Before and After option (7.4). Click on Frame 2 in the Frames panel. Add the second image to the canvas and align it so that the horizontal guideline falls across the eyes of the girl (7.5). Move the new image a few pixels to the right of the first one. Add the rest of the images of the girl to the remaining frames in the same way, aligning them a few pixels to the right of the image in the previous frame. On each frame, move the image of the girl behind the text.

STEP 4 Duplicate the first frame and change the color of the girl to the same one you have used in the rest of the frames.

STEP 5 Still in the Frames panel, Shift + select all frames, then click on the right-arrow button at the top right of the Frames panel to open the Frames panel Options pop-up menu. Choose Properties. When the Frame Delay dialog box opens, enter **40** (7.6).

EXPORTING

STEP 1 Click on the tab of the Optimize panel to access its options and choose Animated GIF for the export file format, WebSnap Adaptive, and 8 colors. Choose File➤Export. In the Export dialog

NOTE

Why do I mention the second state before the first state? The reason is because Fireworks' memory of the user's actions can be too persistent. If you export the whole thing as an animated GIF first and the program doesn't allow you to change the file type to a normal GIF, you can work around this by exporting just one frame of the animation. If you export one frame as a normal GIF, and then try to export the file a second time as an animation, Fireworks may not cooperate. It's a bug, but an elusive one because it doesn't happen every time.

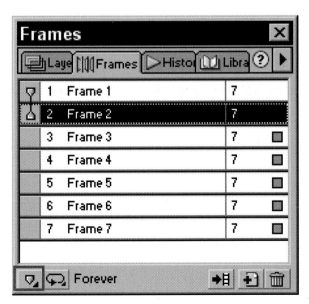

7.4

7.5

7.6

box, give your animation a name and for Save as type, choose Images. The file you have just exported will be the second state of your rollover.

STEP 2 Return to the Optimize panel and change the export file format to GIF. Choose File➤Export. Rename the image and under Save as Type, choose Images Only. Frame 1 will be exported by itself. You'll use this single frame as the first state of your rollover.

ADDING THE ANIMATED ROLLOVER TO YOUR PAGE

STEP 1 Open the single frame you exported in Step two of the last section. While the image is still selected, choose Insert➤Slice from the Insert menu. Click on the drag-and-drop Behavior button in the middle of the slice and choose Add Swap Image Behavior from the menu that opens.

STEP 2 When the Swap Image editor opens, select Image File under Show the swapped image from section of the dialog box (7.7). Click on the folder icon. When the Open dialog box appears, browse to the location of your animation and click on the animation to select it. Click on the Open button to close the Open dialog box. Uncheck the Preload Images box but leave the Restore Image onMouseOut box checked. Click on OK to close the Swap Image editor.

A GIF animation begins to play as soon as the browser loads it. If the viewer waits before mousing

over an animated rollover, he may catch the animation in the middle of the sequence. Disallowing image preloading ensures that the browser begins the animation on the first frame.

STEP 3 Click on the Preview tab at the top of the canvas window and mouse over your animated rollover to test it. Double-check the rollover by previewing it in your browser (File➤Preview in Browser).

TWEENING TO FADE TEXT IN AND OUT

Q. "Okay I'm admitting defeat after trying for 2 days. How do I tween an animation to fade in and out?"

WENDY B.

The new Animation controls in Fireworks 4 make fading objects in and out a cinch. In this exercise we will create a simple banner and animate one of the words in the text. The process may appear a bit intricate, but you'll find it easy to repeat once you understand the principles behind it.

SETTING UP THE BANNER

STEP 1 This banner is full size, so open a new 480×60-pixel canvas. Set the color of the canvas to #6699CC. Type the phrase "To the vector belong the spoils." For the text itself, we use Georgia font, size 32, and color #003366. Before closing the Text Editor, highlight the word *vector* with your cursor and change the color of the word to white. Click OK to close the text editor and choose Commands➤Document➤Center in Document (7.8).

STEP 2 In Fireworks, a string of text is treated as a single object. In order to animate only one word of the string we need to first break the string into separate parts. To do this, select the text string and choose Text➤Convert to Paths; then Modify➤Ungroup. Each letter of the text string is now an independent object. Now we'll regroup the letters into three text objects. Draw a cursor box around the words *To the* and choose Modify➤ group. Using the same method, group the letters of the

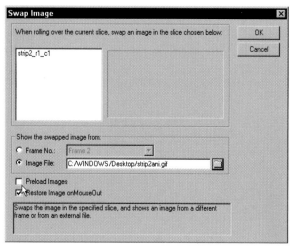

7.7

word *vector*. Last, group the letters in the words *belong the spoils*.

ADDING THE SYMBOL

We'll be animating the word *vector*. Select it with the pointer tool and choose Insert➤Convert to Symbol (7.9). When the Symbol Properties dialog box appears (7.10), give the symbol a name. Select Animation; then click on OK to proceed to the Animate dialog box.

SETTING THE VALUES

STEP 1 After closing the Symbol Properties dialog box, the Animate dialog box appears (7.11). The settings for the fade are set out in Table 7-1. The only default values you'll need to change are the number of frames and the right hand opacity box value.

7-1	FADE SETTINGS
SETTING	VALUE
Frames	5
Move	0
Direction	0
Scale	100%
Opacity	100% to 0%
Rotate	0

When you have entered these values, click OK to close the Animate dialog box. If an alert box that says "The animation of this symbol extends beyond the last frame of the document. Automatically add new frames?" appears, click OK again. This will add new frames with the word *vector* progressively dimmer on consecutive frames.

STEP 2 In the Frames panel, click on the last frame (Frame 5) then on the menu button at the top right of the Frames panel. Choose Add Frames. The Add Frames dialog box appears.

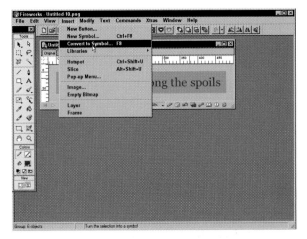

7.8

7.9

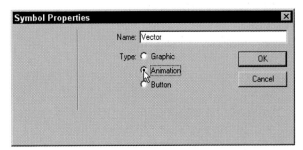

7.10

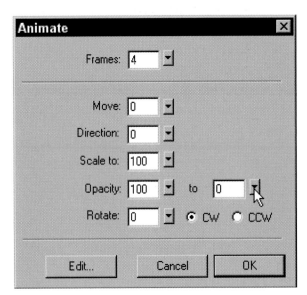

7.11

Accept the default values of "Add 1 frame after the current frame." Click OK. Our animation now has six frames (7.12). Click OK and return to Frame 1.

Select the symbol in Frame 1 and copy it (Edit➤Copy). Paste the symbol into Frame 6. When the alert message appears (as before), click OK to add the extra frames. Open the Object panel and reverse the Opacity settings, changing the first (left-hand) Opacity value to 0% and the second (right-hand) Opacity value to 100% (7.13).

We want the text objects *to the* and *belong the spoils* to appear on every frame, so return to Frame 1 and select them. Click on the button at the top right of the Frames panel to open the Frames panel options menu again, and choose Copy to Frames. Now we're ready to set up the timing of the animation.

Because we've used a limited number of frames to fade the text in and out, we'll need to smooth the motion with speed. Shift + select all the frames in the Frames panel and then open Frames Panel Options pop-up menu again. Select Properties. The Frame Delay dialog box appears. Enter the number 1 and click somewhere outside the dialog box to accept the settings and close the box. Check the results in your browser (File➤ Preview in Browser). The animation is smooth, but it is looping so quickly there is a blinking side effect. Not quite what we had in mind. Refine the effect by changing the timing of Frames 1 and 6 to 50/100 (7.14). That's much better! All that remains is to Optimize the animation and export it for use in your Web page.

BREAKING DOWN

Q. *"I've seen a Java applet that looks like the iris of a lens is opening to reveal an image beneath it. Is there a way to create something like this in Fireworks or is that effect beyond the scope of the program?"*

JEREMY D.

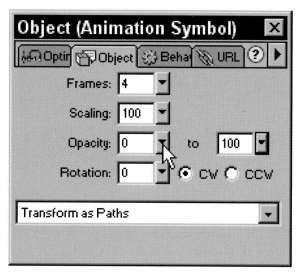

7.12

7.13

Animations that show one image breaking down to reveal another image can be done in Fireworks by using vector shapes, the Eraser tool, the Marquee tools, or combinations of all three. We'll use a vector shape break down technique in this exercise. You'll be surprised by how simple this sort of animation is and by how many variations are possible.

> **TIP**
>
> Frame delays in Fireworks are specified in hundredths of a second. 50/100 displays a frame for half a second.

SETTING UP THE ANIMATION

STEP 1 Load the image you want to animate in Fireworks (7.15). Open the Layers panel Options pop-up menu by clicking on the arrow button at the top right of the panel. Choose New Layer. When the New Layer dialog box opens, enter the word *vector* and click OK to close the dialog box. Reopen the Layers panel Options menu and make sure that Single Layer Editing is checked.

STEP 2 Drag out a rectangle on top of the new layer. The rectangle should completely cover the image on Layer 1. Fill it with a predominant color from the image. Click on the Frames panel tab, then on right-arrow button at the top right of the Frames panel. Choose Duplicate Frame from the pop-up menu. The Duplicate Frame dialog box opens. Select the After Current Frame option and click OK to close the dialog box.

STEP 3 Add a 10-pixel circle to the rectangle on Frame 2 and center it (Commands➤Document➤ Center in Document). Select both the circle and the rectangle and choose Modify➤Combine➤ Punch. This opens a small, circular hole in the blank rectangle that is covering the original image. We want to continue this process, so we'll duplicate Frame 2, using the same frame duplication method we used in Step 2. That will bring our frame count up to three.

7.15

> **NOTE**
>
> The Tiger Lily photo that we have used in this animation is from the U.S. Fish and Wildlife Service, which, along with NASA and NOAA (the U.S. National Oceanic and Atmospheric Administration), is a great source of copyright-free images. Images like this one can be downloaded from the US National Image Library site at *images.fws.gov* or from sites like the Gimp Savvy photo archive at *www.gimp-savvy.com*.

> **TIP**
>
> If you are using a JPEG image for you animation, you will need to take into consideration how it will look when it is exported as a GIF. To prevent blotchy dithering, we have applied a Gaussian blur to the background areas of the photo and have posterized (condensed the brightness variations) the foreground by selecting it with a Marquee tool and applying a watercolor filter.

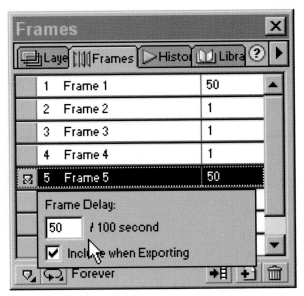

7.14

STEP 4 On Frame 3 , draw a 20 × 20-pixel circle over the punched hole. Choose Command➤ Document➤ Center in Document to center the new circle over the old one. Again, select both the rectangle and the circle and choose Modify➤ Combine➤Punch. Duplicate the frame as we did in Steps 2 and 3.

7.16   **Frame four**

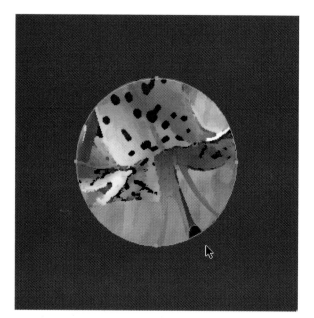

7.17   **Frame eight**

Continue this process for another seven frames, so that there are ten frames in total, each with a progressively larger hole in the rectangle until the image is completely exposed. The punch circles on Frames 3 through 8 are: 40 x 40, 70 x 70 (7.16), 100 x 100, 150 x 150, 200 x 200 (7.17), 250 x 250. With Frame 10 selected in the Frames panel, open the Layers panel and delete the remaining bits of the rectangle on Frame 10 so that the entire original image shows.

SETTING UP THE FRAME DELAYS

We want this animation to fully load before it begins playing and then to play quickly until the final frame. To make the animation work, follow these steps. Open the Frames panel and:

STEP 1 Click on Frame 1.
STEP 2 Click on the right-arrow button at the top right of the Frames panel and choose Properties. Set the Frame delay to 100/100.
STEP 3 Click somewhere outside the panel or press Enter to accept the change.
STEP 4 Shift + select Frames 2 through 8. Click on the arrow button on the Frames panel, and select Properties. Set the Frame delay to 3/100. Though not really necessary, set the delay of Frame 9 to 100/100.
STEP 5 Click on the GIF animation looping button at the bottom of the Frames panel and choose No Looping.
STEP 6 Click on the play icon at the bottom of the canvas window to preview the animation Choose File➤ Preview in Browser to double-check the speed of the animation. Optimize and export the animated GIF.

We've used a large image for this demonstration to make it easier to see in this book. Remember that photos do not compress well as GIFs. The dimensions of an animation of this type must be kept small or the final export file size of the animation will be enormous.

ANIMATING ON A CURVE

Q. *"I want to create a bouncing ball animation. Can I alter the path of an animation to be curved using Fireworks new animation controls or do I have to manipulate individual frames? The manual doesn't seem to specify so I'm assuming linear motion is the only option."*

PETE E.

Animating on a path is not built into Fireworks new Live Animation controls. That doesn't mean an animation can't follow a curve, however. To animate an object along a curve in Fireworks, you need to widen the distance between the object you want to animate and its rotation point. When you convert an object to a symbol in Fireworks, a rotation point is added to the center of the object. This rotation point is like the axle of a wheel. The greater the distance between the axle and the rim of the wheel (the circumference), the larger the diameter of the wheel. To see how we can use this information to animate an object along a curve, let's imagine that the object we want to animate is a piece of chewing gum stuck on a bicycle wheel.

MOVING ON THE ROTATION POINT

STEP 1 Open a 500 × 120-pixel white canvas. Drag a horizontal guideline to the 100-pixel position. This guideline represents the road our bicycle wheel will travel along. Import the bicycle_wheel.png from the Chapter 7 folder on the CD-ROM and place it at the left edge of the canvas, with the rim of the wheel resting on the guideline (7.18).

STEP 2 Draw a red, 12 × 12-pixel circle (to represent the gum) and center it over the axle of the wheel (7.19). Select the wheel and the circle and choose Modify➢ Group. Next, choose Insert➢ Convert to Symbol. When the Symbol Properties dialog box opens, type **wheel_one** in the Name field, for Type select Animation, then click OK to open the Animate dialog box.

STEP 3 In the Animate dialog box, enter 48 for Frames, 415 for Move, 720 for Rotate and select CW for clockwise. Leave the rest of the settings in the Animate dialog box at their default values and click OK. An alert box that says "The animation of this symbol extends beyond the last frame of the document. Automatically add new frames?" appears. Click OK to accept the new frames.

STEP 4 Click on the Onion Skinning icon at the bottom of the Frames panel and when the Onion Skinning dialog box opens, choose Show All Frames. The Onion Skinning dialog box automatically closes. Show All Frames enables us to view the position of the gum (the red circle) as it appears on each frame of the animation (7.20). We've learned that if we stick the gum on the axle, the gum appears to be moving along a horizontal path as the bicycle wheel moves forward on the road (hardly a surprise, as that's what the axle is supposed to do). Next, let's see what happens if we stick the gum on the rim of the wheel instead of on the axle. Close the animation without saving it.

7.18

7.19

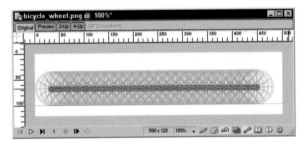

7.20

MOVING ON THE CIRCUMFERENCE

STEP 1 Open a new 500 × 120-pixel white canvas. Drag a horizontal guideline to the 100-pixel position. As we did in the first half of the exercise, import the bicycle_wheel.png from the Chapter 7 folder on the CD-ROM and place it at the left edge of the canvas, with the rim of the wheel resting on the guideline.

STEP 2 Draw a red, 12 × 12-pixel circle (our piece of gum) and center it over the place where the vertical spoke joins the top of the bicycle wheel. The edge of the red circle shouldn't extend outside the edge of the wheel rim but should sit exactly on top of the rim (7.21). Select the wheel and the circle and choose Modify➢ Group. Next, choose Insert➢ Convert to Symbol. When the Symbol Properties dialog box opens, type **wheel_two** in the Name field, for Type, select Animation, then click OK to open the Animate dialog box.

7.21

STEP 3 The settings in the Animate dialog box are exactly the same as before; 48 for Frames, 415 for Move, 720 for Rotate, and select CW. Leave the rest of the settings in the Animate dialog box at their default values and click OK. An alert box that says "The animation of this symbol extends beyond the last frame of the document. Automatically add new frames?" appears. Click OK to accept the new frames.

STEP 4 Click on the Onion Skinning icon at the bottom of the Frames panel and when the Onion Skinning dialog box opens, choose Show All Frames. The Onion Skinning dialog box automatically closes. The red circle appears to be moving forward in a series of arcs (7.22).

STEP 5 Now for some fun. Click on the Color Box in the Canvas Color dialog box to open the Swatches panel. Choose #999999. The wheel image should disappear into the background and leave the red circle visible. Click on the Play button at the bottom of the Canvas window.

We can't show the red circle moving on the page, but we can show you the positions of the red circle on each of the frames (7.23). There's our bouncing ball (er, gum).

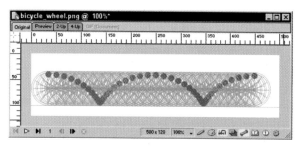

7.22

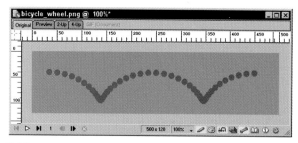

7.23

ASIDE

When the gum is at the top of the arc, both the wheel rotation and the forward movement of the wheel are in the same direction and the gum moves forward fast. When the gum is at the bottom of the arc, the movement of the gum and the movement of the wheel are in opposite directions and the gum is briefly stationary (unless the wheel is skidding). Its path is a smooth arc at the top and pointy at the bottom. The curve is known as a cycloid and has the parametric formula:

$$x = r(\varphi - \sin(\varphi)), \quad y = r(1 - \cos(\varphi))$$

where φ is the rotation angle in radians, and r is the radius of the rotating wheel, or the height of the bounce.

We've used an image of a wheel with a circle attached to it to make this demonstration easy to follow. If you would like to repeat the exercise with your own images, note that the object that you would like to curve or bounce can be attached to an invisible object, like a circle or line with no fill color.

MULTITASKING TEXT TO LOOK LIKE TICKER TAPE

Q. "How do I make a scrolling text animation in a shadow box? I want the text in it to look pixilated, like an old-fashioned ticker tape or theater marquee."

THOMAS A.

One of the more interesting ways to "jazz up" a Web page is to add ticker tape text. There are many Java applets available for this, usually to show news items. If your text information doesn't change very often, animated GIF text is a simpler way to go, with much faster download times and far less risk of crashing the viewer's browser. The ticker tape version we'll walk you through in the following exercise is easily customized for size, font, color, and speed. Making the text move requires only simple tweening. (You'll find a description of tweening in the "Texturing Metals" section of Chapter 6.)

THE SHADOW BOX

STEP 1 Open a 125 × 20-pixel canvas and zoom in 200%. Draw a rectangle slightly larger than the canvas. Add a second, slightly smaller rectangle. Shift + select both rectangles and choose Modify➤Combine➤Punch. The second rectangle is punched through the first, exposing the white canvas beneath. Add a 1-pixel black stroke.

STEP 2 The shadow is next. As commonly used, shadows are gradients composed of many shades of a single color. However, the more colors you use, the larger the file size of the finished graphic. That's not very practical for an animation that requires a large number of frames. To keep the number of colors to a minimum, use pale gray #CCCCCC, set the contrast to 100%, softness to 0,

and width to 4. It's still recognizable as a shadow, but as a hard-edged shadow you'd expect to see produced by a strong light (7.24).

Another trick for keeping the file size down is to use a font that doesn't require anti-aliasing. The font we chose is Sevenet 7. Sevenet 7 was designed for use at very small sizes. When enlarged it has interesting pixelated look, perfect for our ticker tape (7.25).

7.24

7.25

ADDING THE TEXT

STEP 1 Type the string of text you want to animate If you've used Sevenet 7, set it at 8 points with no anti-aliasing and uncheck AutoKern. Accept the text by clicking OK and move the text object over top of the box. Convert the text to a symbol by choosing Insert⇨Convert to Symbol. The Symbol Properties box opens. Select Graphic and click OK to close the Symbol Properties box. The Symbol you created is stored in the Library (7.26). A copy, or "instance" of the symbol, is left on the canvas (7.27).

7.26

7.27

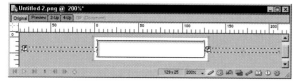

7.28

STEP 2 In the Layers panel, move the text layer below the shadow box layer. Move the text all the way to the right edge of the canvas, so the first letter is behind the right edge of the shadow box. Drag an instance of the text from the Library and move it behind the shadow box. Check in the Info panel to make sure that it is at the same height (the Y value) as the other text and move it all the way to the left, so the last letter (the *s* in News) is behind the left edge of the shadow box (7.28).

ANIMATING THE TEXT

STEP 1 Shift + select both instances of text and choose Modify➤Symbol➤Tween Instances. In the Tween Instances dialog box that appears, choose 51 steps and check Distribute to Frames. If an alert message opens warning that more frames will be added, click OK to accept the additional frames.

STEP 2 Return to Frame 1 and select the shadow box. Choose Modify➤Arrange ➤Bring to Front. Click on the right-arrow button to open the Frames panel Options pop-up menu and choose Copy to Frames. Accept the default setting of All frames and click OK. You can preview the effect by clicking on the play button at the bottom of the document window. The final step is to set up the speed at which the text will move through the shadow box.

SETTING UP THE FRAME DELAYS

Timing is crucial to the success of an animation. Even 53 frames looped at a relatively high speed leave this animation twitching a bit. Pausing the text midway through the box gives the viewer's eyes a rest and, hopefully, makes the animation more interesting. (In case you were curious, using an odd number of frames increases the chance that tweening will create one instance of text squarely in the middle of the box.)

In our example, Frame 27 has the text in the middle of the shadow box. It may be different in yours, and depends on the length of the text string. Click back and forth beginning with Frame 25 to find out for sure. After you discover the right frame, click on the right-arrow button at the top right of the Frames panel and choose Properties from the Options pop-up menu. Set the delay to 300/100. Set all others to 3/100. Change the Export File Type to Animated GIF in the Optimize panel and view the final result in your browser.

If you save a copy of your animation as a PNG and create a library of text symbols, you can quickly create a ticker GIF with new content for your Web page whenever necessary.

ANIMATING TUTORIALS

Q. "I'm building a Web site for a software company and would like to create some animations that demonstrate the way a user might interact with the GUI. You have some on your Playing with Fire site that are similar to what I'd like to end up with. How did you do them?"

MAKI Z.

The GUI animations on the PWF Website were created with screen shots. Screen shots of the interface of a software application are an essential teaching tool for authors and tutorial developers. The value of a screen shot as a teaching tool increases exponentially when you can show the user what happens when he clicks on a button. GUI animations of buttons, tabs, menu, checkboxes are easy to assemble, and because only small areas of the animations need to change, their file sizes can be kept very low. To demonstrate how to assemble a GUI animation, we'll begin with screen shots made in Fireworks 4.

CAPTURING THE SCREEN IMAGES

STEP 1   Pull the set of panels that the Stroke panel is grouped with to the center of the Fireworks desktop and make a screen capture of it. On the PC, this can be done by using Alt + Print Screen. To process the screen capture in Fireworks, choose File➤ New. When the New Document dialog box opens, you'll see that Fireworks has automatically read the dimensions of the screen capture from the clipboard. Click OK to open the canvas then paste in the image from the clipboard (Edit➤ Paste). You can run a dedicated screen capture program like HyperSnap DX if you need to capture the cursor in the screen shot. Crop the screen shot to within 20 pixels of the panel borders and then choose Modify➤Trim canvas (7.29). Minimize the canvas window to get it out of your way.

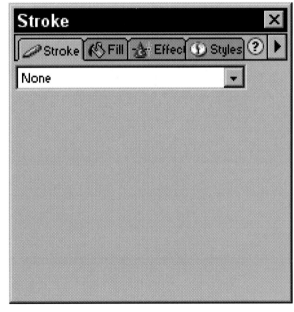

7.29

STEP 2 Turn the cursor capture feature of your screen capture program off and make a screen shot of the drop down menu button (down-arrow) of the Stroke panel in the depressed state (7.30). As in Step 1, crop the image to within 20 pixels of the panel borders and then choose Modify➤Trim canvas. Minimize the canvas window to get it out of your way.

STEP 3 Move the cursor off the button and make screen shots of the Stroke panel with the word *None* highlighted (you need to move your cursor over it), with the word *Basic* highlighted, and the words *Air Brush* highlighted. Crop the images to within 20 pixels of the panel borders and then choose Modify➤Trim canvas. Minimize the canvas windows to get the screen shots out of your way.

STEP 4 Click on the Air Brush option and make a screen shot of the Air Brush pop-up menu. Crop the screen shot to within 20 pixels of the panel borders and then choose Modify➤Trim canvas. Minimize the canvas window to get it out of your way.   Because we want to animate the cursor to emulate the user's cursor movements as he or she interacts with the buttons and menus, we'll also need an image of the pointer cursor. Move the pointer cursor over a section of the panel where the color is solid and make a screen

shot. Crop the screen shot of the pointer cursor, then choose Modify➤ Trim Canvas. Export the cursor image with a transparent background. You should now have six screen captures of the panel and one of the cursor.

DISTRIBUTING THE PREPARED SCREEN SHOTS TO FRAMES

STEP 1 Open the Frames panel and maximize the first screen shot. Click on the right-arrow button to open the Frames panel Options pop-up menu and choose Add Frames. In the Add Frames dialog box, enter 5 for the number of frames and select After current frame (7.31).

STEP 2 Click on Frame 2, copy the panel image from the second screen shot, and paste it in. Repeat the process with Frames 3 through 5, pasting in the panel images from screen shots three through five.

ANIMATING THE CURSOR

The simplest form of animation involves moving a static image, such as the arrow cursor, across the screen. Under some circumstances (such as illustrating the selection of an area with a Marquee tool) this

7.30

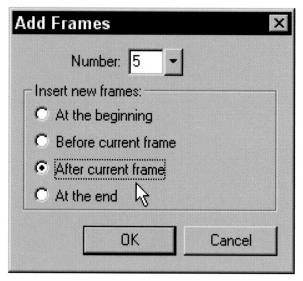

7.31

mechanical motion is appropriate, and we would simply convert the cursor to a Symbol and tween instances of it. In this case, we want the viewer to identify with the imaginary person who's moving the cursor in the animation. Most people make a small, preparatory motion in the direction opposite the one that they want to move the cursor in. Adding this little drift to your cursor animation gives it a more human appearance

STEP 1 Return to Frame 1 and click on the right-arrow button to open the Frames panel Options pop-up menu. Choose Duplicate Frame from the list. Select After Current Frame. The duplicate frame is now Frame 2. Import your cursor image into Frame 2 and place its left edge at the right edge of the panel image (7.32). Duplicate Frame 2 and use your arrow keys to move the cursor closer to the drop-down menu button on the panel image, one pixel down and two or three to the right. The duplicate is now Frame 3.

STEP 2 Duplicate Frame 3 and move the cursor closer to the menu button. Repeat duplicating the frames and moving the cursor until the cursor is over the button (Frame 9). Click on Frame 10. The image on Frame 10 should be the second of the original screen shots. It shows the button in the depressed position (7.33). Copy the cursor image from Frame 9 and paste it into Frame 10. Frames 10 and 11 are the frames where we will add the cursor drift we discussed earlier. Move the cursor image on Frame 10 one pixel to the left.

STEP 3 Frame 11 is the third of our original screen shots, in which the button pops up again after our imaginary Fireworker clicks on it. To complete the cursor drift and heighten the apparent motion of the button, move the cursor image one pixel to the left.

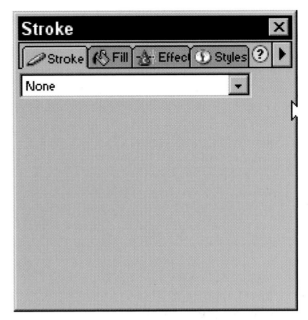

7.32

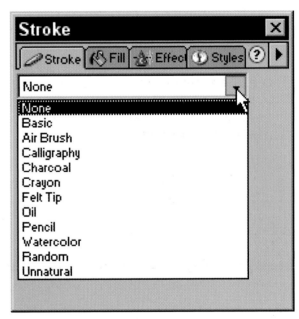

7.33

STEP 4 Duplicate Frame 11 and move the cursor toward the highlighted option in the image of the Stroke panel drop down menu (the line with the word None) (7.34). Duplicate again and move the cursor over the highlighted line. You should now be on Frame 14. Duplicate Frame 14 and move the cursor image down until just the tip of the cursor rests on the highlighted line. Copy the cursor image into Frame 16.

STEP 5 If all has gone well, the Basic option should be highlighted in the image of the panel menu. Move the cursor straight down until it rests on top of the highlighted area. Duplicate Frame 16 and move the cursor image down over the highlighted area until just the tip of the cursor is touching. Copy the cursor image and paste it into Frame 18. Move the cursor down over the highlighted Air Brush line. To create the illusion that the user's mouse button has been released over the highlighted line and is moving quickly away, duplicate Frame 18 and move the cursor image a few pixels to the right. Duplicate again and move the cursor image a few more pixels to the right (7.35).

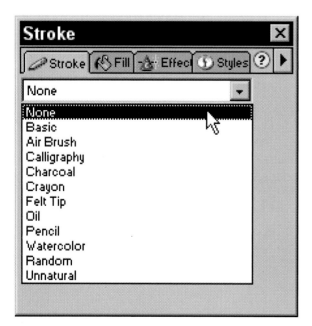

7.34

FRAME	TIMING	COMMENT
1	100/100	slow, to give the viewer a chance to take in the details of the image
2 through 9	1/100	where the cursor approaches the Panel menu button, should be very fast to smooth the motion
10, 11	20/100	needs to pause
12, 13	7/100	needs to be quick
14	100/100	needs to pause a long time so that the viewer can read the menu
15	7/100	
16	100/100	like Frame 14, needs to pause a relatively long time
17	7/100	
18	100/100	
19, 20	1/100	needs to whiz by
21	500/100	the last one needs to pause so that it can be studied, but also so that the animation doesn't begin looping again too quickly

TABLE 7-2   THE FRAME DELAYS

Click on the Play button at the bottom of the canvas window and make any timing adjustments you consider necessary. You can use the techniques you learned in this exercise with any GUI you want to illustrate.

TYPING ANIMATION

Q. "Can you tell me how to animation text in a banner so it looks like flowing across a text box as it is being typed?"

ANDREW K.

This exercise makes use of screen captures of a text box and submit button on a Web page. We'll first build a text form in Dreamweaver, then preview the text form in a browser to make the screen shots. Because this is a banner ad, we'll add a company logo to the animation too. Careful sequencing and timing of the frames will create an illusion of the viewer interacting with the text form in a Web page. Preparing the images

STEP 1   Open a new file in your HTML editor (we used Dreamweaver) and apply a background color to the page Modify➢ Page Properties. Click in the Background color box to open the Color Swatches pop-up and choose #00CCFF. Click OK to close the Page Properties dialog box. Press Enter twice to insert two paragraph breaks. Insert a form field (Field). An alert will pop up asking you if you want to add form tags. Click Yes. Center the Text field by clicking on the Align Center button on the Property inspector. Add a Submit button (Insert➢ Form Object➢ Button). Click on the button and change the Label from Submit to "Go!" Choose Edit➢ Preview in Browser.

STEP 2   When the browser opens with the Web page, resize the browser window until the opening is 400 x 200. Click inside the text field and make a screen shot of the page as the cursor blinks on.

Open a new 234 × 60-pixel canvas in Fireworks and paste the screen shot onto the canvas (Edit➢ Paste). Carefully center the text field and the Go button image on the canvas. Zoom in to 400% and pull horizontal guidelines against the top and bottom edges of the text field. Pull vertical guidelines against the left edge of the text field and the right edge of the button. Export the image using the Exact palette setting, name the file *screenshot1*, and select the white background of the text field as the transparent color (7.36). Once the file is exported, delete the image from the canvas.

STEP 3   Make a second screen shot, this time when the cursor blinks off. Paste the screen shot onto the canvas, zoom in to 400%, and use the guidelines to help you center the text field and button image. Export the image with the Exact palette setting, name the file *screenshot2*, and select the white background of the text field as the transparent color (7.37). When the file has been exported, delete the image from the canvas.

Make a third screen shot, this time while pressing the "Go!" button. Because you don't want the cursor to show in this screen shot, turn off that option in your screen capture program. Paste the screen shot onto the canvas, zoom in to 400%, and use the guidelines to help you center the text field and button image. Export the image with the Exact palette setting, name the file *screenshot3*, and select the white background of the text field as the transparent color (7.38).

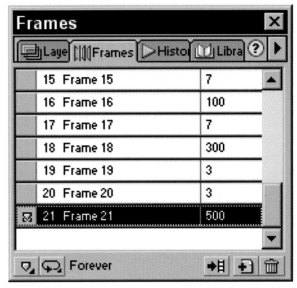

7.35

7.36

7.37

7.38

ASSEMBLING THE FIRST FRAMES

Now that all of our images are prepared, we can begin the more interesting process of assembling the animation.

STEP 1 Open the screenshot1.gif file. Fireworks opens bitmap files on a transparent canvas by default. Change the canvas color to white using Modify➤ Canvas color. Anything behind the text field image will appear as if it is in the text field. You can see the beginnings of the illusion. Click on the right-arrow button at the top right of the Frames panel to open the Frames panel Options pop-up menu. Choose Add Frames. The Add Frames dialog window opens. Enter 1 for the number of frames and select After current frame. Close the Add Frames dialog box by clicking OK.

STEP 2 Import the screenshot2.gif file onto Frame 2. Click on the Onion Skinning button and select Before and After. Zoom in and carefully align the text field and button image with the text field and button image on Frame 1.

STEP 3 Return to Frame 1 and click on the right-arrow button at the top right of the Frames panel. Choose Duplicate Frame and click OK. The Duplicate Frame dialog box opens. Select At the End and click OK. Return to Frame 2 and duplicate it to the end as well. You should now have four frames. Frames 1 and 3 with the cursor image on, and Frames 2 and 4 with the cursor image off.

ADDING THE TEXT

Now we are going to create the illusion of text being typed into the text field image. This part is a bit fussy. We think that when you see how successful the illusion is in the finished animation you'll be quite proud of your accomplishment.

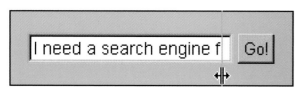

7.39

STEP 1 Duplicate Frame 4 . Click on the Text tool to activate it and click inside the text field of the image. Type the letter **I**. The settings we used are Arial, #000000, 14 pixels, and No Anti-Alias. Click OK to close the Text Editor. Move the letter "I" that you just typed to the inside left edge of the text field image.

STEP 2 Duplicate Frame 5. Click on the letter *I* to reopen the Text Editor. Insert a space after the *I* and type a lower case **n.** Close the Text Editor and duplicate the frame. Click on the text to reopen the Text Editor and type the letter **e** immediately after the *n.* Continue typing out the phrase **I need a search engine for my site**, duplicating the current frame to add new frame after each character.

STEP 3 When you are within one character space of the right end of the text field in the image, stop and place a vertical guideline to the right edge of the last character. In our example, it is the letter *f* of the word for and falls on Frame 23 (7.39). Click on the text field image and choose Modify➤ Arrange➤ Bring to Front.

Duplicate the frame and add the letter *o*. Move the text string to align the right edge of the letter *o* with the guideline. Continue duplicating the frames, adding the next character, and shifting the text string to the right until the complete phrase has been typed in. This way the newly added text appears to be pushing the previous characters left and out of sight in the text field of the image. If we are going to create an illusion, we may as well do it well!

PUSHING THE BUTTON

Now we want to create the illusion of the cursor moving over the Go! button image and clicking on it. We need an image of the black pointer cursor. Open a 50-x-50-pixel, light, gray canvas. Place your cursor on top of the canvas and make a screen shot. Crop the screen shot to within a few pixels of the cursor and choose Modify➤ Trim Canvas. Choose File➤ Export Preview. When the cursor image opens in the Export Preview window, use the Select Transparent Eyedropper to select the gray background of the cursor image for transparency. Export the cursor image, then import it onto the last frame of the typing animation. Place the cursor image at the right side of the canvas (7.40).

STEP 1 Over the next four frames, move the cursor image toward the Go! button. When the cursor image is over the button, delete the text field image and import the third of the screen shots we prepared at the beginning of the exercise, screenshot3.gif. The third screen shot shows the Submit Go! button in the depressed position. Turn on Onion Skinning (Before and After) and carefully align the text field image with the text field image in the previous frame. After the newly imported text field image is properly aligned, select it and choose Modify➤ Arrange➤ Send Backward to move it behind the cursor image (7.41). Move the cursor one pixel to the right and add a new frame.

STEP 2 You may recall that in the introduction of the exercise we mentioned that we were going to include a company logo in the animation. The logo is the soul of this animation. We've used the logo for a nice Website search script called Fluffy Search and features a fluffy, white cloud against a blue background. Fluffy Search is a freeware script so we'll include the URL in case you would like to explore the possibility of adding Fluffy Search to your Website (*www.fluffy.co.uk/fsl*). No doubt you'll want to add your own logo. Choose an image and import it into the new frame (7.42).

TIMING IT RIGHT

The timing of this kind of animation is particularly important, or the illusion that a viewer is interacting with the animation is lost. The motion in the first four frames is the blinking cursor. The default Cursor Blink Rate on a Windows machine (95, 98, NT, Me) is said to be half a second, so 50/100 is about right.

The text needs to move slow enough to be readable, which is much slower than a good typist can type it out. Sacrifice realism for the sake of clarity and set the frame delays to 50/100.

The last text frame before the cursor image enters stage-right needs to pause. A frame delay of 100/100 should be long enough. The cursor frames should be fast to smooth the motion. Set them to 1/100.

The cursor over the depressed button should pause about 50/100s before moving off. The movement of the cursor off the Go! button should be abrupt. However, because it's only one frame, it shouldn't be faster than 20/100.

The logo frame should pause for a long time before the animation begins to play again. (A pause of 500/100 is not too long.)

Preview the animation by clicking on the Play button at the bottom of the canvas window. The final result is an animation that looks deceptively like the user is interacting with the banner.

NOTE

Why make a screen shot of the cursor against a light gray background? We need the background of the cursor image to be transparent. Black cursors have a white border around them. If we shoot the cursor against a white background and use Index transparency, we lose the white border.

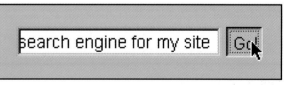

7.40

7.41

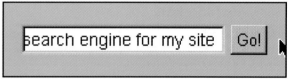

7.42

STOMPING FOOT

Q. *"I've seen an animation of a stomping foot on David's Web compression tools review site. I love it! How was it done?"*

SHARON D.

The animation is of a foot that stomps on and squeezes down the word *graphics*. Our plan of attack in this exercise is to create an initial image, create subsequent images with the text increasingly flattened, export the images as individual GIFs, trim them to the same size, and use these GIFs to create the animation. David created the animation over three years ago when animated GIF programs were rather thin on the ground, but it's still a useful exercise in simple animation.

First, we need a foot. You can draw one, scan one, or find an appropriate image on the Web. The one we used is roughly based on the famous Monty Python stomping foot (7.43).

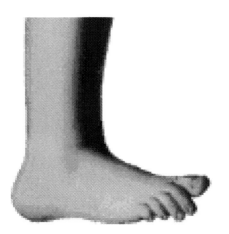

7.43

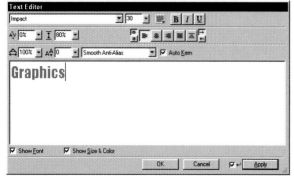

7.44

STEP 1 The image is 140 x 99 pixels. We'll expand the Canvas to 140 x 140 (with the original image at the top and the background set to white) to make room for the text to be squashed by the foot. It is a good idea to increase the screen magnification to 200% to make what we're doing with the graphics easier to see.

STEP 2 Add your text next by typing the word **graphics**. The settings are font size 30 and font color red. We've used the Impact font, but any blocky sans-serif font works would be an equally good choice (7.44).

STEP 3 The text appears in a text layer over the foot image and is set out by the blue border. The appearance of the border indicates that the text is ready for further manipulation. First move the text to the center of the white space below the foot (7.45). The text is wide enough but not as tall as it should be. Choose Modify➤Transform➤ Numeric Transform. When the Transform dialog box opens, uncheck the Constrain Proportions box and set the height to 134 (7.46).

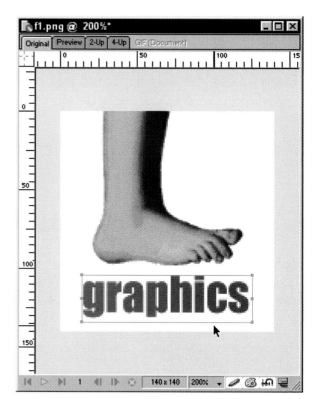

7.45

Accepting the result of these changes gives us the first frame of the animation. Well, nearly. We need to shift the text up under the foot with the up-arrow key, leaving one pixel of white space between the top of the letter *h* and the foot graphic (7.47). More important, we have to trim it to a standard size, which we don't yet know. For now, we'll export it as a GIF by using the Exact palette option.

If you use your own foot image, experiment with the Palette settings to see what looks effective and compresses well by using the Preview Tab on the main image. After the settings are in place, export the file as a GIF File➤Export in the standard way, naming the file *frame1.gif*.

> **STEP 4** Return to the main image to start squeezing the text for the second frame. Use Numerical Transform again and set the height value to 66% because we want the text to start shrinking vertically, and set the width to 105% so that the text gets a bit wider. Again, shift the image up toward the foot, leaving 1 pixel of white space and export the full image as a GIF (7.48). Remember to name the GIF with a different file name. Name this file *frame2.gif*.

The next few steps are easy. Using the same Numerical Transform as before, shift the text toward the foot to leave a one pixel white space, then export the file as a GIF (saving it as *Frame3.gif*). Repeat this process four more times (with consecutive numbers in the names, *frame4.gif* and so on) so that you can assemble the animation from six separate GIF files. Trim the six GIF images to a common size. In this case, a height of 105 pixels is what we choose, because

the final image — with the most squashed text — allows 105 pixels of height before we run out of leg!

FINISHING THE IMAGES

Open the first image and crop it to a height of 105 pixels. Setting a guide one pixel below the bottom of the text (the letter *g*) is a good way to maintain consistency with subsequent images, which we must also

7.47

7.46

7.48

7.49

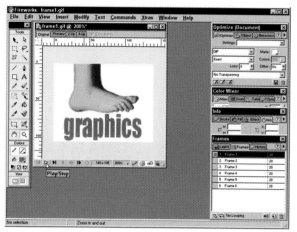

7.50

trim to 140 x 105 pixels. In other words, trim off the top of the leg and the spare white space below the text to fit by using the Crop tool (7.49).

Do the same with the other five GIF images. There are now have six GIFs, each 140 x 105 pixels. We're on the last lap now, creating the animation.

CREATING THE ANIMATION

To begin the animating process, load the first exported cropped GIF image (Frame1.gif) and click on the Frames panel Options pop-up menu.

STEP 1 The open image shows up as Frame 1 in the frames sequence. Add a new frame by using the New Frame button at the bottom right on the Frames panel. (It's the button next to the trash can icon.) Clicking on the New Frame button opens a blank Frame 2.

STEP 2 Open the second GIF image of the sequence, copy it to the clipboard and paste it into frame two. Create a third frame, open the third image in the sequence, copy and paste it, and so on, until we have six frames, all filled.

We can now play the animation by using the Play Button at the bottom of the Image window (7.50). The action is a bit stilted because we are using the default frame delay of 7/100. Double-click on the timing box for Frame 1 and set it to 50/100 (7.51).

Set Frames 2 through 5 to 5/100, and Frame 6 to 80/100. The final step is to click on the GIF animation looping button at the bottom left of the Frames panel and set the looping to Forever.

EXPORTING THE ANIMATION

This last step is easy. In the Optimize panel, select Animated GIF in the Export Format drop-down box (7.52). Set the Palette choice (we've chosen Exact in this instance because it retains the smoothness of the original image we chose, but you should experiment). Also in the Optimize panel, select transparency and choose a Matte Color if your application requires one. To export, choose File➤Export.

And there you have it — a stomping foot. You can find a copy of the animated GIF in the Chapter 7 folder on the CD-ROM.

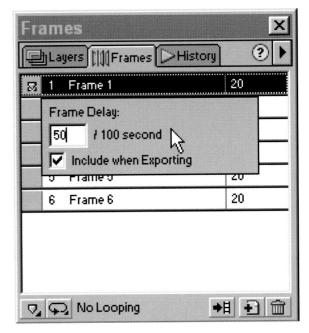

7.51

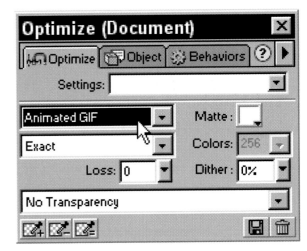

7.52

CHAPTER 8
KEEPING COMPANY WITH OTHER SOFTWARE

Fireworks operates as a fine stand-alone application, but one of its major strengths is its integration with Dreamweaver, Macromedia's flagship Web development program. Dreamweaver is a powerful visual HTML editor and adds industrial-strength JavaScript and DHTML to the Fireworks program's already-significant, built-in capabilities. In this chapter, we explore some the things you can do by using both. We also give a brief look at animating an image in Fireworks with Macromedia Flash and two other useful programs, SWiSH and Ignite. If you don't have copies of these programs, we have provided trial versions of Dreamweaver, Fireworks, SWiSH, and Ignite on the CD-ROM.

"As the Italians say, good company on a journey makes the way seem the shorter."

IZAAK WALTON, FROM *THE COMPLEAT ANGLER*

DISJOINT ROLLOVERS

Q. *"I've done a set of simple rollover icons on my page. Now how do I get them to swap some images on another part of the page?"*

HASS L.

We'll be using three button sets in addition to the graphics for the swap images in this exercise. You'll find copies of them on the CD-ROM located in the back of this book.

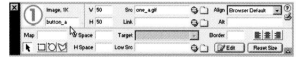

8.1

8.2

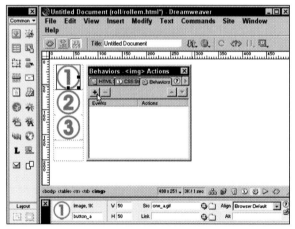

8.3

NOTE

For the image swaps to function properly, each pair of button images and each pair of disjoint rollover images must have the same dimensions.

SETTING UP

STEP 1 Load Dreamweaver and click the Table icon on the Object panel. Add a four-row, one-column table to your page. Place your cursor in the top row and click the Insert Image icon. When the Select Image Source dialog box opens, browse to the one_a.gif file on the CD-ROM. Click the Select button to insert the image. In the Property Inspector, give the button graphic a unique name. As you can see, the figure name is different from the name of the original GIF (8.1).

STEP 2 Insert two_a.gif in the second row of the table and as you did in the last step, give it a unique name. We've used the name button_b. Insert three_a.gif into the third row of the table and give it a unique name (button_c) Insert blank.gif into the fourth row as a kind of place-holder where the text images are swapped. Give it a unique name (blank_text) (8.2).

ADDING THE BEHAVIORS

STEP 1 Click the top button (one_a.gif) then the + button in the Behaviors panel to open the Actions pop-up menu (8.3). Scroll down the menu and choose Swap Image. A dialog box containing a list of the images in your table opens. (Aren't you glad you went to the trouble of adding those unique names for your GIFs?)

The image you have selected is highlighted. To set the source for the image that will be swapped for "button_a," click the Browse button. The Select Image Source dialog box opens. Use the Look in drop-down menu at the top of the Select Image Source dialog box to browse to your image folder, then click one_b.gif to highlight it. Click Select to close the Select Image Source dialog box. That sets the behavior for the button rollover and returns you to the Swap Image dialog box (8.4). Do *not* click the OK button in the Swap Image box yet! That would close the dialog box with only half the job done. You still need to add the Swap Image behavior for the disjoint rollover.

STEP 2 Click the blank_text line in the Swap
Image dialog box to highlight it, then click
Browse. Just as you did in step one, locate the swap
image (in this case, the text_a.gif file) through the
Select Image Source dialog box. Highlight the
image and click Select to close the Select Image
Source dialog box. This adds the behavior that
swaps the dummy image for the first of the disjoint rollovers when the viewer mouses over the
button. *Now* click OK.

 Choose File ➢ Preview in Browser from the
File menu to check your work. If all has gone well,
you should see the button rollover and the first
text image appear below the line of buttons (8.5).

STEP 3 Select the second button, click the + button in the Behaviors panel, and choose Swap
Image from the Actions pop-up menu. You should
see button_b highlighted in the Swap Image dialog box. Click the Browse button and locate the
two_b.gif file. Scroll down to the blank_text line
and highlight it. Click the Browse button to locate
the text_b.gif. Click OK and choose File ➢
Preview in Browser to check your results (8.6).

STEP 4 Select the third button, click the Add
Actions button (+) in the Behaviors panel and
choose Swap Image from the menu. Click the
browse button to locate two_c.gif. Highlight the
"blank_text" line and click the browse button to
locate the text_b.gif. Click OK and preview in
your browser again (8.7).

 Congratulations! You've successfully created a
Dreamweaver 4 disjoint rollover.

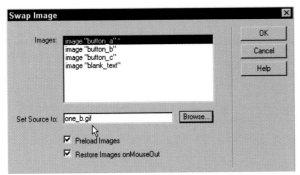

8.4

8.5   8.6

8.7

8.8

SHOW-HIDE LAYERS

Q. "I am very interested in learning how to create a navigation system with fly-out menus, such as the one you did on your Playing with Fire site. Do you mind sharing the secret?"

MICHAEL B.

The only real secret is how easy it is to create this kind of navigation system (created with layers and Show-Hide behaviors), in Dreamweaver.

Before beginning, you need to plan how you want your viewers to navigate through your site. Many people find that drawing a rough diagram of the way the pages will be linked is helpful. After you have a firm plan, set up the basic layout for your index page: header, menu, space for the content, footer, and the like.

DRAWING LAYERS

We have outlined how to attach the behaviors that show and hide the menu parts to hyperlinks. Behaviors can be attached to images, rollovers, or even animations.

STEP 1 After your page layout is complete, click the Draw Layer button in the Objects panel and drag out the layer you want to become visible upon mousing over the trigger (hyperlink one) (8.8). Add a fixed-width table to the layer to constrain text and control image placement (8.9). Add your content to the layer.

STEP 2 Make a note of the layer coordinates in the Inspector window (8.10). Add text and/or images; then set the visibility of the layer to Hidden.

> **TIP**
>
> Adding a temporary background color to the table in a layer makes the layer easier to see while you are switching back and forth between the program window and your browsers to fine-tune its position.

STEP 3 Drag out a second layer for the second hyperlink. Add the table and content; then type the coordinates of the first layer into the Inspector window and press enter. The second layer springs directly over the first. Set visibility to Hidden. Follow the same steps with the rest of the layers until all are drawn, filled with content, and in position. To double-check, count the yellow layer anchors at the top of the Editor window to make sure that the number matches the number of links (8.11).

ATTACHING THE BEHAVIORS

STEP 1 Highlight the first hyperlink; then click the + button in the Behaviors panel. Choose Show-Hide Layers from the Add Actions pop-up menu. The Show-Hide Layer dialog window opens with the first layer selected. Because this is the layer we want to show when hyperlink one is moused over, click the Show button. One at a time, select all the other layers in the list and click the Hide button. When you are finished, click OK to close the dialog box (8.12).

STEP 2 In the Behavior panel, open the Events menu with the arrow button (8.13) and choose onMouseOver from the pop-up menu. If you don't see the button, click the text under Events, and it should appear. Layer 1 is finished. Press F12 on your keyboard or choose Edit ➤ Preview in Browser from the Edit menu to check your work.

STEP 3 Highlight the second hyperlink then click the Add Behaviors button (+). Choose Show-Hide Layers from the Actions pop-up menu. Click Layer 2 to select it, then click the Show button. Select all the other layers one at a time and attach

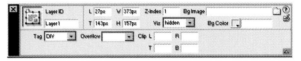

8.10

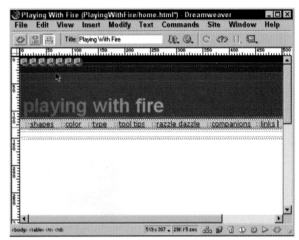

8.11

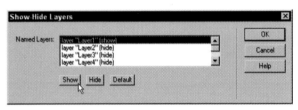

8.12

8.13

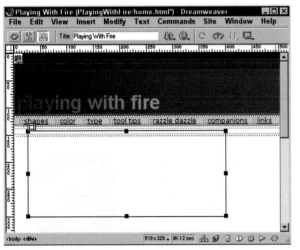

8.9

the hide behavior (8.14). Close the dialog box. Once again, choose onMouseOver from the Events menu. Layer 2 is finished. Test the results in your browsers.

STEP 4 Select the third hyperlink and attach the show behavior to the third layer. Attach the hide behavior to all other layers. Add the onMouseOver event. Continue in this way until all the hyperlinks have the appropriate layers and behaviors attached to them. Test again.

That's all there is to it. Now that you've learned the technique, we'll bet that you'll find many interesting uses for Show-Hide layers.

DHTML ON A TIMELINE

Q. "I am animating image layers via timelines in Dreamweaver. The timelines are triggered by a behavior from an image contained within each of the layers. The problem is that the timeline is only playing once and I'd like them to play every time the viewer clicks the images. Do I need to do a page refresh or something? Has anyone else tried doing this? Man, I hope I can do it, any advice would be really appreciated."

REUBEN S.

Fireworks includes useful tools to add rollovers, image swaps, and GIF animations to your Web site. But compared to the wealth of dynamic interactivity that Dreamweaver offers, Fireworks only scratches the surface. The following tutorial by maestro Lanny Chambers leads you through the creation of a

collection of images, incorporating several advanced illustration techniques; then it shows you how to assemble the pieces in Dreamweaver. You'll animate the images by using layers and Timelines, and apply behaviors that respond to user interaction.

To see the finished project: From the book's CD-ROM, open the file antenna.html in your browser. Click the blinking green light and watch what happens. Are you smiling now? You'll be duplicating this page from scratch, using only the tools built into Fireworks and Dreamweaver. Although the tutorial example is not a simple one, you'll learn dozens of mini techniques that you can apply to your own Web projects. We hope the lesson expands the limits of possibility for you.

CREATING THE PIECES IN FIREWORKS

We'll create the artwork first, then export pieces of it as individual images to be assembled in Dreamweaver.

In this tutorial, we use the X, Y coordinates to refer to the positions of some objects within the Fireworks workspace. Make sure that the Info panel is open (Window ➤ Info), and notice how the numbers in the lower-right quadrant track the position of your cursor in the workspace. Other numbers in this panel describe the selected object's size and position. Dragging, nudging with the arrow keys, or typing new numbers into the Info panel and pressing enter may be used to change the position of an object.

PREPARING THE CANVAS

STEP 1 Create a new document (File ➤ New) with a width of 125 pixels, a height of 400 pixels, and a custom canvas color of #666666. Make sure Snap to

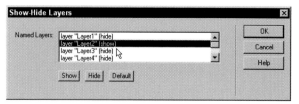

8.14

> **WARNING**
>
> This may not be the best tutorial to try first. Basic familiarity with Fireworks and Dreamweaver is very helpful.

Guides is enabled (View ➢ Guides ➢ Snap to Guides) and that the rulers are visible (View ➢ Rulers), and drag guides to these positions: Vertical guides at 15, 25, 35, 100, and 110 pixels Horizontal guides at 15, 115, 215, 315, 321, 340, 350, 380, and 390 pixels

Watch the numbers in the Info panel to help you position the guides (8.15).

STEP 2 Add two new layers to the document, either by clicking two times on the New/Duplicate Layer icon at the bottom of the Layers panel, or by choosing Insert ➢ Layer. You should now have four layers: the Web Layer and three drawing layers.

STEP 3 In the Layers panel, double-click each drawing layer name and rename them, from top to bottom, Hilites and Shadows, body, and antenna (8.16). (Why "hilites" instead of "highlights?" Hilites fits better within the space allowed for layer names in the panel.) Any time the guides are obstructing your view, hide them by toggling View ➢ Guides ➢ Show Guides. Save the file as antenna.png.

DRAWING THE BODY

STEP 1 For ease of drawing, magnify the workspace to 200% and scroll to the bottom. In the Layers panel, click the body layer to activate it.

STEP 2 Using the Rounded Rectangle Tool, drag out a rounded rectangle, 95 pixels wide and 50 pixels high, starting at X: 14, Y: 340. The rectangle should snap to the guides you made earlier. In the Object panel, set the Roundness to 20. In the Fill panel, set the Fill color to something easy to see, such as #FF0000. (We'll be changing the fill color later.)

STEP 3 Drag out another rounded rectangle measuring, 20 pixels wide and 29 pixels high, starting at X: 15, Y: 321. Set its Roundness to 40. Select both rounded rectangles, then choose Modify ➢ Combine ➢ Union to make them a single object (8.17).

8.16

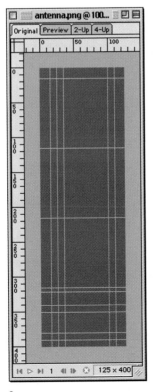

8.15

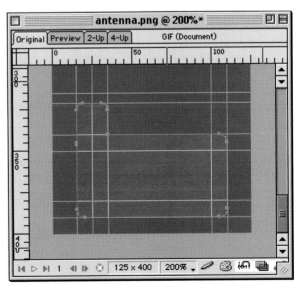

8.17

STEP 4 Widen the radius of the lower-left corner. You could do this by adjusting the Bézier handles, but we'll use a more precise method instead. Using the Subselect tool, move the two points that define this corner so they snap to the guide intersections (8.18).

STEP 5 Using the Ellipse tool, hold down the Shift key and drag out a 20-pixel-diameter circle. Position the circle over the lower-left corner of the rectangle (8.19). Select both objects, then choose Modify ➢ Combine ➢ Union to make them a single object (8.20).

MAKING THE BODY LOOK REALISTIC

STEP 1 In the Fill panel, change the fill to #666666, select the Line-Horiz 4 texture, set its Amount to 25%, and check the Transparent box.

STEP 2 Next, we want to apply a smooth inner bevel and a drop shadow. From the Effect panel drop-down menu, select Bevel and Emboss ➢ Bevel ➢ Inner Bevel ➢ Smooth. Set the Width of the bevel to 10, the Softness to 5 and the Angle to 135. Click somewhere outside the panel to accept the addition of the bevel. Again in the Effect panel drop-down menu, select Shadow and Glow ➢ Shadow ➢ Drop Shadow. Set the shadow Distance to 5, the Opacity to 100%, the Softness to 4 and the Angle to 315 (8.21).

STEP 3 Create a recessed area by dragging out a rounded rectangle 65 pixels wide and 30 pixels high, starting at X: 35, Y: 350. Set the corner roundness of the rectangle to 30 and in the Effect panel, choose Bevel and Emboss ➢ Bevel ➢ Inner Bevel ➢ Smooth. Set the width of the bevel to 5, Contrast 75%, Softness 2, and Angle 135, and change the Button Preset to Inset.

MAKING THE CONTROL BUTTON

STEP 1 Using the Ellipse tool, make the up bezel by dragging out a circle 12 pixels in diameter,

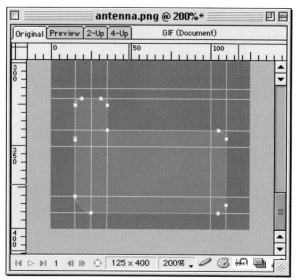

8.18

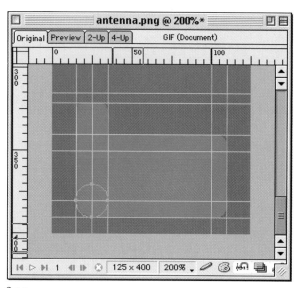

8.19

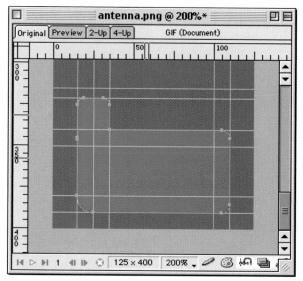

8.20

starting at X: 51, Y: 359. Give it a fill of #666666, a Ring Inner Bevel of Width 3, Contrast 100%, Softness 1, and Angle 135, and a Drop Shadow of Distance 2, Opacity 50%, Softness 2, and Angle 315.

STEP 2 Drag out a circle 6 pixels in diameter for the lighted center, starting at X: 54, Y: 362. Fill it with #006600 and apply a Smooth Inner Bevel of Width 3, Contrast 100%, Softness 3, and Angle 135. The light should be neatly centered on the bezel.

STEP 3 Select both bezel and light and clone them to create the down button. In the Info panel, change the X coordinate from 51 to 72 to shift the bezel and light right of the up button. Select only the down light and change the fill to #660000 (8.22).

DRAWING THE SHINY RING

STEP 1 To draw the shiny ring that appears at the top left of the body where the antenna will be placed, drag out a 20 × 6-pixel rectangle starting at X: 15, Y: 315. Fill with a linear gradient and then edit the gradient (8.23).

STEP 2 Click between the existing color points to add new points; from left to right, the colors are #666666, #FFFFFF, #666666, #CCCCCC, and #666666. Apply a Flat Inner Bevel of Width 1,

Contrast 100%, Softness 2, and Angle 135. Then add a Drop Shadow of Distance 5, Opacity 50%, Softness 5, and Angle 315.

ADDING DEPTH TO THE BODY WITH CUSTOM HILITES AND SHADOWS

STEP 1 Select the body path (but not the recess or buttons) and copy it to the Clipboard. In the Layers panel, click the Hilites and Shadows layer to make it active; paste the body path into the Hilites and Shadows layer. In the Layers panel, lock the body layer by clicking on the pencil next to the "eye" icon. That prevents any accidental changes to the body layer. Remove the Inner Bevel and Drop Shadow effects from the body path you pasted into the Hilites and Shadows layer and in the Fill panel, set the Texture to 0%. Copy the path to the Clipboard. We'll be pasting in again later.

STEP 2 Still in the Hilites and Shadows layer, clone the path (Edit ➤ Clone), then offset the clone two pixels down and to the right by pressing the down-arrow and the right-arrow keys two times each. Select both paths and choose Modify ➤ Combine ➤ Punch to create two highlighted areas. Fill the two

8.22

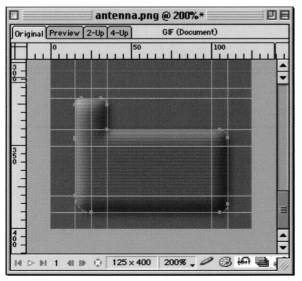

8.21

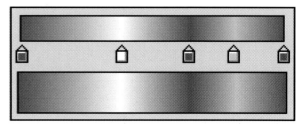

8.23

highlighted areas with white (#FFFFFF) and shift them two pixels down and right with the arrow keys.

STEP 3 Use the Subselect tool and the arrows to move the individual points (8.24). Change the fill to Feather with an amount of 3 and reduce the opacity to 50% in the Layers panel. In the Layers panel, click the eye next to the highlight you just made to hide and protect it.

STEP 4 The shadows are more complicated; they'll need a mask to clip the feathered edges so they won't spill over onto the background.

Paste another copy of the body path into the Hilites and Shadows layer. Clone the path and use the arrow keys to move it up and to the left four pixels. Select both paths and choose Modify ➢ Combine ➢ Punch to create two shadow areas. Fill with black (#000000).

STEP 5 Use the Subselect tool and the keyboard arrows to move individual points (8.25). Change the fill to Feather with an amount of 6 and set the Opacity to 30%.

STEP 6 Paste another copy of the body path over this shadow, select both paths, and choose Modify ➢ Mask ➢ Group as Mask from the menu. Unhide the highlight path and lock the Hilites and Shadows layer. The body is finished.

MAKING THE ILLUMINATED BUTTONS

Because the page is animated by using Dreamweaver layers instead of Fireworks rollovers, exporting is simpler if you create the illuminated buttons in a separate Fireworks document. To make the illuminated buttons, perform the following steps:

STEP 1 Select the bezels and lights (four objects) and copy them to the Clipboard. Open a new Fireworks document (File ➢ New). Accept the suggested size (which will fit the Clipboard contents), and specify a custom canvas color (#666666) by using the Eyedropper on the recessed area around the buttons in antenna.png. Paste the buttons into the new document.

STEP 2 Change the fill for the green and red lights to #00CC00 and #CC0000 respectively, and change their inner bevel contrast to 50%.

STEP 3 To enhance the lights, we'll add a glow to splash some color onto the bezels and add a brighter highlight to intensify the depth of the bevel.

Select the green light and add a Glow effect: Color #00FF00, Width 0, Opacity 50%, Softness 2, and Offset 0. Do the same to the red light but with a color of #FF0000.

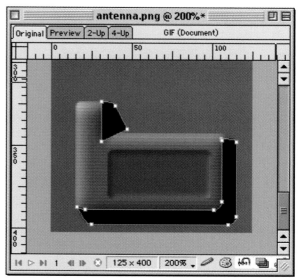

8.24

8.25

STEP 4 For the green light's highlight, drag out a circle with a diameter of 2 pixels, starting at X: 5, Y: 5. Give it a fill of #FFFFFF and a Feather of 1; in the Layers panel, reduce its Opacity to 70%. Clone this circle and change its Y coordinate to 19 in the Info panel to position the clone over the red light; then reduce its opacity to 30% (8.26). Save the file as buttons.png.

8.26

DRAWING THE ANTENNA

STEP 1 The antenna is three similar sections, plus a ball at the top. Using the Rectangle tool, drag out a rectangle 10 pixels wide and 100 pixels high, starting at X: 20, Y: 215. Fill it with the same linear gradient you used for the ring and apply the same drop shadow. If you like, you can copy the ring to the Clipboard and then use Edit ➢ Paste Attributes and remove the bevel.

STEP 2 To make the top end taper, add two points to the top edge by clicking on it with the Pen tool; these new points should be one pixel in from the top corners. Using the Subselect tool, select the corner points and move them down one pixel by pressing the down-arrow key (8.27).

STEP 3 Clone the first section and move it up 100 pixels; in the Info panel, change its width to 8 pixels to make the second section; tap the right-arrow key to center it. Clone, move, and change the width to 6 pixels, and center again to make the third section.

STEP 4 Notice that each section's shadow is unrealistic where it falls on the section below. Change the stacking order by dragging the objects in the Layers panel so the first section is on top and the third section is on the bottom.

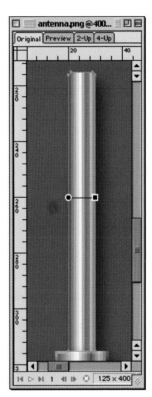

8.27

ADDING THE BALL

STEP 1 Drag out a 10-pixel-diameter circle. Fill it with a radial gradient from #FFFFFF to #666666 and move the gradient's focus up and to the left a few pixels. Apply a Smooth Inner Bevel of Width 5, Contrast 25%, Softness 1, and Angle 135. Then add a Drop Shadow of Distance 5, Opacity 50%, Softness 5, and Angle 315. For an extra highlight, make a circle 3 pixels in diameter with a fill of white and a Feather of 1.

STEP 2 Make sure that the ball is stacked behind the third section (at the bottom of the layer). Then add the shadow the ball casts on the third section by dragging out a rectangle 6 pixels wide and 2 pixels high, fill of #000000, Feather of 1, and Opacity 25%.

The workspace (8.28) and the Layers panel (8.29) (if you've been naming each object) reflects the view and settings you should have. Make sure that you save the PNG file now.

SLICING AND EXPORTING THE IMAGE

STEP 1 Open buttons.png. In the Optimize panel, select GIF, Exact, and No Transparency (8.30).

STEP 2 Drag out a slice over the green button, 18 pixels wide and 16 pixels high; in the Object panel, uncheck the Auto-Name Slices box and name the slice up.gif. Drag out another slice over the red button, 19 pixels wide and 16 pixels high, and name it down.gif. The slices should completely cover the canvas.

STEP 3 Choose File ➢ Export and select Images Only and Export Slices. Click Save to export. Save and close the buttons.png file.

STEP 4 If you closed the antenna.png file, reopen it now. In the Optimize panel, select GIF, Exact, and No Transparency. Drag a guide out of the vertical ruler and drop it at the 40-pixel point to help align your slices.

STEP 5 Drag out a slice 25 pixels wide and 115 pixels high, starting at X: 15, Y: 0. In the Object panel, uncheck the Auto-Name Slices box and name it section3.gif. Clone the slice, and in the Info panel, change the X coordinate to 100 and its Y coordinate to 115; then name it section2.gif. Clone this slice, move the clone to cover the first section, and name it section1.gif. Finally, drag out a slice over the body, 110 pixels wide and 85 pixels high, starting at X: 15, Y: 315. Name this slice body.gif (8.31).

STEP 6 Select File ➢ Export and from the pop-up menus in the Export dialog box, select CSS Layers and Fireworks Slices. Then, uncheck the Trim Images box, specify antenna.htm as the filename, and click Save to Export. Save and close the antenna file. Now it's time to quite Fireworks and head over to Dreamweaver.

ASSEMBLING THE ARTWORK IN DREAMWEAVER

Dreamweaver expands the possibilities for animation and interactivity, allowing you to combine animation and interactivity in ways not possible in Fireworks. In addition to building a page that contains the images we just exported, we will:

- Animate the buttons to look like blinking lights
- Animate the antenna so it raises and lowers on user demand
- Use layers to prevent triggering of inappropriate behaviors

By placing images in layers, you can position them anywhere in the browser window — move them around, make them disappear, or stack them on top of each other. In Dreamweaver, moving layers and changing their visibility are the tools of animation. Timelines control movement and visibility. Behaviors are attached to Timeline frames and to the contents of layers to affect the visibility and actions of other layers. A combination of HTML and JavaScript is known as Dynamic HTML or DHTML. Dreamweaver makes building DHTML pages as simple as possible by writing all of the code for you in the background. Bear in mind that while this tutorial example is small and useless, its implementation is not trivial. When you're finished, use the Code Inspector to examine what Dreamweaver has created for you.

HOW THE ANTENNA WORKS

We use Timelines to tell the browser where to position each antenna section's layer for each frame of the animation cycle. Because a Timeline moves only in one direction, separate Timelines raise and lower the antenna. Each Timeline also triggers several behaviors at the beginning and end of its cycle.

The buttons (green and red lights) blink to indicate when it is the logical choice for user interaction. We use Timelines for this as well because one of the capabilities of Timelines is to hide a layer from view. The dark state of each light is part of the underlying body image, and the illuminated state covers it as required by showing and hiding its layer.

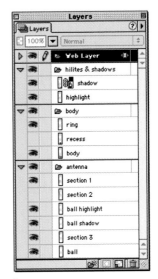

8.29

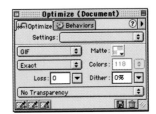

8.30

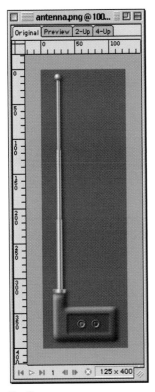

8.28

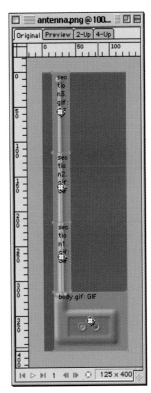

8.31

In Dreamweaver, when you set a layer's visibility to Hidden, its contents disappear, both visually and logically. We take advantage of this to disable the down button while the antenna is not up and waiting to be lowered (that is, when lowering it is not a logical option). We treat the up button similarly. We accomplish this by applying the trigger behaviors for the Timelines to transparent GIFs in layers on top of the buttons, rather than to the buttons themselves, and only exposing them when appropriate. If we attach a behavior to a blinking image, it is only available to click when the image is visible, which makes it a moving target. We could alternate its visibility with another layer containing the dark version of the button, but there would be a flicker in the user's cursor when the layers swap. This solution is simpler and looks better.

Here is a list of behavior components and their functions:

- UpOn: Layer containing up.gif, illuminated green button.
- DownOn: Layer containing down.gif, illuminated red button.
- UpTrigger: Layer containing spacer.gif; clicking stops all Timelines, sets AntennaUp Timeline to first frame, plays AntennaUp Timeline.
- DownTrigger: Layer containing spacer.gif; clicking stops all Timelines, sets AntennaDown Timeline to first frame, plays AntennaDown Timeline.
- AntennaUp: Timeline to raise antenna; first frame hides UpTrigger and UpOn layers to stop blinking and disable green button; last frame stops all Timelines, shows DownTrigger layer to enable red button, plays FlashDown Timeline to flash red button
- AntennaDown: Timeline to lower antenna; first frame hides DownTrigger and DownOn layers to stop blinking and disable red button; last frame stops all Timelines, shows UpTrigger layer to enable green button, plays FlashUp Timeline to flash green button.
- FlashUp: Timeline to flash green button. FlashDown: Timeline to flash red button.

- OnLoad events: Show UpTrigger layer; play FlashUp Timeline when page loads.

If you feel an urge to open the finished version from the CD-ROM again, be my guest!

USING LAYERS

STEP 1 Launch Dreamweaver and open the antenna.htm file you exported from Fireworks earlier. Open the Layers panel (Window ➤ Layers). Change the names of layers section1, section2, and section3 to sect1, sect2, and sect3. Add two layers to hold the button images by using Insert ➤ Layer, and name them UpOn and DownOn.

STEP 2 Using Insert ➤ Image, to place the exported button images into the appropriate layers: up.gif and down.gif into UpOn and DownOn respectively. In the Properties Inspector, resize each layer to match its image's dimensions. Position the UpOn layer at L: 50, T: 358 and the DownOn layer at L: 68, T: 358; then use the Vis field pop-up menu on the Property Inspector to set the visibility of both to Hidden.

STEP 3 Add two more layers to hold transparent GIFs to which behaviors will be attached. Resize each layer to 16 pixels square and insert a single-pixel transparent GIF scaled to 16 × 16. (You'll find one in C:\Program Files\Macromedia\ Dreamweaver 4\Help_sharedassets.) Name the layers UpTrigger and DownTrigger. Position the UpTrigger layer at L: 50, T: 358 and the DownTrigger layer at L: 70, T: 358; then use the Vis field pop-up menu on the Property Inspector to set the visibility of both to Hidden (8.32).

If any layers are in the wrong order, drag them into place in the Layers panel (8.33).

ANIMATING THE BUTTONS

STEP 1 Open the Timelines panel (Window ➤ Timelines), and change the name Timeline 1 to FlashUp. In the Layers panel, click UpOn to select it; then click the fly-out menu in the Timelines panel and choose Add Object. A purple bar labeled UpOn appears with a keyframe circle at each end. Drag the right keyframe circle to Frame 2. Click the Frame 1 keyframe circle, and in the Properties Inspector's Vis field pop-up menu, select Visible. Click the Frame 2 keyframe circle and make sure that the pop-up menu reads Hidden. Check the Autoplay and Loop boxes in the playback options on the Timelines panel (8.34).

STEP 2 In the Timelines panel, choose Add Timeline from the Timelines pop-up menu and change the name Timeline 1 to FlashDown. In the Layers panel, click DownOn to select it; then click the fly-out menu in the Timelines panel and choose Add Object. A purple bar labeled DownOn appears. Drag the right keyframe circle to Frame 2. Click the Frame 1 keyframe circle, and in the Properties Inspector's Vis field pop-up menu, select Visible. Click the Frame 2 keyframe circle and make sure that the pop-up menu reads Hidden. Check the Autoplay box, but not the Loop box.

RAISING THE ANTENNA

STEP 1 In the Properties Inspector, change the T values of the antenna section layers that we labeled sect1 and sect2 to 315. Change the T value of the antenna section layersect3 to 300. That hides the antenna sections behind the body. These layers extend below the bottom of the body, though, so in the document window, change the body layer's background color to #666666 (you can click the Eyedropper on the page background) and drag its bottom edge down to cover the sections.

STEP 2 In the Timelines panel, add another Timeline and name it AntennaUp. In the Layers panel, click sect1 to select it; then drag it into the Timelines panel and drop it when the purple bar appears in animation channel 1. Move the left keyframe to Frame 1, and move the right one to Frame 5. Click the right keyframe, and in the Properties Inspector, change the T value to 215.

STEP 3 Drop layers sect2 and sect3 into animation channels 2 and 3 in the same manner as sect1 and set their right keyframes to Frames 9 and 13, and

8.32

8.33

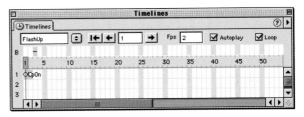

8.34

their T values to 115 and 0 respectively. Slide the red playback head back and forth and verify that the antenna sections work properly. (If they don't, check your keyframe and T value settings carefully.)

ADDING BEHAVIORS

STEP 1 Click in the Behaviors channel above Frame 1 and use Window ➤ Behaviors to open the Behaviors panel. Click the Add Behaviors button (+) and choose Show-Hide Layers from the Actions pop-up menu. The Show-Hide layers dialog box opens. Find UpTrigger in the list of layers names in the dialog box and select it. Click the Hide button. Find and select UpOn from the list of layer names, then click Hide again. Click OK to close the dialog box.

STEP 2 Click in the Behaviors channel above Frame 14, and in the Behaviors panel (8.35),

8.35

add the behavior Timeline ➤ Stop Timeline. Accept the default ALL TIMELINES by clicking OK. Add the behavior Timeline ➤ Play Timeline, select FlashDown from the pop-up menu that appears, and click OK. Add the behavior Show-Hide Layers, select the layer DownTrigger, choose Show, and click OK. In the Timelines panel (8.36), click Frame 1 to set the Timeline at the beginning. Type **15** in the Fps box. Do not check Autoplay or Loop.

LOWERING THE ANTENNA

STEP 1 Add a new Timeline and name it AntennaDown and from the Timelines dropdown menu select AntennaUp. This opens the Antenna Up Timeline. Select sect1 by clicking on its name; the purple bar will turn dark. Click the right-arrow button to open the Timelines panel Options pop-up menu and choose Go to the AntennaDown Timeline and choose Paste from the Timelines panel Options pop-up menu. Do the same for sect2 and sect3.

STEP 2 In AntennaDown, set the keyframes as follows:

- sect1: left keyframe at Frame 9, T = 215; right keyframe at Frame 13, T = 315

NAME:
Lanny Chambers

ORGANIZATION:
website2Go
www.website2go.com
1-877-WEB-2002|
Hobby site: *www.hummingbirds.net*

YOUR COMPUTER:
Macintosh Blue and White G3/350

YOUR CONNECTIVITY TO THE INTERNET:
128K ISDN

PRIMARY APPLICATIONS:
Fireworks, Dreamweaver, Illustrator, Photoshop, QuarkXPress

PERIPHERALS:
Scanner, Wacom Tablet

WORK HISTORY:
I celebrated my midlife crisis by dropping out of business management to pursue graphic design as a freelancer. When Netscape's new table tag made the WWW a viable artistic medium, I began migrating my business away from print. I learned HTML by hand-coding the first serious Web site about hummingbirds (*www.hummingbirds.net*), a significant challenge for a person who resists seriousness at every opportunity.

I began using Fireworks as an alpha tester for Version 1, not too long before the manual was written. I've contributed how-to articles on print and Web design to several online magazines. I worked

- sect2: left keyframe at Frame 5, T = 115; right keyframe at Frame 13, T = 315
- sect3: left keyframe at Frame 1, T = 0; right keyframe at Frame 13, T = 300

STEP 3 In the same manner as for AntennaUp, add these behaviors to AntennaDown:

- Frame 1: Show-Hide Layers, hide DownTrigger and DownOn layers
- Frame 13: Stop Timeline, all Timelines - Play Timeline, FlashUp - Show-Hide Layers, show UpTrigger

In the Timelines panel, click Frame 14 to set the Timeline at the end. Type **15** in the Fps box. Do not check Autoplay or Loop (8.37).

WIRING THE BUTTONS

STEP 1 In the Layers panel, click UpTrigger to select it. In the document window, click the transparent GIF in that layer. In the Behaviors panel, add three behaviors:

- Stop Timeline, all
- Go To Timeline Frame, Timeline AntennaUp, Go to Frame 1 (leave Loop blank)
- Play Timeline, AntennaUp

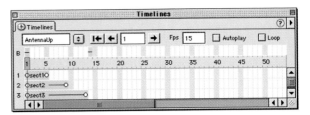

8.36

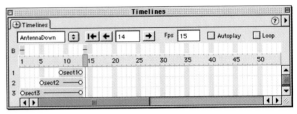

8.37

briefly as art director and chief designer for a local Web hosting company; then I joined website2Go as director of content development. I still do occasional freelance print work, mainly for a high-end audio manufacturer.

WHAT YOU DO IN YOUR LEISURE TIME:

I place tiny numbered aluminum bands on the legs of hummingbirds.

Next, in the Behaviors panel, select each item and change the Event to onClick. Use the up and down buttons to set the order to look like that shown (8.38).

STEP 2 In the Layers panel, click DownTrigger to select it. In the document window, click the transparent GIF in that layer. In the Behaviors panel, add three behaviors:

- Stop Timeline, all
- Go To Timeline Frame, Timeline AntennaDown, Go to Frame 1 (leave Loop blank)
- Play Timeline, AntennaDown. Next, in the Behaviors panel, change each Event to (onClick) by using its drop-down menu. Use the up and down buttons to set the order.

SET THE INITIAL STATE OF THE PAGE

Click in the background of the document window so nothing is selected. In the Behaviors panel, add two behaviors: Show-Hide Layers, show UpTrigger; Play Timeline, FlashUp. Change both events to onLoad (8.39). Save the file. You're done!

8.38

8.39

ANIMATED BANNERS

Q. "I can't seem to find any really good tutorials on how to make a banner ad. I'd like to do it in Flash format. I don't have Flash yet, but I do have SWiSH. Can you help?"

ANDREW T.

We have inside information that Den Laurent of *imagine.co.uk* is fast becoming the Banner Queen of the United Kingdom, so when this next question came up, we knew she was the one to answer it.

Banners come in all shapes and sizes, depending on where they are placed on a page and the guidelines of the site hosting the banner. They can be anything from a little 60 × 40-pixel button to the more common 468 × 60-pixel banners that run across the top of so many sites.

The most important thing you need to know about a banner before you start working on it is its shape and size. If you get these wrong, the hosting site will refuse to use it. Most sites have information pages that tell you what the specifications are for the banners on their site. They'll tell you what shape it needs to be in terms of width and height in pixels, and most sites have weight restrictions too. *Weight* refers to the size in kilobytes of an image: knowing what the maximum is for your banner is important. If it's too heavy, the hosting site won't use it. If the guidelines say your banner should be no more than 10KB and your banner is 11KB, it won't make it onto the site.

The banner in this exercise is going to be at the top of a travel page on a search portal. It must be 468 pixels wide by 60 pixels high and be under 10KB.

PLAN THE MESSAGE

This banner is advertising holidays on the sunny island of Guernsey. Guernsey is a small island in the Channel Islands off the coast of France, but it is part of the United Kingdom. It has lots of sandy beaches and is host to sports from water skiing to powerboat racing. Of course, it also has great seafood. This is far too much to get across in an animated banner, so the first task is to focus in on the core message.

The brief for this banner is to use an image that evokes the feeling of being by the sea, to incorporate the phrase "get away from it all in sunny Guernsey," and (if possible) to create animated text that resembles the motion of the water. I'm going to prepare an image in Fireworks and then import it into SWiSH to create the text effects. If you don't have SWiSH, you'll find a demonstration copy of the program on the CD-ROM.

PREPARE THE BACKGROUND IMAGE IN FIREWORKS

I have an image that has a wonderful sea and sky, which is great for the background of the banner. I need to get it cropped and then stretched to the right size. You'll find a copy of a similar image (sea_sky.png) in the Chapter 8 file on the CD-ROM.

8.40

Open the sea_sky.png file in Fireworks. Exit bitmap mode and then click the Crop tool to activate it. Select the sky and sea and double-click inside the crop marquee (8.40). Adjust the image to the right size for the banner. Select Edit ➤ Image Size and uncheck the Constrain Proportions box; then set the width and height to 468 x 60 pixels. This stretches the image, but I rather like the effect (8.41).

Now we have the background for the banner. Save it as seascape.png. SWiSH can import PNG files; and although seascape.png is 144K, it adds only 2K to the overall file size because SWiSH compresses the image when you export the finished banner.

WORKING IN SWISH

STEP 1 Open SWiSH and click the General tab. set the size of the movie to 468 x 60 pixels and 12 frames per second (8.42).

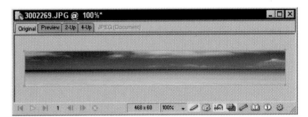

8.41

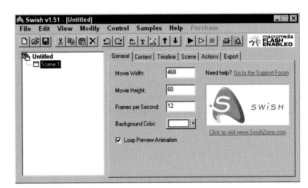

8.42

STEP 2 Click the Content tab and then click the Import button to import seascape.png into SWiSH (8.43). After the file has been imported, you need to click the Add to Scene button to add the image to the movie. If you can't see the movie, select View ➤ Preview to view it.

STEP 3 We'll add the text in two parts — _get away from it all_ and _in sunny Guernsey_ — and add a different effect to each piece of text (8.44). To add text, click the Insert Text button on the toolbar, and the Text panel appears. Type **Get away from it all** in the Text window, then choose a font and a color. The font you choose can have an effect on the file size, so experimenting with different fonts is worthwhile. Blocky sans serif fonts are usually a good choice. Checking the Export as Shapes box can also help to make savings on file size too.

Click the Insert Text button again to add the second piece of text, _in sunny Guernsey,_ in the same way.

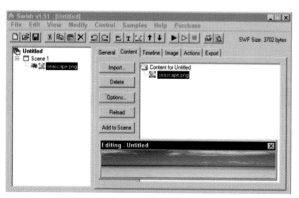

8.43

8.44

ADDING THE FIRST TEXT EFFECT

STEP 1 SWiSH shows both pieces of text in the movie, one on top of the other, so you'll need to hide the text you are not working on. In the left pane of the program window, click the eye icon of the text object that you want to hide (8.45). Click the Timeline tab to open the Timelines panel, and put your cursor in the first frame of the text layer. Click the Add Effect button. Choose 3D Spin from Effect pop-up menu. The 3D Spin Effect dialog box opens.

Imagine that you are standing at the waterfront, gazing down at the reflection of a boat on the sea. The reflection grows and shrinks with the movement of the water. That's the effect you want to evoke with the text here.

STEP 2 In the 3D Spin Effect dialog box, set the Spin Axis for the text to Horizontal and select Invisible for Begin with. Enter 180° in the Rotate by field. Check the Cascading Spin box so that the effect is displayed letter by letter instead of displaying the text as a whole. Check the Include spaces and new lines box (so that the effect calculates the spaces between the words) and select Forward for the direction from which the text appears. Set the Start Scale Factor to 30% and the End Scale Factor to 130% and Alpha Fade to 100% (8.46).

STEP 3 Each letter appears on screen at 30% of its size, scales up to 130% of its size, and rotates to 180° before disappearing. This creates a ripple-like reflection in the water. To preview the effect, click the Play Movie button on the toolbar. Click the Stop Movie button on the toolbar to go back to editing the movie (8.47).

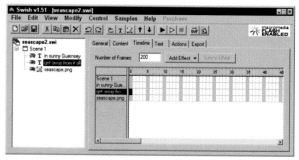

8.45

STEP 4 Click the eye icon to hide the *get away from it all* layer and click the eye icon of the *in sunny Guernsey* layer to show it.

ADDING THE SECOND TEXT EFFECT

You can use effects like Show, Hide, Fade In, and Fade Out to blend effects together. In this case, we don't need to use them for the first piece of text because the first piece of text removes itself from the screen. So, select the right frame for the second piece of text and add an effect. We'll introduce the second part of the animation on Frame 30 in the *in sunny Guernsey* layer (8.48).

SETTING THE SCALE CHARACTERS EFFECT

STEP 1 Click the Timeline tab and then the Add Effect button. Choose Scale Characters from the Add Effect pop-up menu. This effect makes the letters appear at 300% of their normal size and

transparent (8.49). As the letters scale down to their normal size, they become opaque. The letters come in one by one, overlapping each other as they arrive on screen. When the Scale Characters dialog box opens, set the Scale characters by option to 30% and the Fade characters by option to 100%. Check the Include spaces and new lines box and the Add Characters and Forward boxes.

8.47

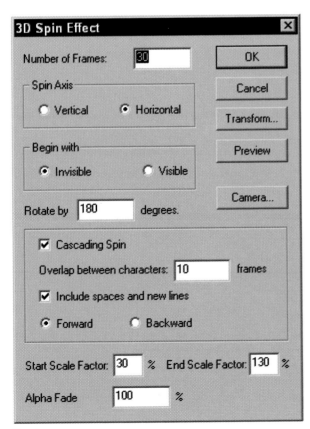

8.48

8.46

8.49

STEP 2 Click the preview button in the Scale Characters dialog box to see how the effect looks. We see that 30% was too small a scale setting. It just isn't that interesting. Let's try it at 300%. Yes, that's the look we want. The letters look a sail rippling in the fresh, sea air. You can also control how much the letters overlap by changing the number in the Overlap between characters box. Beware: If you set this number too high, the text won't come in character by character but all at once (8.50). Click the OK button to close the Scale Characters dialog box.

EXPORTING THE SWF FILE

STEP 1 Click the Export tab. Check both the Clip Objects to Movie Window box and the Export All Text as Shapes box. Don't check the Offset Movie to Suit Movie Clip box because you might get some odd effects, such as your movie running partially off screen. Check the Loop Movie box, but uncheck the Show Menu box. Your project doesn't need a menu because it is a banner. Leave the other settings as they are and click the SWF button on the toolbar to export the movie (8.51).

8.50

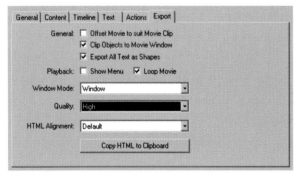

8.51

Check to see if the banner is under 10K. If the banner is over 10K, you'll need to make it smaller. Some text effects take up a lot of space, so you may need to try another version of the banner using different effects. Or you may need to simplify the effects you have, perhaps making them shorter by adjusting the number of frames they take to complete or removing any transformations you've added, like scaling or rotating the letters. If the file is only just over the limit, say 11K, you could try choosing a different font. Small and easy changes like font size can sometimes save you 2-3K.

STEP 2 If you are using images in your banner, you can adjust how much compression SWiSH applies to the image. Click the Content tab, select the image, and on the Content panel, click the Options button. Doing this lets you set the compression level SWiSH uses when you export your movie.

After you have your banner at the right weight, it's ready to go the site it will be hosted on. You also need to provide the URL that your banner points to. Most sites that host banner ads will want to add that link themselves so that they can track how many click-throughs your banner generates. If they don't do this, you could add an action to your banner that would redirect the user to the target site when they click the banner. It's important to check the policies out with the hosting site first though.

STEP 3 To add an action in SWiSH, select the object you want to make clickable. (It might be a piece of text or maybe the background image.) Click the Actions tab and on the Actions panel, click the Add Action button. Choose On Release and then click the Add Action button again and choose GoTo URL. Add the Web address in the URL box. Now when you export the movie, it has a link to the site embedded in it.

FLASH SPLASH

Wanda Cumming' award-winning Creative Solutions design site is a perfect example of what design teachers have been telling us for years: "Have something to communicate; then deliver it as simply as you can." We've asked Wanda to lead us through the steps she took to create her simple but effective splash page at *www.creativesolutions.ns.ca/*.

SETTING UP

Go to Modify ➤ Movie and set the frame rate to 12 fps, the standard for Web animation and the default for Flash. To accommodate an approximate aspect ratio across browsers (see the sidebar "Exporting Flash movie" for more information), fill in the screen dimensions of 620 x 310 pixels and choose the background color. In this case, #006666.

UTILIZING FRAMES, KEYFRAMES, AND TEXT

Now you'll need to begin entering the text. Just a few words on fonts: You'll keep your file size down considerably by not breaking type apart by instead using the text in its original form. When a Flash movie is exported, it sends the outline information for the font with it, so whenever you use an *e*, for example, it uses the same information each time, thereby reducing the memory required. If you break your type apart or create outlines for your text, the movie will need to calculate the information each time, thereby increasing the file size. The more fonts you use, the greater your file size increases, because Flash must send the outline information for each font.

STEP 1   Select Ctrl, and in the Timeline above the teal area (the Stage), select the first frame then click and drag to Frame 4. Choose Insert ➤ keyframe. This gives a fraction of a second lead time, but is also a good habit to develop because it allows you to insert frames at the beginning of your movie if you need to. This movie begins on Frame 4.

EXPORTING FLASH MOVIES

When exporting Flash movies, you can specify absolute pixels or let the movie scale according to a viewer's resolution. The latter will cause the movie to run a little slower, but it allows the movie to fill the window in a more customized way; it's neither too small nor too large, and scrolling is not required. If you decide to use absolute values for your movie dimensions, you'll need to consider aspect ratio. Because browsers use fixed-pixel dimensions for their menus and toolbars, the content portion of the window will vary at different resolutions. The following are resolutions and their approximate maximum content areas:

Internet Explorer:

640×480 — 620×318	1024×768 — 1004×606
800×600 — 780×438	1280×1024 — 1260×862

Netscape Navigator:

640×480 — 620×302	1024×768 — 1004×590
800×600 — 780×422	1280×1024 — 1260×846

Keyframes are where changes in the animation are defined and are unlike basic frames, which can appear in multiples between two keyframes. The frames between keyframes can also be tweened. Flash automatically creates the changes between the two specified keyframes. These areas are highlighted in light blue (tweened motion) or light green (tweened shape). Some of the text is tweened later in the tutorial, but for now, static text appears across multiple frames.

STEP 2   Double-click the default layer name in the Timeline, (Layer 1), and name it *effective*. It is a good practice to use names that makes layers easily identifiable to you or someone else later when revisions are necessary.

Select the Text tool (8.52). Click the upper-left area of the stage and drag to the right, creating enough room to type **effective.** Ctrl + T brings up the Character panel. I've used Frutiger Roman, 28 pt, flush left, black (8.53). Substitutions for Frutiger Roman might be Myriad Roman, Swiss 721 BT, or Zurich BT.

STEP 3 In the Timeline, extend the frames to Frame 9 with a new keyframe at the end (Press Ctrl, drag, insert keyframe). This leaves the *effective* text in place up to and including the new keyframe.

With the new keyframe selected in the Timeline, select the Type tool and position the word *communication* just below the word *effective.* Use Frutiger Roman, 36 pt, flush left, white.

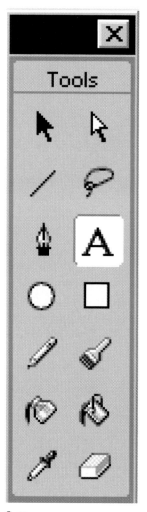

8.52

Extend the frames once again with a new keyframe at Frame 14. This leaves both *effective* and *communication* in place, and the word *gets* can now be added. With the new keyframe still selected, select the Type tool and position *gets* on the stage. Use Frutiger Roman, 28 pt, flush left, black.

Extend the frames with a new keyframe at Frame 19. Click the text tool and type the word **results**. Use Frutiger Roman, 36 pt, flush left, yellow (8.54).

SYMBOLS AND TWEENING

STEP 1 Select all four words and convert them to a Symbol (Insert ➤ Convert to Symbol). Name the symbol *effective* and, for Behavior, choose Graphic. Symbols are stored in the Library, where they can be called upon for future use. Like fonts, symbols can also keep memory size down because their information is stored once, but can be used

> **NOTE**
>
> Flash Player movies send data over a network connection by streaming it sequentially, frame by frame. When the visitor's Flash Player (plug-in or Active-X control) receives the data for a single frame, it is able to display it immediately without waiting for the subsequent frames to load. When this data is received at about the same frame rate per second as specified in Flash (12 fps), the movie will play smoothly and without interruption. For example, a 28 Kbps modem can receive approximately 3600 bytes of data per second. Some of this connection is taken up with "network overhead" to identify items and their placement. If we specify 12 frames per second and the total bytes used is less than 3600 bytes within that 12-frame section (remembering to allow for network overhead), the movie will stream smoothly and without interruption on a 28Kbps modem. To check the number of bytes being used, check Generate size report when exporting your movie.

multiple times. This symbol is not needed again. I've converted the four words to a symbol for tweening purposes.

STEP 2 Extend the frames with a new keyframe at Frame 32. On the Timeline, select all frames (Shift + select), including the start and end keyframes, 19 and 32. To tween, open the Frames panel and choose Tweening ➢ Motion. No rotation, scaling, and the like are needed, so deselect those options.

STEP 3 We want this symbol to fade to invisible, so you'll need to alter the attributes in the frame where it fades away. Flash tweens the frames between 19 and 32.

On the Timeline, select Frame 32. Choose Modify ➢ Instance. Click the Effect panel tab and choose Alpha from the drop-down list that appears. Move the Opacity slider to 0%, making the symbol completely transparent.

Now is a good time to check your work. To play your movie, press return or enter. Spotting errors on the fly saves possible headaches later. When you've

finished amazing yourself with your creation, move along to the next step.

LAYERS

Because tweened symbols must have their own dedicated layers, you'll need to add another layer to continue.

STEP 1 In the Timeline, below the layer named *effective,* find the small Page icon with a plus sign. Click it once to add another layer. Layer 2 appears above the layer named *effective.* Double-click the words *Layer 2* and rename the layer *you have.*

You'll notice a pencil icon on the layer, which means that it is the active layer. Watching for the pencil before placing items on the stage is a good habit to develop to ensure that you're putting the items on the layer you'd intended. Insert a new frame (Frame 33) on this layer and make it a keyframe.

Type the words **you have** on the stage. The settings are Frutiger Roman, 28 pt, flush left, black. We'll be applying an effect to the text later, so convert it to a symbol (Insert ➢ Convert to Symbol). Name the symbol *you have* and click the Graphic radio button.

STEP 2 Extend the frames, with a keyframe at Frame 38. Select Frames 33 through 38 inclusive, and choose Modify ➢ Frames (or use Ctrl+L). Again, no scaling, rotation, and the like are necessary, so deselect them (8.55).

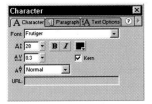

8.53

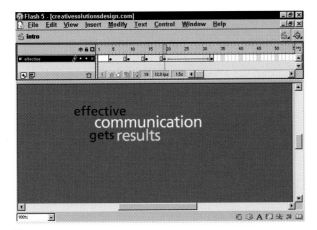

8.54

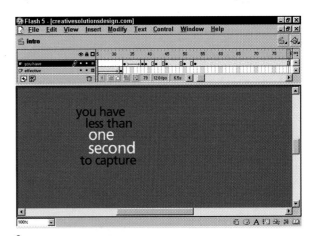

8.55

Because we'd like this to fade in instead of out, select Frame 33 and click the symbol *you have.* Choose Modify ➢ Instance. Click the Effects tab and choose Alpha. Reduce the opacity to 0%.

STEP 3 On the same layer (because no new symbols are tweened on this layer), select Frame 33 and insert a new keyframe (Frame 39).

Extend the frames with a new keyframe at Frame 42. Type the text ***than.*** Use Frutiger Roman, 28 pt, flush left, black.

Extend the frames with a new keyframe at Frame 45. Type the text **one second**. Use Frutiger Roman, 36 pt, flush left, white.

Extend the frames with a new keyframe at Frame 50. Type the text **to.** Frutiger Roman, 28 pt, flush left, black.

Extend the frames with a new keyframe at Frame 53. Type the text **capture.** Use Frutiger Roman, 28 pt, flush left, black. Extend these frames to Frame 79; no keyframe is necessary.

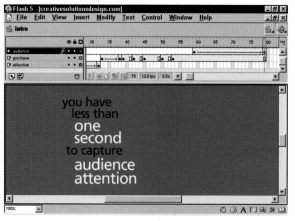

8.56

The next phrase needs to be tweened and faded in, so a new symbol, and therefore new layer, is necessary. Create a new layer and call it *audience.* The fade in causes a lapse in the presence of the new symbol, so overlapping the Timeline with the previous layer synchronizes it a little better.

STEP 4 Select Frame 59 and enter a keyframe. On the stage, type the text **audience attention.** Use Frutiger Roman, 36 pt, flush left, white. Convert it to a symbol (F8) and call it *audience.*

Enter a keyframe at Frame 79. Select Frames 59 through 79, inclusive, and choose Modify ➢ Frame(or use Ctrl+F).

Select Frame 59 and choose Modify ➢ Instance (or use Ctrl+I). In the Effect panel, choose Alpha and set the opacity to 0% (8.56).

Now for the litmus test. Check your movie by pressing enter.

CREATING THE ILLUSTRATION

There are many ways to approach illustration in Flash. In this case, the drawing was created from start to finish by using Flash illustration tools (the paintbrush and the eraser). However, illustration skills are not required to accomplish this. We might consider scanning a high-contrast, abstract photograph of a face, using Fireworks to give it a line-art effect, and exporting it as a SWF file for Flash. A drawing can also be created as vector line art in Freehand and exported in SWF format. For programs that support drag and drop, you may elect to simply drag the image onto the stage. The options are many — the choice is yours.

For the purpose of this exercise (and for those who feel that they have no digital illustration skills whatsoever), let's assume that we've scanned a high-contrast photograph on a white background, tweaked it in Fireworks until we were happy with it, and exported it in SWF format (File ➢ Export ➢ Save as Type ➢ Macromedia Flash SWF).

STEP 1 Before importing the file, create a new layer for the image and call it *face.* Use Ctrl+R to import the SWF file you've created, and the image automatically appears center screen on the layer called *face.* Notice that all frames on the layer *face* are now gray. Because Flash understands Frame 1 to be the last specified keyframe, it inserts the SWF file in that frame, and the image continues to play till the end of the movie (8.57).

For now, click the image and delete it. Notice that all frames have returned to white, signifying that they're empty. Not to worry: Your image has not fallen into a black hole — it has been stored automatically in the movie's library.

Combining simultaneous actions offers visual sophistication and emphasizes a point. Part of *creativesolutionsdesign.com*'s visual message is that visual communications must be clear and concise to capture audience attention. The face itself is a symbolic representation of the audience, and the simultaneous appearance of the face and the words *audience attention* packs the symbolism with a little more punch. The fade-in, therefore, begins at Frame 59, in unison with the fade-in for *audience attention.*

STEP 2 Insert a keyframe at Frame 59 on the layer *face.* To access the SWF file again, use Ctrl-+. Flash has given the SWF file a default name of *Bitmap 1.* Subsequent bitmap imports would be named *Bitmap 2* and so on. Change the filename to *face* or some other recognizable name.

STEP 3 Click the thumbnail image in the Library panel (8.58) and drag it onto the stage. Should scaling be required, right-click (choose Scale) and drag the square handles to the scale required. If you prefer to enter fixed scaling percentages, use Ctrl+Alt+I. Click the Transform tab and enter the desired variables. When you've finished scaling and positioning the image, click outside the image area and press Escape (8.59).

Now that the line drawing is scaled and positioned, we can begin to remove the white background area and do further touchups. We'll want to do this for two reasons:

■ We don't want the white background there; only the eyes and mouth need to be animated, and the surrounding pixels are in the way.

■ The extra pixels surrounding the eyes, nose, and mouth create a larger file size.

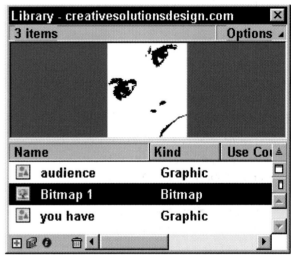

8.58

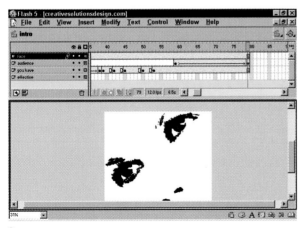

8.57

8.59

STEP 4 One way to remove the surrounding white area is with the Eraser tool. However, Flash has some wonderful selection tools that expedite the process and spare you from eraser-tool tedium. Before we begin selecting pixels, we'll need to literally break them apart. Select the line drawing with the Arrow tool. To break the pixels apart, use Ctrl+B. Click an area outside of the image or press Escape to deselect the image.

STEP 5 Click the Lasso tool and note the group of options that appear at the bottom of the Toolbox. You'll find a Magic Wand and, to the right of the wand, the Magic Wand Properties button (noted with an ellipsis, three dots, to signify more information to come). After you've clicked the Magic Wand, click the Magic Wand Properties button. It offers several selection options. The Threshold tells the Magic Wand how many colors or shades it should consider in its process. In this case, we want it to include only one, so enter *1*. This is also a fairly complicated drawing, and we'd like to get in as closely as possible to the pixels, so select *pixels.* Click OK.

STEP 6 Back to the drawing board. Now when you move your cursor over the white area on the stage, the Magic Wand appears. Click the white background area once and press Delete. If you look closely, there seems still to be a white halo around the black areas.

The selection has not gotten as close to the pixels as we would like. Using the Magic Wand and the same properties, use Shift + select all black pixels (8.60) to remove the halo. You may have to zoom in by using the Magnifier tool (type M to select the Magnifier tool, or use Ctrl+).

The following can be done in a number of steps, perhaps doing one eye, then the other eye, then the nose parts, and the mouth. We assume, however, that you've managed to Shift+ select all black pixels with the Magic Wand.

STEP 7 Now cut (use Ctrl+X). You'll want to paste these black pixels back on the stage in a moment. For now, you'll see the halo areas on the stage (8.61). To eradicate these offenders, click the Subselect tool in the toolbox to activate it, and drag over the whole area where the halo appears and let go. Handles outlines the halo areas. Press Delete.

Place the black pixels back in their original position, just choose Edit ➢ Paste in Place. If any other halo portions remain, drag the Eraser tool over the portions you'd like removed. Another option is to add a small black stroke around the selected area by clicking the Ink Bottle tool along on the edge. Use Ctrl+Alt+I, to bring up the Info panel; click the Stroke tab to access the Stroke panel options and specify a stroke width.

To emphasize the eyes and give them a bit more dimension, use the Paint Bucket tool to fill the enclosed areas with white. To select a fill, simply click in the color well in the Toolbox and,

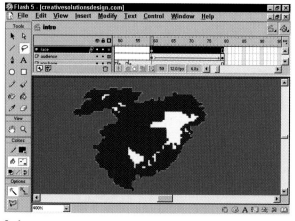

8.60

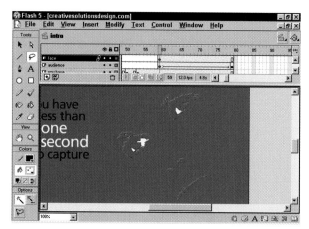

8.61

when the palette opens, click the white swatch with the Color Picker. Any areas that are not enclosed needs to be painted in with the Paintbrush tool.

ANIMATING THE ILLUSTRATION

Don't forget that this entire image fades in simultaneously with *audience attention.* In the Timeline, Frames 59 through 79 should all be gray on the layer *face,* indicating that the illustration is static or unchanged throughout.

STEP 1 Use the Arrow tool to draw a selection box around the illustration on the stage and convert it to a symbol. Call the symbol *face.* Insert a keyframe on layer *face* at Frame 79. Select Frame 59 and change the effect to Alpha, 0%. Tween Frames 59 through 79 inclusive. Fade-in accomplished. Now you're ready to blink those eyes!

Try to think of animation as a stack of images, one on top of the next — we create the illusion of motion by subtly altering one action from the next. Remember the old-fashioned flip books? It is exactly like that. You might want to find a friend who is not the least bit self-conscious and doesn't mind you studying his or her movements intensely. Have your friend blink very slowly so you can get an idea of what happens when we blink our eyes. Try to imagine this as a sequence of steps. Because such a blink happens very quickly, it is not necessary to have every microscopic movement illustrated.

This is very much a gradual process — don't worry if you don't get each frame correct in the blink of an eye. (Pardon the pun.) You might even want to sketch the steps on tracing paper and scan them in, but I've had more success by using the Onion Skinning features in Flash and altering the existing pixels, rather than attempting to match one scan convincingly to the next. Try scaling and skewing, adding a few pixels here and there until you have it right. Believe it or not, this is a simple sequence of nine frames. What goes up must come down. When an eye closes, it opens again. Hopefully. Some of these frames, as a result, are

the same at either end. There are actually only four more frames to illustrate (8.62–8.64)!

STEP 2 On the layer *face* in the Timeline, with Frame 79 selected, Ctrl+drag to Frame 80 and choose Insert ➢ keyframe. This action inserts a new keyframe, leaving the illustration in place in Frame 79 and duplicating it in the next frame. Break it apart by using (Ctrl+B).

Notice that because we've duplicated the frame, tweening is active on Frame 80 but is not necessary because each of the frames is manipulated manually, frame by frame. Press Ctrl+F, and select

8.62

8.63

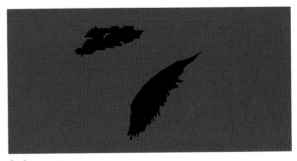

8.64

None for tweening to turn it off. Press Escape to deselect all.

STEP 3 Frames 79 and 80 are identical. To create a foundation, which you can change in Frame 81, Ctrl+drag to Frame 81 and choose Insert ➤ Keyframe. Continue this process until you've completed the illustrations as they appear in Frame 84.

STEP 4 Now for the easy part! Insert three blank keyframes (press F7) for Frames 85 through 88 inclusive. Select Frame 83 and choose Edit ➤ Copy Frames. Click the blank keyframe on Frame 85 and choose Edit ➤ Paste Frames.

Repeating this process, copy Frame 82 and paste it into Frame 86, copy Frame 81 and paste it into Frame 87, and copy Frame 80 and paste it into Frame 88. Presto! Go and get yourself that chocolate reward.

REACHING THE HOME STRETCH

STEP 1 To fade the face out to nothing, select Frame 79 on the layer *face* and make sure that the *face* symbol is selected on the stage. Copy the frame (Edit ➤ Copy Frames).

Create a new layer and call it *fade out*. Insert a keyframe at Frame 89 on the new layer and choose Edit ➤ Paste in Place to paste in the copy of Frame 79. Extend the frames with a new keyframe at Frame 100 and tween the frames. Modify the symbol on Frame 100 so its Alpha effect is 0%.

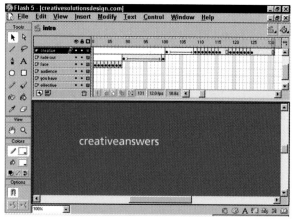

8.65

STEP 2 Now you'll turn the mouth into the letter *C*. Create another new layer and call it *creative* (8.65). Insert a blank keyframe at Frame 101. Because the face is still stored in memory from your last copy command, you can do another Paste in Place (Edit ➤ Paste in Place) on Frame 101. Break the image apart and remove the eyes and nose portions of the drawing.

STEP 3 Extend the frames with a blank keyframe at Frame 109. Type a letter **c** on the stage. Use Frutiger Roman, 28 pt, flush left, yellow. There should be nothing in this frame but the letter *c* and nothing in Frame 101 but the mouth. On the layer *creative*, select Frames 101 through 109 inclusive and tween. In the Frame panel, choose Shape from the Tweening drop-down menu, rather than Motion, for Blend, and choose Distributive.

STEP 4 Extend keyframe 109 to another keyframe at 110 and turn the tweening off. Add a new keyframe for each letter until the word *creative* is spelled out. To allow for a time stall between the two words, *creative* and *solutions,* add three frames to the last *e* in creative and repeat the process of adding a new keyframe for each letter in the word *solutions.* After the last *s* in *answers,* add six frames to allow *creative answers* to register mentally.

STEP 5 Create a new layer and call it *solutions,* repeating the same process as in Step 4, until the words *creativesolutions* have been spelled out. Again, extend the frames at the end (Alt-drag the keyframe to the final frame of the sequence) to allow time to let the idea register. This process ends at approximately Frame 156. There, select the final text and convert it to a symbol (Insert ➤ Convert to Symbol) called *solutions.* Copy the symbol.

The next new layer, *logo resize,* houses the scaled and repositioned logo.

STEP 6 Create a new keyframe at 157 and Paste in Place (Edit ➤ Paste in Place). Extend the frames, with a new keyframe at Frame 167. Reduce the logo symbol and tween the motion between Frames 157 and 167 inclusive — be sure to select the Scale box in the tweening palette this time. Add frames to Frame 170. Select the scaled logo and copy.

STEP 7 Add a new layer and name it *to scene 2,* create a keyframe at Frame 171 (8.66) and Paste in Place. Extend by two more frames. Add a new keyframe at 174 and type the word **design**, using a paler yellow and a typesize equal to the now-reduced version of *creativesolutions.* Extend by two more frames. Add a new keyframe at 177.

Use the circle tool to create a small 3D ball, filling it with a yellow to black radial fill (gradient fill, "round" rather than linear), with no stroke (outline) so that it appears to have dimension. Extend by two more frames. Add a new keyframe at 180. Again, using a typesize equal to the now-reduced version of *creativesolutions,* but this time in white, type the word **com**. Extend by two more frames. Extend the keyframe from Frame 182 to 183, leaving all components of the logo in place at Frame 182, but allowing for a new keyframe with the same components at Frame 183. This is necessary because it is the last frame of the scene and it needs an "action" to describe what it should do next. Be sure that keyframe 183 is selected on the *to scene 2* layer. To embed an action in this frame (noted with a small "a" on top of the dot in the timeline), Ctl+Alt+A on a PC (Cmd+Opt+A on a Mac) for the Action panel. Double-click the "Go To" action. Fill in the number 2 for Scene. (Be sure to name your next scene "2" though, or ensure that whatever you fill in here is applied as the same name in the next scene.) Fill in 1 for the Frame field (provided your next scene begins at Frame 1). Bravo!

STEP 8 Extend the keyframe from Frame 182 to 183, leaving the whole logo in place at Frame 182 but allowing for a new keyframe at 183. This is necessary because it is the last frame of the scene, and it needs an action to describe what it should do next.

To embed an action in a frame, use Ctrl+Alt+A on a PC, (or Cmd+Opt+A on Mac) to arrive at the Action panel. With keyframe 183 selected, double-click the Go To action (8.67). Fill in the number 2 for Scene. (Be sure to name your next scene 2 though — or ensure that whatever the name or number is here, you apply to the next scene.) Fill in 1 for the Frame field (8.68).

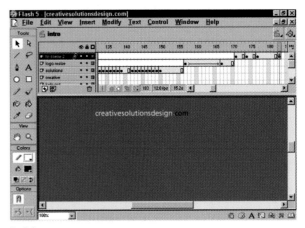

8.66

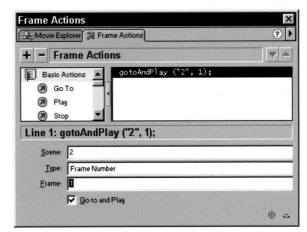

8.67

8.68

IGNITE WIPE ANIMATION

Q. "There is a kind of divider bar on the Apple Web site that shows news flashes. How can I do something like that for my site?"

TIM M.

8.69

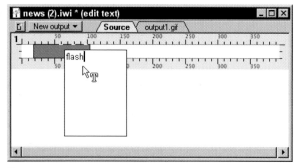

8.70

8.71

If you don't need to display a huge number of "flashes," this can be done as a quickly-cycling GIF animation. The secret to doing it well is advance planning of the sequence.

Film animators use something called a storyboard for planning out a sequence of film. A *storyboard* is a series of sketches representing the *keyframes* (frames that mark important visual transitions) of the animation. Ignite is a great program to use for this type of animation because it allows you to create keyframes, then the "tween" frames, and view them all at once as you are setting up the frame delays. You'll find a trial copy of Ignite (PC only) on the CD-ROM in the back of this book. You need to install Ignite before beginning this exercise.

This project requires a large number of frames. To minimize the file size, we limit the number of colors to three and use a squarish font that doesn't require much anti-aliasing.

STEP 1 Begin with a simple drawing of two lines and a rectangle (8.69). You can find a copy of the one we imported from Fireworks, called ignite.gif, in the Chapter 8 folder of the CD-ROM.

Open the graphic in Ignite, and then click next to the word *Frames* on the Inspector panel, (the context-sensitive panel on the left of the main window), type in the number **56**, and press Enter (8.70). Click the graphic to highlight it; then click the Duplicate button in the Inspector panel to distribute it to all the frames.

NAME:
Wanda Cummings

ORGANIZATION:
Creative Solutions Design and Marketing
45 Vimy Avenue, Suite 1020
Halifax, Nova Scotia, Canada B3M 4C5
902-443-6197

THE KIND OF COMPUTER(S) YOU WORK ON:
Anything with a keyboard.

YOUR CONNECTIVITY TO THE INTERNET:
Cable modem, when it's working.

PRIMARY APPLICATIONS:
Flash, GoLive, Quark, Freehand, Illustrator, Photoshop, Acrobat, Fontographer, MS Office, FileMaker Pro. Oh, and coffee.

PERIPHERALS:
Well, they pretty much visit friends a lot of the time, but when they are here, they would be a scanner, printer, CD-RW, Zip drive, printer, Web cam, and telephone. Did I mention telephone?

WORK HISTORY:
I started out in print more than 20 years ago (and have the scars to prove it) in the days of phototypesetters, drafting boards, tape, wax, and x-acto knives. I even learned how to lay beds of lead type from a man who had already been a typographer for 50 years by the time I was just starting out, and as a result, I have a fascination with and love for typography. I've had the distinct pleasure of working in print houses, design

STEP 2 Click the Text button on the Edit bar, then click the rectangle in the image. A pop-up text box appears. Type the word **flash** into the pop-up text box; then click outside the text box to accept the changes. Use your arrow keys to center the text on the rectangle. Next, we'll modify the text by using the Text properties on the Inspector panel (8.71).

STEP 3 Click to the right of the word *Size* on the Inspector panel and change the value to 22. Center the text again, if necessary. Click to the right of the word *Font* on the Inspector panel and choose a font from the drop-down list that appears in the Inspector panel. We've used a font called Bank Gothic. Other good ones might be Russell Square or Copperplate Gothic.

Click the color patch next to the word *Color* on the Inspector panel. The Color Picker window opens, allowing you to either type in the RGB value of your color (use the Eyedropper to select it from the color wheel) or scroll down the list of Web-safe colors and click a color to select it (8.72). We'll choose white so that the image shows up better. Last, click next to the word *Anti-alias* on the Inspector panel and reduce the amount of anti-alias to somewhere between 10 and 30 percent (8.73). With the text still highlighted, click the Duplicate button on the Inspector panel to distribute the text to all frames.

houses, agencies, and my own one-horse show in the capacity of designer, writer, illustrator, instructor, computer fixer-upper, and garbage emptier. I'm currently writing my own book; other articles can be found at digital-web.com, webreview.com, and webreference.com.

FAVORITE PLEASURE:
Coffee. Definitely coffee. And trains. :)

TIP

To make auditing your work as you go easier, click on the New Output button at the top of the canvas and select a format. (You can change it later.) This step allows you to toggle back and forth between the working and output windows.

TIP

When modifying height and width or x and y positions, notice that clicking on either one of them shows a link between the two with a little padlock button. When the lock button is down, it maintains the aspect ratio. To make a modification without changing the other property, click on the padlock so the button is in the raised position.

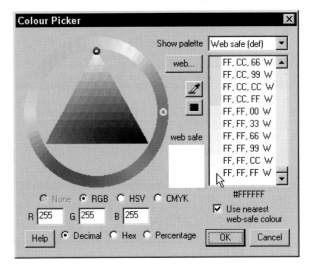

8.72

8.73

PREPARING FOR THE STORYBOARDING

STEP 1 You are now ready to begin setting up the cells of the animation. Type a string of text on top of the long blank area of the graphic in Frame 1 (8.74). Select the text, then click the Duplicate button on the Inspector panel. Scroll down to Frame 7. Select the text in Frame 7; then click the Stop Duplication Here button on the Inspector panel.

STEP 2 Type a new text string on Frame 8. Check the X and Y positions in the Inspector. If they are not the same as the first one, either nudge the text string into position by using the arrow keys or click the X and Y values in the Inspector window and enter the correct coordinates. With the text still selected, click the Duplicate button on the Inspector panel. Scroll down to Frame 14, click the text, and then click the Stop Duplication Here button, also on the Inspector panel.

STEP 3 Type a new text string on Frame 15; then adjust the X and Y coordinates. Highlight the text and click the Duplicate button. Repeat this process five more times, dropping down seven frames each time, stopping the duplication, typing in a

8.74

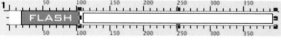

8.75

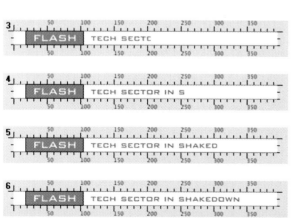

8.76

new headline, adjusting the X and Y coordinates, highlighting the text and then duplicating it.

STEP 4 One more thing to add to the frames. Drag a white rectangle over the text in the first frame (8.75). The text needs to be covered, but be careful not to white-out the top and bottom lines. If you create a GIF output at this point, you can toggle back and forth between the source and output files to double-check. We use the white rectangle to cover and uncover the headline texts in the on the frames of the animation.

PREPARING TO ANIMATE

The ruler around the objects on the canvas is marked off in 10-pixel ticks with markers every 50 pixels. We'll use the 50-pixel marks to measure how far to slide the rectangle over the text on each frame.

STEP 1 Copy the white rectangle from Frame 1 and paste it into Frames 8, 15, 22, 29, 36, 43, and 50. The first instance of each headline should now be in white.

Scroll back up to Frame 2 and paste the rectangle into it. Use your right-arrow key to move the rectangle 50 pixels to the right. If you want to speed up the process, choose File ➢ Options to open the Options window File ➢ Options, click the Editing tab, and set the nudge distance to 50 pixels.

STEP 2 Copy the nudged rectangle from Frame 2 and paste it into Frames 9, 16, 23, 30, 37, 44, and 51.

Scroll back up to Frame 3 and paste the rectangle into it. Use your right-arrow key to nudge the rectangle 50 pixels to the right. That should leave it close to the 200-pixel mark.

STEP 3 Copy the nudged rectangle from Frame 3 and paste it into Frames 10, 17, 24, 31, 38, 45, and 52.

8.77

Scroll back up to Frame 4 and paste that same rectangle in. Nudge it 50 pixels to the right (or to about the 250-pixel mark).

STEP 4 Copy the rectangle from Frame 4 and paste it into Frames 11, 18, 25, 32, 39, 46, and 53.

Scroll back up to Frame 5 and paste the rectangle in. Nudge it 50 pixels to the right and copy it.

STEP 5 Paste the rectangle into Frames 12, 19, 26, 33, 40, 47, and 54. Scroll back up to Frame 6 and paste the rectangle into it. Nudge the rectangle 50 pixels to the right and copy it. Paste the rectangle into Frames 13, 20, 27, 34, 41, 48, and 55 (8.76).

SEQUENCING

Here is where Ignite really shines. Click View ➢ Animation to open the Animator. For special frame-editing functions (such as Select all, Reverse Selected, Copy Frames to End, and deleting or setting frame delays), click the Actions button in the Animator (8.77).

STEP 1 Let's add some custom frame delays to the default ones. In the Animator (the window titled GIF animation), click the Actions button and choose Select all from the drop-down list. Then click the Actions button again and choose Frame delays. In the window that opens, select the radio button opposite "Change frame delays to." Type **3000 ms** in the box next to Change frame delays to and click OK (8.78). You can also access the Change frame delays to dialog box by clicking on the frame you want to change in the Sequencer window and then on the little plus button next to the number box. To see how this works, select the first frame and click the + button and type **4000 ms** into the Change frame delays to box.

The headlines need to pause long enough to be able to read them. The other frames need to be quite fast to smooth the motion. Our preference is to create a pause between each loop of the animation. We've used a 4000 ms pause on the first frame. Frames 7, 14, 21, 28, 35, 42, 49, and 56 — which display the full headlines — are set to 3000 ms. We'll set all the others to 5 ms.

STEP 2 To preview your animation as you work on the timing, choose Outputs ➢ Play Animation. When you are satisfied with your work and are ready to export, review the GIF optimization values in the Inspector panel (8.79) and double-check your animation in Browser Preview. We've used the suggested optimization settings. To export, click the Save This Output button in the Inspector panel window.

STEP 3 If you use your animation in a Fireworks document, change the Max BBP to 256, change the GIF frames setting to Full Frames, 0% Web Safe, no dithering, and disable Area Include. Export, and then import into Fireworks.

And that brings the animation exercise to a successful conclusion. Ignite is a very efficient animation program and there are occasions when you will use it in preference to Fireworks.

8.78

8.79

WHAT'S ON THE CD-ROM?

This appendix provides you with information on the contents of the companion CD that accompanies this book. Unless otherwise stated, versions for both Macintosh and PC are included. Here is what you'll find:

- Macromedia Dreamweaver 4 (trial)
- Macromedia Fireworks 4 (trial)
- Macromedia Flash 5 (trial)
- Adobe Acrobat Reader 4.0
- Amphisoft Filters, from Ilya Razmanov (freeware)
- Eye Candy 4000, from Alien Skin Software (demo)
- Ignite 2, from Fluffy Clouds Ltd. (trial, PC)
- Screen Ruler, from Micro Fox Software (shareware)
- Style Master 1.9 CSS Editor, from Western Civilisation pty. ltd. (demo, Mac)
- SWiSH v1.51, from Harrow Productions (trial, PC)
- TopStyle Pro 2.0, from Bradbury Software LLC (trial version, PC)
- Fireworks Commands by Brian Baker (freeware)
- Fireworks commands from Amelia Productions (freeware)
- PDF of this book
- A mini Website linking to all the images required for the tutorials in the book, plus custom Styles, Gradients and Textures for Fireworks

SYSTEM REQUIREMENTS

Make sure that your computer meets the minimum system requirements listed in this section. If your computer doesn't match up to most of these requirements, you may have a problem using the contents of the CD.

For Microsoft Windows 95/98/NT version 4.0, 2000 or later:

- PC with an Intel Pentium processor (Pentium II recommended)
- At least 64MB of available RAM
- 800 x 600, 256-color display (1024 x 768, millions of colors recommended)
- 80MB of available hard disk
- Adobe Type Manager Version 4 or later with Type 1 fonts

For Macintosh:

- Mac OS 8.6 or 9.X
- Power Macintosh Processor (G3 or higher recommended)
- 64MB of available RAM
- 800 x 600, 256-color display (1024 x 768, millions of colors recommended)
- 80MB of available hard disk
- Adobe Type Manager Version 4 or later with Type1 fonts

USING THE CD WITH MICROSOFT WINDOWS

To install the items from the CD to your hard drive, follow these steps:

STEP 1 Insert the CD into your computer's CD-ROM drive.

STEP 2 Click Start ➢ Run.

STEP 3 In the dialog box that appears, type d:\setup.exe, where d is the letter of your CD-ROM drive.

STEP 4 Click OK.

USING THE CD WITH MAC OS

To install the items from the CD to your hard drive, follow these steps:

STEP 1 Insert the CD into your computer's CD-ROM drive.

STEP 2 Double-click the CD icon to show the CD's contents.

STEP 3 Double-click the Read Me First icon.

STEP 4 With the programs that come with installer programs, you simply open the program's folder on the CD and double-click the icon with the words Install or Installer.

WHAT'S ON THE CD

The CD-ROM contains the image files for the tutorials in the book, applications, plug-ins, accessories, and an electronic version of the book. Following is a summary of the contents of the CD-ROM arranged by category.

IMAGE FILES AND FIREWORKS GOODIES

We've included a mini Website on the CD-ROM to present all the images required for the tutorials in the book, along with some custom Styles, Gradients and Textures for Fireworks. To access the mini Website, insert the CD into your CD-ROM drive. Locate the index.html file and double click on its icon to open the index.html file in your browser. You'll see a Web page with tabs that you can click on to open the chapter files. Clicking the Ch02 tab, for example, will open a new page called Ch02: Coloring Your Web. The links to the Zip files of the images to complete Eddie Traversa's Painting with Light tutorial (abstract1.jpg, hand_pose.jpg, futureman_pose.jpg and abstract_9.jpg) are embedded on the page. Click on the links to access the ZIP files, then unzip the files to a folder on your hard drive. To open the unzipped images in Fireworks, choose File ➢ Open, then browse to the folder you have deposited them in. Click on the image file and then click OK. The image you have selected opens in Fireworks on a new canvas.

APPLICATIONS

The following applications are on the CD-ROM:

Shareware programs are fully functional, free trial versions of copyrighted programs. If you like particular programs, register with their authors for a nominal fee and receive licenses, enhanced versions, and technical support.

Freeware programs are free, copyrighted games, applications, and utilities. You can copy them to as many PCs as you like — free — but they have no technical support.

Trial, demo, or evaluation versions are usually limited either by time or functionality (such as being unable to save projects).

The following Web Authoring tools will assist you in developing Web pages.

■ **Macromedia Dreamweaver 4:** *For Mac OS 8.6 or later and Windows 95/98/NT version 4.0, 2000 or later. Trial version*
Macromedia Dreamweaver 4 is the premier Web site authoring program. Whether you use Dreamweaver's visual layout tools or its text-editing environment, the intuitive Macromedia User Interface makes it easy. For more information: *www.macromedia.com/software/dreamweaver/*

■ **Macromedia Fireworks 4:** *For Mac OS 8.6 or later and Windows 95/98/NT version 4.0, 2000 or later. Trial version*
In Fireworks, create, edit, and animate Web graphics using a complete set of bitmap and vector tools. Launch and edit Fireworks graphics from inside Dreamweaver or Macromedia Flash. For more information: *www.macromedia.com/software/fireworks/*

■ **Macromedia Flash 5:** *For Mac OS 8.6 or later and Windows 95/98/NT version 4.0, 2000 or later. Trial version*
Macromedia Flash 5 fuses the precision and flexibility of vector graphics with bitmaps, audio, animation, and advanced interactivity to create brilliant and effective Web experiences that attract and engage visitors.

■ **Ignite 2**: *Windows 95/98/NT version 4.0, 2000 or later. Trial version*
Whether you want to produce fast downloading GIFs or JPEGs, make optimized animated GIFs, chop up images for use in tables or use Web safe colors and more than 1300 hybrid colors Web safe in your images, Ignite 2 will do it all for you and much more.

■ **Style Master 1.9 CSS Editor:** *For MacOS 8 or later, Minimum 5MB RAM memory allocated to Style Master. Demo version*
Style Master 1.9 supports all of CSS1 and CSS2, the complete style sheets standard from the World Wide Web Consortium.

■ **SWiSH v1.51:** *Windows 95/98/NT version 4.0, 2000 or later. Trial version*
Make text explode, move, drop, rise, weave, distort and much much more . . . simply and quickly!

■ **TopStyle Pro 2.0:** *Windows 95/98/NT version 4.0, 2000 or later. Trial version*
The award-winning cascading style sheet editor for Windows. TopStyle's powerful style checker validates against multiple CSS implementations, alerting you not only to invalid entries in your style sheets, but also to bugs in popular browsers that may affect their display.

■ **Screen Ruler:** *MacOS 8 or later. Windows 95/98/NT version 4.0, 2000 or later. Demo version*
Screen Ruler is a great virtual ruler ready to be dragged around on your computer screen. This application is very useful for measuring objects in Pixels, Inches, Picas, Centimeters, and Percentage of Length.

PLUG-INS AND ACCESSORIES

■ **Amphisoft Filters:** *Windows 95/98/NT version 4.0, 2000 or later. Freeware*
A set of powerful, fully functional plug-in filters that enable you to tackle extraordinary special effects. Generously provided by Ilya Razmanov (a.k.a. Ilyich the Toad) from Moscow. Watch out for this lad, he's *very* good.

- **Eye Candy 4000:** *MacOS 8 or later. Windows 95/98/NT version 4.0, 2000 or later. Demo version* Twenty-three time-saving filters that will fortify any user's creativity. Eye Candy is the only filter set on the market that combines practical effects like shadows, bevels, and glows with stunning effects like Chrome, Fire, Smoke, and Wood.
- **Adobe Acrobat Reader 4.0:** *MacOS 8 or later. Windows 95/98/NT version 4.0, 2000 or later. Freeware* Adobe Acrobat Reader is free software that lets you view and print Adobe Portable Document Format (PDF) files.

ELECTRONIC VERSION OF PLAYING WITH FIRE

The complete (and searchable) text of this book is on the CD-ROM in Adobe's Portable Document Format (PDF), readable with the Adobe Acrobat Reader (also included). For more information on Adobe Acrobat Reader, go to *www.adobe.com*.

TROUBLESHOOTING

If you have difficulty installing or using the CD-ROM programs, try the following solutions:

- **Turn off any anti-virus software that you may have running.** Installers sometimes mimic virus activity and can make your computer incorrectly believe that a virus is infecting it. (Be sure to turn the anti-virus software back on later.)
- **Close all running programs.** The more programs you're running, the less memory is available to other programs. Installers also typically update files and programs; if you keep other programs running, installation may not work properly.

If you still have trouble with the CD, please call the Hungry Minds Customer Care phone number: (800) 762-2974. Outside the United States, call (317) 572-3993. Hungry Minds will provide technical support only for installation and other general quality control items; for technical support on the applications themselves, consult the program's vendor or author.

INDEX

ABOUT THE AUTHORS

Linda Rathgeber is an accomplished writer, Web developer, and Macromedia Evangelist who coaches newcomers in the use of Macromedia's Dreamweaver and Fireworks programs. She is a former editor, layout and graphic artist for the *Holistic Resource Magazine*, and a contributing writer to such diverse publications as *Woman's World* and *Dream Quarterly International*. Since turning freelance, her graphic work has been featured by independent film company King Pictures, in numerous book ads for author Bill Stott, and on the companion CD of Joseph W. Lowery's *Fireworks 3 Bible*. Linda is also the creative director of Oztex Alliance. She lives in Austin, Texas with a monitor pet named Missy and a couple of Dell PCs. She can be reached at *www.playingwithfire.com*.

David C. Nicholls is a brilliant photographer, and an expert on graphics compression software (for which he has written numerous reviews). His Web development company is a member of a consortium refurbishing the Australian government's AusAID site.

COLOPHON

This book was produced electronically in Indianapolis, Indiana. Microsoft Word 97 was used for word processing; design and layout were produced using QuarkXPress 4.11 and Abobe Photoshop 5.5 on Power Macintosh computers. The typeface families used are Chicago Laser, Minion, Myriad, Myriad Multiple Master, Prestige Elite, Symbol, Trajan, and Zapf Dingbats.

Acquisitions Editor: **Michael Roney**
Project Editor: **Mica Johnson**
Technical Editors: **Richard Gaskin, Sean Mahoney**
Copy Editors: **Beth Parlon, Diana Conover**
Special Help: **Angela Langford**
Production Coordinator: **Dale White**
Graphics and Production Specialists: **Sean Decker, Joyce Haughey, LeAndra Johnson, Gabriele McCann, Jill Piscitelli, Heather Pope, Betty Schulte, Laurie Stevens**
Quality Control Specialists: **Susan Moritz, Carl Pierce, Charles Spencer**
Proofreading: **Sossity R. Smith**
Indexing: **Rebecca R. Plunkett**

END-USER LICENSE AGREEMENT

READ THIS. You should carefully read these terms and conditions before opening the software packet(s) included with this book ("Book"). This is a license agreement ("Agreement") between you and Hungry Minds, Inc. ("HMI"). By opening the accompanying software packet(s), you acknowledge that you have read and accept the following terms and conditions. If you do not agree and do not want to be bound by such terms and conditions, promptly return the Book and the unopened software packet(s) to the place you obtained them for a full refund.

1. **License Grant.** HMI grants to you (either an individual or entity) a nonexclusive license to use one copy of the enclosed software program(s) (collectively, the "Software") solely for your own personal or business purposes on a single computer (whether a standard computer or a workstation component of a multi-user network). The Software is in use on a computer when it is loaded into temporary memory (RAM) or installed into permanent memory (hard disk, CD-ROM, or other storage device). HMI reserves all rights not expressly granted herein.

2. **Ownership.** HMI is the owner of all right, title, and interest, including copyright, in and to the compilation of the Software recorded on the disk(s) or CD-ROM ("Software Media"). Copyright to the individual programs recorded on the Software Media is owned by the author or other authorized copyright owner of each program. Ownership of the Software and all proprietary rights relating thereto remain with HMI and its licensers.

3. **Restrictions On Use and Transfer.**
   (a) You may only (i) make one copy of the Software for backup or archival purposes, or (ii) transfer the Software to a single hard disk, provided that you keep the original for backup or archival purposes. You may not (i) rent or lease the Software, (ii) copy or reproduce the Software through a LAN or other network system or through any computer subscriber system or bulletin-board system, or (iii) modify, adapt, or create derivative works based on the Software.
   (b) You may not reverse engineer, decompile, or disassemble the Software. You may transfer the Software and user documentation on a permanent basis, provided that the transferee agrees to accept the terms and conditions of this Agreement and you retain no copies. If the Software is an update or has been updated, any transfer must include the most recent update and all prior versions.

4. **Restrictions on Use of Individual Programs.** You must follow the individual requirements and restrictions detailed for each individual program in the Appendix of this Book. These limitations are also contained in the individual license agreements recorded on the Software Media. These limitations may include a requirement that after using the program for a specified period of time, the user must pay a registration fee or discontinue use. By opening the Software packet(s), you will be agreeing to abide by the licenses and restrictions for these individual programs that are detailed in Appendix and on the Software Media. None of the material on this Software Media or listed in this Book may ever be redistributed, in original or modified form, for commercial purposes.

5. **Limited Warranty.**

   (a) HMI warrants that the Software and Software Media are free from defects in materials and workmanship under normal use for a period of sixty (60) days from the date of purchase of this Book. If HMI receives notification within the warranty period of defects in materials or workmanship, HMI will replace the defective Software Media.

   (b) **HMI AND THE AUTHOR OF THE BOOK DISCLAIM ALL OTHER WARRANTIES, EXPRESS OR IMPLIED, INCLUDING WITHOUT LIMITATION IMPLIED WARRANTIES OF MERCHANTABILITY AND FITNESS FOR A PARTICULAR PURPOSE, WITH RESPECT TO THE SOFTWARE, THE PROGRAMS, THE SOURCE CODE CONTAINED THEREIN, AND/OR THE TECHNIQUES DESCRIBED IN THIS BOOK. HMI DOES NOT WARRANT THAT THE FUNCTIONS CONTAINED IN THE SOFTWARE WILL MEET YOUR REQUIREMENTS OR THAT THE OPERATION OF THE SOFTWARE WILL BE ERROR FREE.**

   (c) This limited warranty gives you specific legal rights, and you may have other rights that vary from jurisdiction to jurisdiction.

6. **Remedies.**

   (a) HMI's entire liability and your exclusive remedy for defects in materials and workmanship shall be limited to replacement of the Software Media, which may be returned to HMI with a copy of your receipt at the following address: Software Media Fulfillment Department, Attn.: *Playing with Fire*, Hungry Minds, Inc., 10475 Crosspoint Blvd., Indianapolis, IN 46256, or call 1-800-762-2974. Please allow four to six weeks for delivery. This Limited Warranty is void if failure of the Software Media has resulted from accident, abuse, or misapplication. Any replacement Software Media will be warranted for the remainder of the original warranty period or thirty (30) days, whichever is longer.

   (b) In no event shall HMI or the author be liable for any damages whatsoever (including without limitation damages for loss of business profits, business interruption, loss of business information, or any other pecuniary loss) arising from the use of or inability to use the Book or the Software, even if HMI has been advised of the possibility of such damages.

(c)   Because some jurisdictions do not allow the exclusion or limitation of liability for consequential or incidental damages, the above limitation or exclusion may not apply to you.

6.   **U.S. Government Restricted Rights.** Use, duplication, or disclosure of the Software for or on behalf of the United States of America, its agencies and/or instrumentalities (the "U.S. Government") is subject to restrictions as stated in paragraph (c)(1)(ii) of the Rights in Technical Data and Computer Software clause of DFARS 252.227-7013, or subparagraphs (c) (1) and (2) of the Commercial Computer Software - Restricted Rights clause at FAR 52.227-19, and in similar clauses in the NASA FAR supplement, as applicable.

7.   **General.** This Agreement constitutes the entire understanding of the parties and revokes and supersedes all prior agreements, oral or written, between them and may not be modified or amended except in a writing signed by both parties hereto that specifically refers to this Agreement. This Agreement shall take precedence over any other documents that may be in conflict herewith. If any one or more provisions contained in this Agreement are held by any court or tribunal to be invalid, illegal, or otherwise unenforceable, each and every other provision shall remain in full force and effect.

CD-ROM INSTALLATION INSTRUCTIONS

To install the items from the CD-ROM to your hard drive, follow these steps:

1. **Insert the CD-ROM into your computer's CD-ROM drive.**
2. **Click Start ➢ Run.**
3. **In the dialog box that appears, type** D:\SETUP.EXE.
   Replace *D:* with the drive letter for your CD-ROM drive, if needed.
4. **Click OK.**
   A License Agreement window appears.
5. **Read through the license agreement and then click the Accept button if you want to use the CD-ROM. After you click Accept, you are never bothered by the License Agreement window again.**
   The CD-ROM interface Welcome screen appears.
6. **Click anywhere on the Welcome screen to enter the interface.**
   The next screen lists categories for the software on the CD-ROM.
7. **To view the items within a category, just click the category's name.**
   A list of programs in the category appears.
8. **For more information about a program, click the program's name.**
9. **If you don't want to install the program, click the Go Back button to return to the previous screen.**
   You can always return to the previous screen by clicking the Go Back button. This feature enables you to browse the different categories and products and decide what you want to install.
10. **To install a program, click the appropriate Install button.**
    The CD-ROM interface drops to the background while the CD-ROM installs the program you chose.
11. **To install other items, repeat steps 7 through 10.**
12. **When you finish installing programs, click the Quit button to close the interface.**
    You can eject the CD-ROM now. Carefully place it back in the plastic jacket of the book for safekeeping.

To run some of the programs on the *Playing with Fire* CD-ROM, you need to leave the CD-ROM in the CD-ROM drive.